Dr. Wilfred Funk at Your Elbow. . . .

While you use this book you will have one of the world's greatest authorities on words at your elbow. Dr. Funk, noted author of eleven books and for many years president of Funk & Wagnalls Company, publishers of dictionaries and encyclopedias, combines a vast scholarly background with a unique ability to entertain while teaching. For many years he wrote the monthly feature "It Pays to Increase Your Word Power" for the *Reader's Digest*, and his *30 Days to a More Powerful Vocabulary* written with Norman Lewis has already sold more than two and a half million copies. But more important—his books have helped millions of men and women gain a richer life through a richer knowledge of words and how to use them more effectively.

SIX WEEKS TO WORDS OF POWER
was originally published by
Funk & Wagnalls Company.

Books by Wilfred Funk

Six Weeks to Words of Power
30 Days To A More Powerful Vocabulary

Published by POCKET BOOKS

Six Weeks To
WORDS OF POWER

▲▲▲

Wilfred Funk

LITT. D.

PUBLISHED BY POCKET BOOKS NEW YORK

SIX WEEKS TO WORDS OF POWER

Wilfred Funk edition published 1953

POCKET BOOK edition published March, 1955

27th printing.....................November, 1975

This POCKET BOOK edition includes every word contained
in the original, higher-priced edition. It is printed from
brand-new plates made from completely reset, clear, easy-to-
read type. POCKET BOOK editions are published by POCKET
BOOKS, a division of Simon & Schuster, Inc., 630 Fifth
Avenue, New York, N.Y. 10020. Trademarks registered
in the United States and other countries.

Standard Book Number: 671-80420-0.

Printed in the U.S.A.

CONTENTS

Contents

Six Weeks To

WORDS OF
POWER

INTRODUCTION

1. It Pays to Increase Your Word Power

THERE are perhaps only a few hundred "power words" in our language. But they are the words that make our language work.

I have tried to gather the best of them in this small volume. They are not *all* here, of course. For one thing, such common "power words" as *punch, cut, kick, shout,* are known to every literate person and are therefore naturally omitted from these pages. And, in the second place, another author might make slightly different selections from those I have made. No one of us learns a word under precisely the same circumstances. And each one of us has surrounded a word with different connotations. For this reason, it is always possible that you may receive no great impact from a word that hits me with unbelievable force.

But the heart of the "power vocabulary" is in this present book just the same. And if these words are learned they can almost perform miracles for your speech and in your writing.

Success and vocabulary go hand in hand. This has been proved so often that it no longer admits of argument.

I have done vocabulary testing for innumerable business concerns. Almost without exception the results were a remarkable indication of the salaries received. Even the vocabularies and the pay of the secretaries of executives usually followed the same ascending scale as that of the positions of the bosses whom they served. In one outfit that I remember well, the two lowest-paid girls were poorest in vocabulary.

Why shouldn't this be so?

Our knowledge of words is all that makes it possible for us to understand our associates or our friends. And it is only by words that we can impart ideas to others. Or command them to do our wishes. More important than this, we think with words. We can't think without them!

Said the great American educator, Dr. John Dewey: "Thought is impossible without words."

Said Thomas Sheridan, British actor of 200 years ago: "There is such an intimate connection between ideas and words that whatever deficiency or fault there may be in the one necessarily affects the other."

It follows then almost like a law of mathematics that the more words you know the more clearly and powerfully you will think. And, also, the more ideas you will invite into your mind. The world has suddenly discovered these truths and has become word-conscious as never before. It has awakened to the overwhelming power of words.

Without words the wheels of business would stop spinning. Without words we would still be savages. The accumulated knowledge of medicine, of philosophy, of the sciences, of the lifework of the great dead, could not have been passed on except by the magic of words. Without them we would be like the ants whose pattern of living has remained unchanged for millions of years.

And another tribute to the "power words" lies in this strange circumstance. When words fail, wars begin; but nowadays war planes often drop words instead of bombs. In some nations men are jailed for not listening to the right words on the air, and they are shot for listening to the wrong ones. When wars finally end we settle our disputes with words.

This is why people everywhere have long since come to recognize the importance of words in the lesser departments of life. Vocabulary tests are being used more and more as adjuncts in grading the ability of people. Personnel directors are using them to weed out applicants. They are a final hurdle that our army boys must pass in order to qualify for officer training. As a captain in charge of training once wrote to me: "If a GI hasn't an adequate vocabulary he won't understand what we are trying to teach him." And, of course, colleges employ these vocabulary quizzes as a major factor in their aptitude tests.

And anent this, here is an amazing discovery that was made in one university. The story is told by William D. Templeman, former professor of English at the University of Illinois.

At this institution the freshmen were subjected to a variety of aptitude tryouts. One of these was a 29-word VOCABULARY test. After some years of testing, the faculty thought that it might be interesting to find out whether the results of any of these tests might give a clue to the future scholastic standing of the students. To the surprise of those who conducted the investigation it was found that the unbelievably brief vocabulary test of 29 words was the most accurate prediction of the future general semester point average of the students for all courses. This led Dr. Templeman to say: "Mr. and Mrs. Parent and Mr. High School Principal, if you want your child to achieve success with his studies in college, look to his vocabulary!"

Of course, there are other ways to success in life besides building one's vocabulary. But there is none that is easier.

Just remember that educators tell us that the reading ability of people across the nation is that of 7th-grade pupils. Surveys show that the average person cannot understand material written above the level of 12- or 14-year-old children. So what simpler way is there to avoid competition than by raising your own vocabulary above this common level?

One pleasant and encouraging part about this is that it is so easy to do. And it takes so very little time. A few minutes a day is enough.

It is true that you don't cover a prodigious number of

words in this book. But they are "power words" of a high level. They are the mainspring words of our speech. And the odd thing is that with each one of these words that you learn, hundreds of simpler words will almost automatically be understandable to you and will become a living part of your vocabulary. You will notice this as soon as you begin. And before you finish you will have increased your word supply by many thousands of terms.

One reason for your swift accrual of word power will be that your attitude toward words will have suddenly changed. You will become enthusiastic about them. You will be curious about them. You will no longer pass over the unfamiliar ones. You won't be happy if you do. They will challenge you to discover their meanings.

This book, then, can be your first step toward forming a new and helpful habit—the habit of adding to your word supply. And the funny thing is, if you form a habit like this, the habit will turn around and take care of you and your work will become almost effortless.

May I add one small note to this introduction?

You will first be faced with verbs, the mainsprings of our language. Then will follow the nouns that are the building blocks of our thoughts. Then come the adjectives, the pigments that give color to our sentences. And to a minor extent, you will encounter those modifiers called adverbs. The other parts of speech, prepositions, conjunctions, and such, can hardly be ranked as words of power.

2. Let's Test Your Vocabulary

BEFORE you start this pleasant six weeks' trip it will help if you will first find out what your present vocabulary level is. This will be an interesting experiment for you to make, and it shouldn't take you more than 20 minutes to do. It should be fun, too. And the rest of this book is going to be laid out as nearly like a game as possible.

When you have finished this chapter you will have a fairly accurate idea about your word level. You will be able to detect the weak points in your vocabulary. And it is just these weak points that this book has been designed to straighten out.

And here is a statement that may startle you and show you why it is so critically important that you should start now.

If you are over 25 years old your vocabulary is already 95 percent complete as far as you are concerned. Only 5 percent more will be added during the remainder of your lifetime—*unless YOU do something about it*. And together with this, bear in mind, as I have told you, that the active vocabulary of the average adult, coast to coast, is not much larger than that of a child 12 years old.

What inadequate equipment that is with which to face the modern world! For, unless you are willing to acquaint yourself with words and to draw upon the beauty and the immeasurable power of the English language, you will not be well prepared to meet the competition of the new, difficult, and most complicated era that we are facing.

There are a very few fortunate people who learn early in life the secret power of words. Those who have gone ahead discovered it long since; they made use of it and they won what they wanted by using it. This may be why men within your own circle, who do not seem as bright as you, may be getting ahead of you.

But this magic power is no longer a secret and the techniques for acquiring it have long since been devised.

With this very volume that you hold in your hands you will be able to equip yourself with a richer vocabulary, and you can do it in those odd moments of the day that you usually waste if you will only make a plan and set a date. And the date is set and the plan is laid out for you in this book.

If you are young it will be easy for you to do. But never give age as an excuse. You *can* teach an old dog new tricks. This is the scientific discovery made by Dr. Irving Lorge, a brilliant psychologist at Columbia University. By a series of tests he has proved that older people lose nothing in mental power if they will keep up their active interests. They lose slightly in speed. Yes. But he showed that the ability of the mind to think and create, barring illness, is with you until the age of 90 and past. Your body gets old, Dr. Lorge says, but not your mind if you care to use it. The mind never retires!

There are a host of dramatic instances in history that point up this fact.

Rodin, the sculptor, did some of his finest work after 70. Michelangelo was 70 when he painted the frescoes in the Sistine Chapel. Verdi composed the opera *Otello* at 75 and *Falstaff* at 80; and also Anatole France at 80 and Thomas Hardy at 88 were in the full flush of literary creation; while at 98 Titian painted the *Battle of Lepanto*. As a matter of true fact, 5 percent of all of the works of genius have been done after the age of 80.

So neither age nor youth is left with a shred of excuse for lack of performance in any field controlled by the mind. Both can continue to advance their knowledge through the years. And, in the present instance, both can profit so greatly by word study and can get such keen enjoyment out of acquiring the art of superior self-expression. For nothing can make a man feel more confident than a mastery of his native speech. On the other hand, nothing can give a man such a sense of inferiority as a stammering incompetence in the use of words.

Now may I speak of the technique of learning new words?

When you come across a new word, you will do well, of course, to copy it down in a blank book and to indicate its pronunciation, with a rhyming word if necessary. And then you should write down its most common meaning and the sentence in which you first noted the word. And, finally, you should try to use the word, if it is not too difficult, in a letter or in conversation.

But while all these moves are useful, they are of secondary importance. Words learned by memory and rote are slippery eels that are apt to slide out of your mind back into the sea of forgetfulness.

The matter of first importance in vocabulary building is *to have a burning intellectual curiosity about things*—to develop new and wider interests. You will learn and remember words best when you are reading about a subject that absorbs you, for then you will wish to know what the writer is talking about. You learn and remember words when you want and *need* to know their meanings. Here is the new idea in vocabulary building, and the techniques of this book are based on this new approach.

Now you are ready for your tests. When you have finished, why not try them on one or more of your friends? It may entertain them and they will probably enjoy finding out how *they* stand.

RULES:

The rules for taking these tests are simple and are the same for all five.

You will notice that there are 10 key words in each test, printed in small capitals. After each key word there are four words or phrases lettered A, B, C, and D. Check that word or phrase that you think is *nearest in meaning* to the key word. Let's set up a sample.

COURAGEOUS—A: strong. B: cowardly. C: brave. D: cruel.

In this case you, the reader, would mark "brave" as being nearest in meaning to "courageous."

Because of the different age groups that will take these tests, no arbitrary time limit has been set. But since you want to get an honest appraisal of your vocabulary it would be unfair to yourself to take an unreasonable length of time. You either know these words or you don't, and fussing won't help. And please don't do too much guessing.

After you have finished these 5 tests turn to page 11–12 and check your results against the correct answers that are given there.

TEST 1

(1) DETRIMENTAL—A: depressing. B: increasing. C: injurious. D: complaining.

(2) SUBJUGATE—A: to substitute. B: to subdue. C: to yield. D: to battle.

(3) CHASTISE—A: to make pure. B: to punish. C: to reward. D: to pursue.

(4) TANTALIZE—A: to flatter. B: to tease or torment. C: to experiment. D: to hesitate.

(5) STANCH—A: standing on end. B: a bad odor. C: firm and steady. D: tight shut.

(6) INDICT—A: to write down. B: to charge with crime. C: to command. D: to point out.

(7) INFLEXIBLE—A: complicated. B: bending. C: tightly woven. D: firm.

(8) AUDACIOUS—A: brilliant. B: bold. C: powerful. D: frightening.

(9) EROSION—A: a bursting. B: a wearing away. C: a heavy stain. D: a slope.

(10) INCESSANT—A: uncertain. B: unceasing. C: occasional. D: irritating.

Do you have the feeling that you did fairly well with the first test? You should have, as the meanings of the first group of words are known to most literate people.

Now try the following test. These words are a little harder.

TEST 2

(1) INFRACTION—A: an interruption. B: a fracture. C: a delay. D: a violation.

(2) TORRID—A: coarse. B: extremely hot. C: hurried. D: angry.

(3) EXUDE—A: discharge slowly. B: dry out. C: boast. D: flatter.

(4) IMMUNE—A: silent. B: protected against disease. C: stubborn. D: imprisoned.

(5) TERSE—A: provoked. B: tense. C: brief. D: serious.

(6) NETTLE—A: to catch. B: to vex. C: to prick. D: to deceive.

(7) LAGGARD—A: careless. B: slow. C: untidy. D: lazy.

(8) ALIENATE—A: to make friendly. B: to travel widely. C: to make hostile. D: to ban.

(9) FEIGN—A: to pretend. B: to disdain. C: to flatter. D: to be favorably disposed.

(10) RAVAGE—A: to enrage. B: to plunder. C: to be devious. D: to tempt.

Here is a still harder list. If you are an average adult the odds are that you will miss about one third of these words.

TEST 3

(1) PREVARICATION—A: confusion. B: wandering around. C: a deviation from the truth. D: an act of delay.

(2) BERSERK—A: hairy. B: in a frenzy. C: foreign. D: disheveled.

(3) PUNITIVE—A: punishing. B: incidental. C: strong. D: deceptive.

(4) VAUNTED—A: greatly desired. B: boasted. C: powerful. D: empty.

(5) ALTERCATE—A: to occur in turns. B: to dispute angrily. C: to agree. D: to change.

(6) INVEIGLE—A: to provoke. B: to corrupt with money. C: to bulldoze. D: to entice.

(7) IMPETUOSITY—A: peevishness. B: rash and sudden haste. C: great anger. D: persistence.

(8) ARROGANT—A: claiming without right. B: uninterested in others. C: proud and disdainful. D: towering.

(9) EULOGY—A: high praise. B: criticism. C: hope. D: a lament for the dead.

(10) EVOCATION—A: a cancellation. B: a creation. C: a calling forth. D: a hobby.

The pressure is being put on you now. The words in this group are still more difficult. If you do reasonably well with this test you can rank yourself as having a superior vocabulary.

TEST 4

(1) CONTRAVENE—A: to obstruct or prevent. B: to bring about an agreement. C: to disown. D: to hold of less importance.

(2) IMPERTURBABLE—A: incapable of being agitated. B: worthy of trust. C: greatly disturbed. D: mysterious.

(3) PEREMPTORY—A: uncertain. B: angry. C: decisive. D: noisy.

(4) RECANT—A: to remember. B: to describe an event. C: to apologize. D: to disavow and retract.

(5) EXPEDITE—A: to be cautious. B: to delay. C: to make easy. D: to experiment.

(6) DEIGN—A: to consider worthy. B: to condescend. C: to despise. D: to refuse.

(7) EXCULPATE—A: to absolve from blame. B: to behead. C: to accuse. D: to torture.

(8) INEFFABLE—A: unutterable. B: sinful. C: heavenly. D: breathless.

(9) IMMOLATE—A: to try to excel. B: to sacrifice. C: to persecute. D: to calm.

(10) LIBIDINOUS—A: involving damaging statements. B: wild. C: lustful. D: impulsive.

Now you have arrived at a group of top-level words. If you should be completely successful with them you might as well put this book down. You won't need it. It will prove that you have an extraordinary vocabulary. Don't worry for the present, however, if these words are unfamiliar to you or even if you miss them all. Not more than one in a hundred knows them. As you go on with your word study you may be surprised to find words of this type eventually becoming a part of your vocabulary.

TEST 5

(1) TURGID—A: rough. B: roiled and muddy. C: swollen. D: thick.

(2) RODOMONTADE—A: overornate writing. B: lofty bragging. C: deafening clamor. D: burlesque.

(3) SUPEREROGATION—A: something superfluous. B: triumph. C: a cross-examination. D: conceit.

(4) EUPHORIA—A: feeling of well-being. B: state of unconsciousness. C: loss of memory. D: exhaustion.

(5) EXIGUOUS—A: hard to understand. B: winding. C: shrewd. D: slender or scanty.

(6) PREDILECTION—A: a definite order. B: a prophecy. C: an advancement in position. D: a preference.

(7) ARTIFACTS—A: fiction. B: conspiracies. C: things made by primitive peoples. D: frank statements.

(8) POLITY—A: methods of government. B: courtesy. C: freedom. D: trickery.

(9) PLETHORA—A: epidemic. B: confusion. C: excess. D: punishment.

(10) GLABROUS—A: romantic. B: shining. C: sticky. D: without hair.

The meanings of the words in the first test are known to almost all literate adults. About three out of four adults will know the words in Test 2. Two out of three persons are familiar with the terms in Test 3, while only one person out of eight will have a perfect score in Test 4. We are not rating you on Test 5. It is of exceptional difficulty.

ANSWERS:

Test 1:   1—C; 2—B; 3—B; 4—B; 5—C; 6—B; 7—D; 8—B; 9—B; 10—B.

Test 2:   1—D; 2—B; 3—A; 4—B; 5—C; 6—B; 7—B; 8—C; 9—A; 10—B.

Test 3:   1—C; 2—B; 3—A; 4—B; 5—B; 6—D; 7—B; 8—C;
              9—A; 10—C.

Test 4:   1—A; 2—A; 3—C; 4—D; 5—C; 6—B; 7—A; 8—A;
              9—B; 10—C.

Test 5:   1—C; 2—B; 3—A; 4—A; 5—D; 6—D; 7—C; 8—A;
              9—C; 10—D.

YOUR VOCABULARY RATINGS

Test 1:   10-9 correct—excellent
              8-7 correct—good to fair
              6 and under—poor

Test 2:   10-8 correct—excellent
              7-6 correct—good to fair
              5 and under—poor

Test 3:   10-7 correct—excellent
              6-5 correct—good to fair
              4 and under—poor

Test 4:   10-6 correct—excellent
              5-4 correct—good
              3 and under—fair to poor

If you are excellent or good to fair in Tests 1 and 2, and
good to fair or poor in Tests 3 and 4, your vocabulary is
about average.

Now count the total number of correct answers that you
have gotten in the above list of 40 words and then look
below for your vocabulary rating.

> 40-37 correct—extraordinary
> 36-33 correct—excellent
> 32-26 correct—good to fair
> 25 and under—poor

The readings of these tests will give you a helpful
picture of your present vocabulary standing. The chapters
that follow will bring about a revolution in your word
power that will truly astonish you.

PRONUNCIATION KEY

THE pronunciation system in this book is as simple as it is humanly possible to make it. Only two diacritical marks are used over the vowels: the macron (‑) or long mark and the breve (˘) or short mark—and these only when necessary.

The pronunciation of the word *ignominious*, for instance, will be given as ig nō min' Ĭ us. There you have the long and the short marks. The accent on the *min'* indicates that that syllable receives the stress.

Where the pronunciation of the vowel is obvious it is left unmarked. Everyone knows, for instance, that, unless otherwise indicated, a vowel between consonants is short. For example, the *a*'s in the syllables *mat* and *man* would naturally be short. In like fashion, when we record the pronunciation of *salacious* as să lay' shus the *u* in *shus* is short.

Where there is a division among the authorities as to the value of the vowel the reader is left on his own. The first syllable of the word *repugnant*, for instance, can be shown as rē pug'nant, rĕ pug'nant, or ruh pug'nant. In this volume such a vowel will be given without a diacritical mark as re pug'nant. Authorities can be found to back any one of these three pronunciations.

FIRST WEEK

Thought is impossible without
words.   JOHN DEWEY

1. Verbs That Deal with Human Traits

WE WILL start our trip with verbs, for verbs are the
little power units that make sentences move.

It is perfectly possible, of course, to write an intelligible
sentence without a verb. We can say: "Tonight at the
Orpheum Theater the world-famous actress Lita Leffing-
well in person." But the verbs are all implied, just the
same.

If you have power verbs at your command you can give a
tremendous impact to your sentences. They will travel
with the speed of a bullet and will penetrate deep into
their target.

A single example will help point up these statements.
Which of these two sentences, for instance, hits hardest?

"I have a hearty dislike for crime."

"I abhor crime."

That one word *abhor* takes the place of five weaker words.

So it is wise to pick your verbs well. And in the opening
chapters of this book you will meet the most forceful
ones in the English language.

14

I. We will first consider 10 verbs that have to do with human traits. It may help you to remember these words if we don't give you their precise meanings right away. It will be better if you discover them for yourself.

The words in question are printed in small capitals. After them are given four choices, lettered A, B, C, and D. It is your job to check that one of the four choices which you think is *nearest in meaning* to the key word.

Now let's ask you a question. What do human beings do?

(1) LANGUISH (lang′gwish)—A: they cry. B: flirt. C: linger behind others. D: become weak.

(2) COMMISERATE (kŏ miz′ur ate)—A: they suffer. B: sympathize. C: complain. D: weep.

(3) ABHOR (ab hore′)—A: they are afraid. B: run away. C: detest. D: tremble.

(4) GORMANDIZE (gore′man dize)—A: they brag. B: exaggerate. C: torture. D: eat voraciously.

(5) CONDONE (kŭn dōn′)—A: they show sympathy. B: are sorrowful. C: complain. D: forgive.

(6) IMPORTUNE (im pore tune′)—A: they ask ceaselessly. B: flatter. C: are overhumble. D: forbid.

(7) GROVEL (grŭv′ul *or* grov′ul)—A: they grumble. B: crawl at someone's feet. C: twist and turn. D: burrow in the ground.

(8) COVET (kuv′it)—A: they fear. B: flirt. C: hide. D: desire intensely.

(9) MALINGER (mă ling′gur)—A. they are tardy. B: angry. C: feign sickness. D: injure others.

(10) EXPIATE (ex′ pĭ ate)—A: they explain carefully. B: long for. C: atone for. D: talk too much.

Answers: 1—D; 2—B; 3—C; 4—D; 5—D; 6—A; 7—B; 8—D; 9—C; 10—C.

II. Now we will indicate the correct meanings of these words by descriptive sentences.

(1) They grow pale and weak, often because they are hopelessly in love. They *languish*.

(2) They sympathize with the sorrows and misfortunes of others. They *commiserate*.

(3) They hate and loathe crime. They *abhor* it.

(4) They are piggish when they sit at the dinner table. They *gormandize*.

(5) They are kind in their attitude toward the sins of others. They *condone* them.

(6) They trouble others with their repeated demands. They *importune* people.

(7) They are abjectly humble and literally crawl at the feet of others. They *grovel*.

(8) They are envious and wickedly long for the possessions of others. They *covet* them.

(9) They act sick so that they can get out of work and other responsibilities. They *malinger*.

(10) They have to pay for their sins by serving time. They often *expiate* their crimes in jail.

III. Let's make a third try and see how familiar you are with these words. Read the following descriptions and place the proper verb after each one. The sentences do not appear in the same order as in the first two lists, by the way. The key letter should help you enough so that you won't have to refer to Section I.

1. eat too much   go_____

2. tire people out urging them to do something
   or asking them for something   i_____

3. atone for sins   e_____

4. crawl at someone's feet in a low and abject way   gr_____

5. fade away and grow weak and thin, especially
   for love · l_____

6. feel hate and disgust for something · · · · · · a_____

7. feel compassion and sympathy for someone · com_____

8. long intensely for something that belongs
   to another · c_____

9. act sick in order to get sympathy or to
   avoid work · mal_____

10. forgive another's sins or shortcomings · · · · · c_____

Answers: 1—gormandize; 2—importune; 3—expiate; 4—grovel; 5—languish; 6—abhor; 7—commiserate; 8—covet;
9—malinger; 10—condone.

IV. Now these words will be paired with other words or phrases
either similar or nearly opposite in meaning. It is your job to
tell which.

(1) condone—unforgiving	Same	Opposite
(2) gormandize—gorge	Same	Opposite
(3) covet—crave	Same	Opposite
(4) importune—urge	Same	Opposite
(5) languish—grow fat	Same	Opposite
(6) expiate—never pay the penalty	Same	Opposite
(7) grovel—crawl in abject humility	Same	Opposite
(8) malinger—brag of one's health	Same	Opposite
(9) abhor—loathe	Same	Opposite
(10) commiserate—be unsympathetic	Same	Opposite

Answers: 1—Opposite; 2—Same; 3—Same; 4—Same; 5—Opposite; 6—Opposite; 7—Same; 8—Opposite; 9—
Same; 10—Opposite.

V. By this time you probably have a fairly good grasp of the meanings of these 10 words. Can you fit them into sentences? Some of the words will be in different tenses, or even in different speech forms, as *grovels, importuning*.

(1) Even with his vicious criminal record he has still succeeded in keeping out of jail. He hasn't had to _____ his sins.

(2) He _____ with his friend in his great sorrow.

(3) She is bitterly jealous and _____ her sister's wealth.

(4) There are those who eat with discretion and those who _____.

(5) When the clerk telephoned that he was sick everyone knew that he was _____.

(6) It is nauseating to see the humiliating way he _____ before his boss.

(7) The merciful often _____ the sins of the weak.

(8) He kept _____ me until I finally said "yes."

(9) The pure in heart _____ evil.

(10) It was sad to see him grow pale and wan, _____ from love.

Answers: 1—expiate; 2—commiserates; 3—covets; 4—gormandize; 5—malingering; 6—grovels; 7—condone; 8—importuning; 9—abhor; 10—languishing.

These are 10 powerful verbs and you will already have been helped by having added them to your vocabulary. There may be two or three that will elude you, and, as you go along, there will surely be others that, for some reason, won't stick in your mind. It might help if you start to make a list of these slippery ones and review them from time to time.

With words we govern men.

DISRAELI

2. These Are Your Verbs of Denial

YOU CAN'T seal off words into watertight compartments. In many cases their meanings overlap other fields. But it is often possible to group them in a rough way. There are many verbs, for example, that deny, dismiss, and exclude.

I. Here are a few very usable ones. Again we will keep their exact meanings concealed from you for a time, unless you already know them. Check that one of the four choices A, B, C, and D you think is *nearest in meaning* to the key word.

(1) ABJURE (ab jŏor')—A: to loathe. B: to irritate. C: to renounce and forswear. D: to curse.

(2) OSTRACIZE (os'tră size)—A: to criticize bitterly. B: to destroy. C: to struggle against. D: to exclude socially.

(3) REPUDIATE (rē pū'dē ate)—A: to be ashamed. B: to refuse to acknowledge. C: to challenge. D: to fight against.

(4) PROSCRIBE (prō scribe')—A: to prohibit. B: to dismiss. C: to arrest. D: to damage.

(5) NULLIFY (nul'ĭ fī)—A: to confuse. B: to make useless. C: to make numb. D: to conquer.

(6) CONFUTE (kon fūt')—A: to embarrass. B: to prove to be wrong. C: to face with a crime. D: to destroy one's reputation.

(7) RESCIND (rē sind')—A: to retreat. B: to banish. C: to repeal, as a law. D: to give up.

Answers: 1—C; 2—D; 3—B; 4—A; 5—B; 6—B; 7—C.

II. The meanings of these words will become clearer if they are put in sentences. The tenses of the verbs will sometimes be different.

(1) The astronomer Galileo was forced to *abjure* his theory of the rotation of the earth.

(2) After he was involved in scandal he was *ostracized*.

(3) The nation *repudiated* its debts.

(4) Dancing and smoking are *proscribed* by this sect.

(5) His dissipated ways have *nullified* all the good the doctors have done him.

(6) I will confess that your sound argument *confutes* my statement.

(7) The town council plans to *rescind* the objectionable traffic law.

III. We can look at these 7 words in another way. You may have a friend of the following type. What did your friend do?

(1) He *abjured* his sinful ways.

(2) He *ostracized* his dishonest neighbor.

(3) He *repudiated* his debts.

(4) He *proscribed* card playing in his home.

(5) He *nullified* the good effects of his diet.

(6) He *confuted* his critics.

(7) He *rescinded* the orders he had given.

IV. The meanings of the 7 words that we have given you are rather clipped. Even a single word is apt to spread over quite a bit of territory, and it will be wise if we cover each one a little more fully.

Also, words are much like people: the more you know about them the better you can understand them. And so, beyond their present-day meanings, we plan to give you the family history of each one and to tell you where it comes from.

(1)   ABJURE: To disclaim; to refuse; to renounce and forswear under oath; to recant. This word comes from the Latin *adjuro*, "to deny on oath."

(2)   OSTRACIZE: To exclude from all intercourse and social favors; to banish from all privileges. From the Greek *ostrikon*, "a shell." Shells were used as voting tablets on which the Greeks wrote the names of such citizens they wished to banish.

(3)   REPUDIATE: To refuse to acknowledge; to disclaim; to renounce; to disown. The Latin *repudiatus*, from *repudium*, "a divorce."

(4)   PROSCRIBE: To prohibit; to put outside the law. The Latin *proscribo*, "to outlaw."

(5)   NULLIFY: To make useless; to deprive of effect. From the Late Latin *nullifico*, "to make into nothing."

(6)   CONFUTE: To prove to be wrong; to refute an argument and prove it false. The Latin *confuto*, "to silence."

(7)   RESCIND: To repeal; to annul; to cancel; to abolish. The Latin *rescindo*, "to cut back," or "to abrogate a law."

V. How many of the words do you remember?

1. ab_____   4. pro_____
2. os_____   5. n_____
3. re_____   6. c_____
       7. r_____

Only 7 words have been covered in this chapter. But they are words of significance and force. Each one of them that is new to you will open another door in your mind through which ideas can pass.

Let's use another figure of speech. Words are like atoms. The hidden power within men, for good and for evil, is almost without limit. The secrets of releasing this power have been discovered, and you can now use this power to help yourself and to help others.

> Language! The blood of the
> soul! OLIVER WENDELL HOLMES

3. Verbs of General Value

BEAR this in mind. Power in words will, of course, be of untold value to the young. But age itself can become an asset if you acquire a masterful vocabulary. If you are old, you are rich in life. If you are rich in language also, you can make yourself fascinating to others. An older man or woman who is a virtuoso in conversation can command any group. Vocabulary is more important to age than to youth. We demand so little of youth. We demand so much of age.

I. The 10 verbs that follow are verbs of great force. The modern sentences in which they have been placed will suggest their meanings.

(1) "They are *arrogating* to themselves the attributes of God Almighty."—John D. Rockefeller, Jr.

(2) "This cheap and sensational literature will *vitiate* the reading habits of our children."—Frank J. Meyers.

(3) "He attempted to make a gracious speech in reply but was *stultified* by his timidity."—I. Ogden Woodruff.

(4) "He seemed almost determined to *alienate* my affections."—John Haynes Holmes.

(5) "Every family was *aggrieved* by the new and extortionate taxes."—James Truslow Adams.

(6) "They were so badly nourished that both intelligence and energy were *blighted*."—Louis Bromfield.

(7) "If they practice what they preach they will *confound* the critics of free private enterprise."—H. W. Prentis, Jr.

(8) "Nothing can *countervail* our march to victory."—Winston Churchill.

(9) "Man may, in a measure, *denude* his heart of dreams." —William Henry Boddy.

(10) "I *disdain* to drape grim reality with pretty phrases." —Edmund Wilson.

II. The familiar words will, of course, present no problems. But have you now been brought near enough to the meanings of the unfamiliar ones, if any, to do well with the coming test? Refer to the sentences in Section I when you need to.

Check that one of the three choices which you think is *nearest in meaning* to the key word.

(1) ARROGATING (ar'ō gate ing)—A: questioning. B: bragging. C: claiming unreasonably.

(2) VITIATE (vish'ĭ ate)—A: to spoil. B: to wipe out. C: to encourage.

(3) STULTIFIED (stŭl' tĭ fied)—A: stopped entirely. B: made to appear foolish. C: made angry.

(4) ALIENATE (ale'yen ate)—A: to make stronger. B: to hold on to. C: to estrange.

(5) AGGRIEVED (ă greev'd')—A: enraged. B: ruined. C: unjustly injured.

(6) CONFOUND (kon fownd')—A: to overwhelm. B: to irritate. C: to encourage.

(7) BLIGHTED (blīt'ed)—A: impaired. B: sharpened. C: made strong.

(8) DENUDE (dē nūde')—A: to fill full. B: to strip. C: to deceive.

(9) COUNTERVAIL (kown tur vale')—A: to thwart. B: to help. C: to announce.

(10) DISDAIN (dis dane')—A: to try. B: to hope. C: to scorn.

Answers: 1—C; 2—A; 3—B; 4—C; 5—C; 6—A; 7—A; 8—B; 9—A; 10—C.

III. Will these phrases help you recall the words?

1. made to appear foolish   s_____

2. counteract or thwart   c_____

3. oppressed or unfairly injured   a_____

4. impair in quality or spoil   v_____

5. claiming presumptuously   a_____

6. withered   b_____

7. estrange   a_____

8. perplex or overwhelm   c_____

9. scorn   d_____

10. strip   d_____

Answers: 1—stultified; 2—countervail; 3—aggrieved; 4—vitiate; 5—arrogating; 6—blighted; 7—alienate; 8—confound; 9—disdain; 10—denude.

IV. In the following sentences which of the words are used incorrectly and which correctly?

(1) Anyone who is *stultified* is stilted.   True   False

(2) Things that *vitiate* are helpful.   True   False

(3) Anything that we *disdain* we consider unworthy of us.   True   False

(4) When you *confound* a person you throw him into confusion.   True   False

(5) We try to *alienate* those we love.   True   False

(6) When we *denude* a person we deceive him.   True   False

(7) Those who are *aggrieved* are hurt unfairly.   True   False

(8) Things that are *blighted* are withered. True False

(9) When people are *arrogating* they are asking
   questions. True False

(10) Those who *countervail* wish to help. True False

Answers: 1—False; 2—False; 3—True; 4—True; 5—False;
      6—False; 7—True; 8—True; 9—False; 10—False.

V. We are now due for definitions.

(1) ARROGATING: Taking or claiming unreasonably; ascribing
   proudly and presumptuously; usurping.

(2) VITIATE: To impair the quality or make impure; to spoil.

(3) STULTIFIED: Made to appear foolish; reduce to foolishness;
   made futile.

(4) ALIENATE: To estrange; to separate, as though foreign or
   alien; to make a stranger of; to exclude from confidence
   and attachment.

(5) AGGRIEVED: Subjected to ill treatment; unjustly injured;
   oppressed.

(6) CONFOUND: Overwhelm; discomfort; perplex; throw into
   confusion; defeat.

(7) BLIGHTED: Caused to decay; ruined; frustrated; withered;
   impaired or destroyed.

(8) DENUDE: Strip the covering from; lay bare.

(9) COUNTERVAIL: Offset; oppose with equal power; counteract;
   prevail against; thwart.

(10) DISDAIN: To scorn; to consider unworthy; to think unsuit-
   able and beneath one.

If you take the trouble to learn words of this type, you will
find that your reading will inevitably and mathemat-
ically move to a higher level. A person's vocabulary must
grow with him or he cannot grow.

> Each word was at first a stroke of
> genius.   EMERSON

4. One-Syllable Verbs of Power

WE SPEAK of the "English" language and we have a feeling that it is largely based on Anglo-Saxon, or, as it is now called, Old English. But there are truly very few words that trace their beginnings to England.

More than 60 percent of our speech comes to us either directly from Latin and Greco-Latin or through a Romance language such as French, which, of course, is of Latin parentage.

Words from the Latin are often longer and more "literary" than others. We have, for instance, the Old English verb *walk* and its Latin counterpart *perambulate*. True, these are synonyms, but synonyms never mean *exactly* the same thing. You *walk* downtown but you *perambulate* around a garden. "Perambulate" has the idea of "ramble" in it. And, in like fashion, *poor* and *impecunious* are similar but not identical in meaning.

The Old English noun *home* is much simpler than the Latin-derived word *residence*, and it is always preferable to use a plain and simple word when possible. But again, these two words are not precisely the same in meaning. We say "Home Sweet Home" but not "Residence Sweet Residence."

Pairs such as these are synonyms but synonyms are not *identical* and, therefore, each one has its place and its value in our language.

Has it already occurred to you that when we come to our one-syllable words we begin to find a scattering of German, Dutch, and Old English roots? You will discover a few such in the following list. They are often words of unusual strength. You can feel their impact when you merely say *flaunt*, *flout*, *flail*, and *flay* out loud. As a matter of fact, all the words below pack an extraordinary punch.

I. Try your wings and see if you can pick that one of the four choices which is nearest in meaning to the key word.

(1) FLAUNT (flawnt)—A: to scoff at. B: to beat with a rod. C: to praise unduly. D: to make a gaudy display.

(2) FLOUT (flout)—A: to whip or flog. B: to treat with contempt. C: to cry out. D: to show off.

(3) FLAY (flay)—A: to spread out. B: to ravel at the edge. C: to make tired. D: to criticize severely.

(4) FLAIL (flail)—A: to thrash about. B: to beat. C: to strip the skin off. D: to be scared.

(5) PRATE (prate)—A: to talk foolishly. B: to parade up and down. C: to spread out thin. D: to flatter.

(6) RAIL (rail)—A: to laugh uproariously. B: to tear down. C: to utter loud complaints. D: to send to prison.

(7) WREAK (reek)—A: to be wringing wet. B: to emit evil smells. C: to split wide open. D: to inflict as vengeance.

(8) RAZE (raze)—A: to destroy utterly. B: to build up. C: to make fun of. D: to harvest.

(9) CLOY (cloy)—A: to make fun of. B: to tire, as with too much sweet. C: to flirt. D: to stick together.

(10) FOIST (foist)—A: to lift up. B: to drench. C: to palm off slyly. D: to scorn.

Answers: 1—D; 2—B; 3—D; 4—B; 5—A; 6—C; 7—D; 8—A; 9—B; 10—C.

II. Here are the true meanings of these words. When you

(1) *flaunt* your wealth before others, you are making a vulgar display of it.

(2) *flout* the opinions of another, you are scoffing and treating them with scorn.

(3) *flay* a person, you are criticizing him bitterly and without mercy.

(4) *flail* a horse, you are flogging him.

(5) *prate* about your virtues, you are babbling in a foolish and vain fashion.

(6) *rail* against fate, you are complaining in a loud and angry manner.

(7) *wreak* ruin on an enemy, you are usually inflicting the damage in a spirit of vengeance.

(8) *raze* a building, you utterly demolish it and level it to the ground.

(9) *cloy* your taste with jam, you have sickened of it.

(10) *foist* a fake coin on another, you are palming it off slyly as though it were worth something.

III. Some of these words are rightly paired with identifying words and phrases. Some are incorrectly paired. It is up to you to straighten them out.

1. flail	*a.*	beat
2. raze	*b.*	complain loudly
3. flout	*c.*	make a vulgar display
4. flaunt	*d.*	treat with scorn
5. foist	*e.*	palm something off
6. rail	*f.*	demolish
7. cloy	*g.*	tire, as with too much sweet
8. flay	*h.*	get revenge
9. prate	*i.*	criticize without mercy
10. wreak	*j.*	babble

Answers: 1—*a*; 2—*f*; 3—*d*; 4—*c*; 5—*e*; 6—*b*; 7—*g*; 8—*i*; 9—*j*; 10—*h*.

IV. Can you place each of the 10 words in its proper sentence? The tenses of the verbs will sometimes be changed.

(1) He was cruel to animals and would continually _____ his donkey.

(2) A vain man will often _____ his success in the face of everyone.

(3) She was a jealous woman and persistently tried to _____ ruin on her rival.

(4) The art dealer tried to _____ a fake painting on the customer.

(5) My taste for the theater has been _____ by too frequent attendance.

(6) They foolishly ignored and _____ the wise advice that they had received.

(7) The enemy bombed the city until they _____ it, with not one building left.

(8) We humans are apt to _____ bitterly at our hard luck instead of philosophically accepting it.

(9) Some mothers _____ about the cleverness of their children until it becomes sickening.

(10) I have never heard a man _____ another in such a vicious and angry fashion.

Answers: 1—flail; 2—flaunt; 3—wreak; 4—foist; 5—cloyed; 6—flouted; 7—razed; 8—rail; 9—prate; 10—flay.

V. How many of these verbs can you remember?

f. . . .	r. . . .
f. . . .	w. . . .
f. . . .	r. . . .
f. . . .	c. . . .
p. . . .	f. . . .

Don't be disheartened if you miss three or four. It would be remarkable if you recalled them all. It will help you if you say them out loud to yourself. And also if you write them down. Then you will be using eye and ear memories.

Every word that you learn will help us who are your friends to know you better, for your vocabulary is *you.* Your words are your personality. If you are poor in words, your personality will seem colorless and we won't be able to see the true you. After all, the ability to speak and to write superior English is the first mark of an educated man, and your investment of time for acquiring this skill will be supremely worthwhile, whether for grace of conversation or for salesmanship, whether for dollar value or for social value.

Syllables govern the world.

SELDEN

5. Verbs of Action

VERBS of true action are always interesting. They imply motion, decision, and such. They indicate that things are happening. They give power to our sentences and they are the dynamos that turn the wheels of language. If you read words such as these out loud, you can almost feel their physical impact.

I. Consider the following list. Several of these words may already be a part of your vocabulary. But sometimes we forget to use them.

     (1) DEVASTATE (dev′as tate)

     (2) ENJOIN (en join′)

 (3) INSTIGATE (in'stĭ gate)

 (4) EFFECTUATE (ĕf fek' tū ate)

 (5) EXPEDITE (ex' pĕ dite)

 (6) PREEMPT (prē empt')

 (7) COERCE (kō urse')

 (8) EXTIRPATE (ex'stir pate)

 (9) COMMANDEER (kom an deer')

 (10) EMBROIL (em broil')

II. Let's put these 10 words to work.

(1) Soldiers are supposed to destroy. They bombard towns, dynamite buildings, and set fire to them. It is their business to lay waste and to *devastate* the countryside.

(2) A criminal can have had an honest change of heart. He may have decided that crookedness doesn't pay out. The judge will *enjoin* him to avoid dishonesty.

(3) There are those saboteurs who wish to overthrow our type of government. They work hard to incite division in our ranks. They conspire to *instigate* revolution.

(4) Many leaders in the field of education are making an effort to improve the methods now being used in our schools and colleges. They are trying to *effectuate* a change.

(5) When you are in a hurry and wish to get service in a restaurant sometimes a tip will help to *expedite* matters.

(6) You are planning to buy a certain desirable plot on which to build a factory. Watch out. Your competitor may get there first and *preempt* the land.

(7) When you want a man to do some certain thing you usually have to win him over by tact. You rarely can *coerce* him.

(8) Gambling is rife in your town. Criticism is reaching high places and reputations are being blackened. The decent businessmen have determined to *extirpate* crime.

(9) If a war is on and the government has asked your factory to turn over its material to the army, you had better comply or they may *commandeer* your products.

(10) If you are an outsider it is part of wisdom not to take sides in a family dispute. As sure as you do, it will *embroil* you.

III. Can you recall the words and put them into sentences? This may not be easy to do. And if you can do it without referring to Section II you are an exception. The sentences will not appear in the same order as before.

(1) As sure as you take part in that dispute it will e_____ you.

(2) Watch out, or some early arrival will p_____ your favorite chair.

(3) The better element among the sportsmen are bound to e_____ crookedness from basketball.

(4) It seems that each year a hurricane is fated to d_____ the island.

(5) The citizens are dissatisfied with the police force and wish to ef_____ a reform.

(6) I e_____ you to change your ways.

(7) The agitators are trying to i_____ a strike.

(8) Tell the waitress you are in a hurry and that will e_____ matters.

(9) In times of war the government will sometimes c_____ the services of your employees.

(10) You'll never get him to do that disagreeable job unless you c_____ him.

Answers:　1—embroil; 2—preempt; 3—extirpate; 4—devastate; 5—effectuate; 6—enjoin; 7—instigate; 8—expedite; 9—commandeer; 10—coerce.

IV. At this point we are going to ask you to write a synonym or a synonymous phrase after each of these words, which are probably becoming familiar to you. What you write down may not be worded in precisely the same fashion as the answers below, but you will be able to judge whether your words or phrases are sufficiently close in meaning to the key words.

(1) devastate . . . . . .   (6) preempt . . . .
(2) enjoin . . . .   (7) coerce . . . .
(3) instigate . . . . . .   (8) extirpate . . . . . .
(4) effectuate . . . . .   (9) commandeer . . . . .
(5) expedite . . . . . .   (10) embroil . . . .

Answers: 1—lay waste; 2—urge; 3—goad to action; 4—bring about; 5—speed up; 6—acquire beforehand; 7—force; 8—root out; 9—seize for military or public use; 10—involve.

V. After the previous and most difficult test it might be restful to try something entirely different. Can you identify these 8 new words that end in *"ate"*? They are not all words of exceptional power.

1. resign from a kingship   a_____
2. tell or relate   n_____
3. clear from suspicion   v_____
4. blot out completely   o_____
5. set apart for a solemn purpose   d_____
6. command with authority   d_____
7. start a sudden and premature action   p_____
8. vie with   e_____

Answers: 1—abdicate; 2—narrate; 3—vindicate; 4—obliterate; 5—dedicate; 6—dictate; 7—precipitate; 8—emulate.

VI. Now it will help to keep these 8 words in your mind if you will try to use them in sentences. The order of the 8 words, of course, is changed.

(1) Let us _____ our lives to serving our country.

(2) We should honor the memory and _____ the virtues of George Washington.

(3) The conqueror will _____ his terms to the defeated enemy.

(4) There are dramatic occasions when a king has been forced to _____ his throne.

(5) He was able to _____ his honor and good name.

(6) The criminal tried to _____ every trace of evidence of his crime.

(7) This drastic and unfair law will _____ riots.

(8) He loved to _____ the story of his adventurous life.

Answers: 1—dedicate; 2—emulate; 3—dictate; 4—abdicate; 5—vindicate; 6—obliterate; 7—precipitate; 8—narrate.

Better review the words in this chapter and in those that have gone before. And as you read on, pay close attention, too, to those ahead, since at several points in this book you are going to be asked about them.

> Words are the instruments that
> make thought possible.   JUDD

6.   Verbs That Suggest Violence

WORDS are warm and alive to the fingertips. We humans invent them, so they inherit all our traits, all our oddities and quirks, all the good and evil that we have in us. There are words of kindness, such as *love, mercy, compassion, chivalry*. And there are words of destructive force such as those that follow.

Often the meaning of a word becomes clearer if we learn the history behind it, if we trace it to its origin. Some of the words that you will find in this book will be strangers, others mere acquaintances. Why not make them all your intimate friends? Words are like people: the more you know about their past lives, the better you will understand them.

Most of our English words, as we know, come from other languages, the majority from the ancient Latin.

I. What can we discover about the 8 violent words given below?

(1) LACERATE (las′ŭr ate) (5) EXTORT (ex tort′)

(2) RAVAGE (rav′ĭj) (6) SABOTAGE (să′bō tahzh)

(3) DECIMATE (des′ĭ mate) (7) JEOPARDIZE (jep′urd ize)

(4) SUBVERT (sub vert′) (8) DECAPITATE (dē cap′ĭ tate)

(1) LACERATE—The word *laceratus* appears in Latin and gives us a valuable English term. It comes from the verb *lacoro* that means "to tear." That is, your skin can be torn roughly by a nail. In similar fashion, your feelings can be "torn" too. What does a neighbor do when she hurts and wounds your feelings deeply?

She *lacerates* them.

(2) RAVAGE—Here we face a more complicated history. Sometimes the words that come down to us from other languages broaden in their meanings and change in their spellings. This has happened to the Latin word *rapio*. This term first meant simply "to seize"; then, "to snatch away by force"; then, in war, "to plunder." In French the word became *ravir*, and entered our language as *ravage*. So what do enemy troops do when they lay waste to a country?

They *ravage* it.

(3) DECIMATE—If there was a mutiny in a Roman army, it was the standard punishment to take one out of every ten soldiers and put him to death. In Latin *decem* meant "ten," and *decimo*, "to take a tenth," which is what they did when they punished the boys. This bred the word *deci-*

matus, which is very close to the English word that we are
considering. So what does an army do to the forces of the
enemy when it destroys a large part of them?

It *decimates* them.

(4) SUBVERT—At this point we come to a word that we took
over almost bodily from the Latin term *subverto*, "overthrow." This parent word breaks up into the Latin parts,
sub, "under," and *verto*, "to turn." When revolutionists
"turn under" the institutions of a country, when they
overthrow and destroy its political structure, what do
they do to that nation?

They *subvert* it.

(5) EXTORT—Here again we are considering an English word
taken, almost letter for letter, from the classics. In Latin
extortus meant "twisted out," and so "wrested away,"
usually by force. How do the police under a dictatorship
"twist out" or gain a confession from a prisoner?

They *extort* the confession.

(6) SABOTAGE—The French word *sabot* means the wooden shoe
or shoes bought by the peasants who couldn't afford leather
ones. The French turned *sabot* into the verb *saboter*, which
means "to do work badly" or "to destroy a plant or
machinery wilfully so as to win a strike." Why this
meaning grew out of the word for "shoe" we don't know.
In similar circumstances what do we say that our American
workers do to their employer's property?

They *sabotage* it.

(7) JEOPARDIZE—In Old French the words *jeu parti* meant, in
the field of sports, "game divided"—that is, an even or
equally divided game. When a game is even, each player
feels that he is in danger of losing, and for this reason the
words *jeu parti* also grew to mean "uncertainty," and
finally these words became *jeopardy* and *jeopardize* in
English, and the English word grew stronger with the
years. Now when soldiers enter a dangerous battle

They *jeopardize* their lives.

(8) DECAPITATE—In Latin the word *decapito* splits into *de*, "off,"

and *caput,* "head," or "off with his head." In China what
do the executioners usually do to their victim?

They *decapitate* him.

II. You have met 8 words and some of them may possibly be
new to you. Here is a little test that may help to fix them in
your mind. Each word or phrase in the second column applies
to one particular word in the first column. See if you can pair
them off. Refer back as little as possible to Section I.

1. lacerate	*a.* to overthrow
2. ravage	*b.* to chop someone's head off
3. decimate	*c.* to damage an employer's plant
4. subvert	*d.* to tear roughly
5. extort	*e.* to kill a large part of the enemy
6. decapitate	*f.* to place in danger
7. jeopardize	*g.* to lay waste or destroy
8. sabotage	*h.* to obtain from a person by violence

Answers: 1—*d;* 2—*g;* 3—*e;* 4—*a;* 5—*h;* 6—*b;* 7—*f;* 8—*c.*

III. Now to turn this around another way. Each of the following
sentences identifies a word in the above list. The order of the
words is changed. Try to fill in the blank space with the word
that will give sense to the sentence. The tense of the verb may
be changed, as *subvert* to *subverts* or *subverted.* You are helped
with telltale initial letters.

(1) The racketeer, at the point of a gun, e_____ money from
his victim.

(2) The strikers were bitter and s_____ the factory.

(3) Attila, the Hun, r_____ the villages as he marched
through with his destroying hordes.

(4) In Old England the executioners often d_____ a criminal.

(5) The slaughter was great as the defenders d_____ the
invaders.

(6) Mountain climbers continually j_____ their lives.

(7) The rough edges of sarcasm are apt to l_____ the feelings of a sensitive person.

(8) The communists plan to s_____ the government.

Answers: 1—extorted; 2—sabotaged; 3—ravaged; 4—decapitated; 5—decimated; 6—jeopardize; 7—lacerate; 8—subvert.

IV. One good way to build a vocabulary is to change words to other parts of speech. Can you transfer these verbs into their noun forms? Two of them do not change at all.

(1) lacerate	(5) extort
(2) ravage	(6) decapitate
(3) decimate	(7) jeopardize
(4) subvert	(8) sabotage

Answers: 1—laceration; 2—ravage; 3—decimation; 4—subversion; 5—extortion; 6—decapitation; 7—jeopardy; 8—sabotage.

V. Cover the foregoing list with your hand or with a piece of paper and see how many of these eight words you can recall.

1. l_____	5. e_____
2. r_____	6. d_____
3. d_____	7. j_____
4. s_____	8. s_____

Now check your results against Section IV. If you tripped up on two or three of them don't worry. It all takes time.

Before you end the chapter, review the words in Section I. Then look away from the page and see how many you can remember and say out loud with their proper pronunciations.

VI. There are other verbs of action that can be included in this group, verbs that are filled with dynamite. There is *bludgeon*, for instance, that means to strike with a short club or, figuratively, to use violent arguments or criticisms, as, "You can

neither *bludgeon* nor cajole a person into accepting this truth."
Garrotte, glutted, and *writhe* are three other violent terms, *garrotte*
meaning to strangle or throttle in order to rob; *glutted* meaning
filled to excess, as, "They were *glutted* with victory"; and *writhe,*
of course, meaning to twist and contort.

Here is an amusing and provocative side light on words. I
have found if you wish to give vocabulary tests to others,
you will soon discover that most people are loath to
expose themselves to the challenge. They seem to guess
in advance that when they get through you are going to
know a little too much about their intellectual level. And
they are right, for vocabulary is a telltale of I.Q.

But however eager you are to improve your vocabulary,
don't hurry too much about adding to your word supply.
If you make hard work of it you may tire of it and it
might be just as well to quit for a while when it stops being
fun.

Of course this all depends on your type of mind. You
may be the tireless student who enjoys setting himself or
herself a difficult chore. But on the whole, it is best to
pick up this work much as a woman does her knitting.
If you will do this regularly for a few minutes each day
you will accomplish wonders.

> Most men paint, fish or collect
> stamps. My hobby is the dictio-
> nary.   ASHURST

7. Verbs for Everyday Use

THE OLD-FASHIONED method of building a vocabulary was by rote. The spelling and the pronunciation of a
new word were taught, the dictionary definition was
given, and the pupil was then asked to commit these items
to memory by repetition.

This plan is not without its value. Memorizing and repetition must be a part of the scheme, but if these are used alone the words are apt to be soon forgotten.

In this book, as far as possible, the indirect method is being used. When a new word is met you will be asked to some extent to guess at its meaning. Gradually the significance of the new term will dawn on you, and when you approach it this way the chances that it will stay with you are much greater. And from then on you will be surprised how often you will come upon these same words in your daily reading.

I. The words in this chapter are going to be introduced to you first in sentences. Read them out loud in their context and see if you don't get at least a glimmer of the meanings of those that are unfamiliar to you.

(1) They *aver* (ă vur′) that they have been faithful and have carried out the orders.

(2) In order to gain votes the politicians *pander* (pan′dur) to the greed of the people.

(3) He is *beset* (be set′) on every side with trouble.

(4) A judge will often *adjure* (ă jŏŏr′) the prisoner to lead a better life.

(5) Years of failure began to toughen him and *inure* (in yŏŏr′) him to disappointment.

(6) Look out or she will use her charms to *inveigle* (in vā′g′l) you into marriage against your will.

(7) They have honest-appearing faces but their actions *belie* (be lie′) their looks.

(8) It was an awesome sight to watch Vesuvius *disgorge* (dis gorj′) its smoke and molten lava.

(9) The reporters planned to *accost* (ă cost′) the Senator as soon as he came out of the White House.

(10) It was beautiful to see the diamond *coruscate* (kor′ us kate) in the light.

(11) Your food is so hearty that if I eat any more it will *satiate* (say'shi ate) me.

(12) He was only suspected of tax fraud but this new evidence will surely *incriminate* (in krim'i nate) him.

II. Some of these words were probably old friends of yours to begin with. Others were mere acquaintances. A few, perhaps, complete strangers. But by the time you finish this chapter they should all be a part of your working vocabulary.

We will try these words from another angle.

Listed below are the twelve words you have just covered. After each word are four choices lettered A, B, C, and D. It is your job to check that one of the four lettered words or phrases you believe to be *nearest in meaning* to the key word. Three of each of the four choices are wrong. One is correct. It will help you if you refer to Section I.

(1) AVER—A: to deny. B: to assert. C: to lie. D: to delay.

(2) PANDER A: to bog. B: to minister to the passions of others for profit. C: to mumble incoherently. D: to hate and loathe.

(3) BESET—A: to be stubborn. B: to conquer. C: to be bothered and harassed. D: to guarantee.

(4) ADJURE—A: to swear to. B: to detest. C: to bring to an end. D: to entreat earnestly.

(5) INURE—A: to harden. B: to flatter. C: to grow fat. D: to demand.

(6) INVEIGLE—A: to act the fool. B: to entice. C: to tell an untruth. D: to surrender.

(7) BELIE—A: to recline. B: to wheedle. C: to trust. D: to prove false.

(8) DISGORGE—A: to grow fat. B: to abhor. C: to eject. D: to confess.

(9) ACCOST—A: to speak to first. B: to pay for. C: to insult. D: to strike.

(10) CORUSCATE—A: to dance. B: to get rusty. C: to shout. D: to sparkle.

(11) SATIATE—A: to be gracious. B: to gratify beyond the natural desire. C: to waver or be uncertain. D: to be hungry.

(12) INCRIMINATE—A: to overcome. B: to treat unfairly. C: to injure purposely. D: to involve criminally.

Answers: 1—B; 2—B; 3—C; 4—D; 5—A; 6—B; 7—D; 8—C; 9—A; 10—D; 11—B; 12—D.

III. The meanings of the words that have been indicated are correct but somewhat limited in scope. Most words have a variety of meanings and the more meanings you know the more valuable the words become to you. We will now cover the above words again in a more expansive way.

(1) AVER: To declare positively; to assert formally; to affirm confidently from positive knowledge as "I *aver* that my motives are sincere."

(2) PANDER: To minister to the passions and prejudices of others, usually for personal profit, as "The religious charlatan *panders* to the fears of the people."

(3) BESET: Harassed; embarrassed; attacked on all sides; hemmed in; encompassed, as "Millions in India are *beset* by starvation and abject poverty."

(4) ADJURE: To earnestly entreat; to urge; to appeal to; to solemnly command, as "We *adjure* you not to criticize our actions until you hear our side of the story."

(5) INURE: To harden or toughen; to become habituated or accustomed to, as "The inhabitants of the arctic are *inured* to cold."

(6) INVEIGLE: To beguile; to wheedle; to persuade by deception or flattery, as "The agent *inveigled* his client into an unwise investment."

(7) BELIE: To give the lie to; to show to be wrong; to misrepresent, as "His brave front *belied* his cowardly heart."

(8) DISGORGE: To eject or to vomit, as a volcano that *disgorges* molten lava; also a gambler may be forced to *disgorge* his ill-gotten gains.

(9) ACCOST: To come up and speak to first; to approach and address with a remark, as "He was a friendly man who was apt to *accost* any stranger."

(10) CORUSCATE: To give out sparkles of light; to flash or glitter, as "The dowager fairly *coruscated* with jewels."

(11) SATIATE: To fill to repletion; to satisfy beyond the natural desire; to disgust and weary with too much, as "The little boy became *satiated* with sweets."

(12) INCRIMINATE: To connect with crime or to charge with crime; to show to be guilty, as "He refused to answer as he claimed it might *incriminate* him."

IV. Now let's return to the 12 words that we started this chapter with. Are you familiar enough with them to recognize them from the descriptions given below? Incidentally, they will be presented in a different order. Each phrase refers to one of the words you have had. Try to complete the assignment without referring back to the other Sections. The initial letters will help you. Sometimes the words will appear in a different form, as *belie, belies, belied,* or *belying.*

(1) He has suffered so long that he has become used to pain. "He is i_____ to pain."

(2) He has eaten so much food that he feels stuffed and uncomfortable. "He is s_____ with food."

(3) He wheedled the man into buying the worthless stock. "He i_____ the man into buying."

(4) He was investigated and his crime was discovered. "The evidence was i_____."

(5) He gained his office by making promises that appealed to the greed of the people. "He p_____ to the passions of the people."

(6) He solemnly commanded the young man to mend his ways. "He a_____ the young man to mend his ways."

(7) He asserted positively that he had paid the bill. "He a_____ that he had paid the bill."

(8) He saw the icicles, like so many gems, sparkling in the sun. "He saw the icicles c_____ in the sun."

(9) He slapped the man on the back and spoke to him. "He a_____ the man."

(10) He made the thief give up his gains. "He made the thief d_____ his gains."

(11) His brash manner covered up his natural shyness. "His bold manner b_____ his shyness."

(12) He was surrounded and harassed by a gang of hoodlums. "He was b_____ by hoodlums."

Answers: 1—inured; 2—satiated; 3—inveigled; 4—incriminating; 5—pandered; 6—adjured; 7—averred; 8—coruscating; 9—accosted; 10—disgorge; 11—belied; 12—beset.

V. Did you notice in Section IV that the proper word often made the sentence shorter? A shorter sentence usually gains in power.

These 12 words that you are becoming familiar with are not all easy. It will take several rehearsals to make them stick. We will walk up to them from another angle.

(1) Do you normally *aver* that something is so when you are not sure?   Yes   No

(2) Is a charlatan apt to *pander* to the prejudices of people?   Yes   No

(3) When you are surrounded by difficulties are you *beset?*   Yes   No

(4) When you are *inured* to cold are you sensitive to it?   Yes   No

(5) When your deeds *belie* your high moral attitude do they confirm it?   Yes   No

(6) When a salesman *inveigles* you into buying an article is he apt to be cheating you?   Yes   No

(7) When you *accost* a man do you generally pass him by without speaking?   Yes   No

(8) You are *satiated* with food. Have you had too much?   Yes   No

(9) When you *adjure* a person are you entreating him earnestly?   Yes   No

(10) When an object *coruscates* is it dull and lifeless?   Yes   No

(11) If you are *incriminated* are you involved in crime?   Yes   No

(12) When you *disgorge* something do you swallow it?   Yes   No

Answers: 1—No; 2—Yes; 3—Yes; 4—No; 5—No; 6—Yes; 7—No; 8—Yes; 9—Yes; 10—No; 11—Yes; 12—No.

VI. Here's a restful chapter ending for you and a change of pace to try your wits. The word *run* is said to have more than 832 different meanings in noun and verb forms. For instance: He makes a *run* in baseball. I've *run* behind in my work. Can you write 10 more sentences with 10 other meanings of *run* in them? Cover up the 10 suggestions below.

(1) . . . .   (6) . . . .
(2) . . . .   (7) . . . .
(3) . . . .   (8) . . . .
(4) . . . .   (9) . . . .
(5) . . . .   (10) . . . .

     (1) A clock will *run*.
     (2) I *run* you down.
     (3) You *run* up a bill.
     (4) I'll give you the *run* of the house.
     (5) She has a *run* in her stocking.

(6) They *run* the scales on the piano.

(7) These colors will *run*.

(8) He plans to *run* for office.

(9) He knows how to *run* a business.

(10) There was a *run* on the bank.

All of this proves that we are still poor in speech if we know only one meaning of a word. Not every word has more than one meaning. But most of them have, and if these meanings are known to us this knowledge will bring us power.

Increasing your knowledge of words, as you are now doing, means mental growth. Every term that you add to your word supply opens a new door in your mind for ideas to enter.

There are those who still think that words are largely literary tools for professional writers. As a matter of true fact, word study is a very practical, hardheaded business, since a wide vocabulary and worldly success go hand in hand. New words bring new friends, new interests, new power. They are so intimately tied up with success that we often speak of the two as though they were one and the same thing.

FIRST INTERMISSION

Stories behind Words

DO YOU really want to add to your word supply? You must, or you wouldn't have sought out this book in the first place. And if you were not serious you would never have persisted up to the present point.

Then if you are earnest in your intent, try to become inordinately curious about words. Even develop a self-conscious interest in them for a while.

It's too bad that we learn to read when we are so young. It makes us take words for granted. And yet words are exciting little things and fairly wriggling with life. Let's pick up one, turn it over, and examine it.

Here is the word *love*, for instance. What is *love?* How would you define it? Is it the strange black hieroglyphics printed on this page? Or is it an emotion? Is it rather a "noun" as the grammar teachers tell us? Is it something I have just said? The sound that hits your ears? An idea in my mind? In your mind? In many minds? Is *love* really a "word"? Or just a meaning?

Yes, we forget that there is nothing so filled with mystery as a word. We are apt to think that words just happen like Topsy in *Uncle Tom's Cabin*. And yet each one has a romantic history behind it of birth, of life, and sometimes even of death. If we follow that history far enough we will usually discover that a poetic picture lies behind that word somewhere in the past. If you will search for these pictures the study of words becomes an enthralling and most important adventure, and you will find your vocabulary growing apace.

Shall we trace a few of these word histories? Though some of them may read like fiction, they are still true.

Have you ever heard a girl friend remark: "My dear, I ran across her yesterday and she was wearing the most *tawdry* outfit I have ever seen?"

Of course, the catty word *tawdry* meant that the poor victim had on a dress, hat, and such that were showy and gaudy. They were without either taste or elegance.

All right. Where did this word TAWDRY come from?

During the seventh century in England there lived a pious young girl whose Saxon name was Aethelthryth. As she grew older Aethelthryth heard the call of religion. As the the wife of the King of Northumberland, she founded a famous monastery at Ely and later became its abbess.

This holy woman had had one vanity in her childhood. She had loved beautiful necklaces and would borrow them and try them on secretly before the looking glasses of that day. In later life Aethelthryth was stricken with a throat disease, probably cancer, and she blamed her sickness on her one worldly vanity.

After her death the abbess became known as Saint Audrey shortened from her Latin name Etheldreda. Centuries later the 17th of October, her birthday, came to be celebrated by a fair where vanity scarves called "St. Audrey's laces" were sold. And as time went on the scarves were produced in quantity and became cheap in quality.

The local yokels clipped "St. Audrey's laces" to "tawdry laces." In our modern word *tawdry* the initial letter "*t*" is all that is now left of the poor saint!

Again, you, of course, know the word *maudlin*. It now applies most often to those women who cry easily at the movies—or over a sentimental play or book or any other slightly sad occasion. Such women boil at a low temperature. The history of this word explains its meaning.

The term MAUDLIN goes back to the Mary Magdalene of Bible fame who was freed of the seven devils by Jesus. In religious art Mary Magdalene was usually pictured by classical painters with eyes swollen and red from weeping for her sins.

Little by little the pronunciation changed from Magdalene, by way of the Old French Madelaine, to *maudlin*, and gradually the meaning changed too and, in the end, was applied to those who shed tears over little or nothing.

Thus the spelling and pronunciation of MAUDLIN (mawd'lin) are not too strange. The present college in Oxford University in England that we Americans would call "Magdalene" (mag'dă lin) from its spelling is pronounced "Maudlin" College by the British.

And once again would it surprise you to know that *glamour* and *grammar* were, at the beginning, one and the same word? That the "glamour" girl of today was named after the dull Latin "grammar" you used to thumb your way through in school?

We will trace it back to its beginning.

All through the ages there has been a mystery attached to words. The ancient Egyptian priests kept the art of reading and writing as a secret of the temple. It gave them power. The people around them looked upon these skills with superstitious awe. Even in eighteenth-century England illiteracy was common and the ability to read and write was regarded with a fishy eye. In the minds of the peasants this tricky knowledge was tied up to black magic.

In those early days Latin was the language of the cultured few. The intellectuals conversed and wrote social letters to each other in that dead tongue. But the masses thought that this knowledge of Latin and Latin grammar had something to do with the devil himself.

As the years went by the letter "*r*" in the mysterious word *grammar* changed to "*l*," as "*r*" often does in the mutations of language. Other modifications crept in and a new word *glamour* was born that carried with it some of the scary and mystic overtones that people attached to the word *grammar*. For the word GLAMOUR at its birth meant "magic," a "spell or charm." Now the meaning has been modified and the Hollywood starlet who has *glamour* casts a spell over men instead of over Latin grammar!

Let's flash these word pictures more swiftly on the screen. There is, for example, that gay *carnival*, just preceding Lent, you may have gone to in New Orleans. The word CARNIVAL eventually traces back to the Late Latin *carnelevarium*, from *caro*, "flesh," and *levo*, "to take away." The revel is over, the lean fast days have come, and there is no more meat-eating for a while.

When you say that a man looks CRESTFALLEN you are talking about a rooster who has lost a cockfight and whose "crest" is really "fallen." Then there is the PRECOCIOUS child, and *precocious*, in Latin, means "baked ahead of time," so, if you don't like the child you can call him "half baked"!

Suppose you were to speak of a man as *puny*. You would mean that he was slight and inferior. Well, PUNY is a modification of the French word *puis*, which means "after," and *né*, which means "born," and if you pronounce these words in the French way they sound like our *puny*. So if you are *puisné* and *puny* you look as insignificant and helpless as you did right after you were born.

And there is that *gossamer*like dress that the women wear that is made of a very thin gauzelike fabric. The word GOSSAMER comes from the Middle English *guss-sommer*, the November season in Old England called "goose summer" when they plucked the geese and the air was full of feathers.

And then there is the word TRIVIAL, almost directly from the Latin *tri via*, or "three roads." You see, where those roads joined in Roman days the women would meet on the way to market. Quite unlike the girls of today, they would stop and gossip and talk of *trivial* things!

Yes, this language of ours is full of excitement and beauty. It is the richest and proudest language in history. In the year 1789 a wise Frenchman prophesied that English would one day become the universal language. How right he was.

Two thirds of the world's correspondence is now written in English. One half of the world's newspapers are printed in it. Three quarters of the world's broadcasts are delivered in English. And this language with all its imagination, flexibility, and daring is ours almost for the asking.

Let's make a small daily program so that we will become masters of our native speech. It is the most distinguished badge of culture we can wear. And it will be power at our tongue's end.

SECOND WEEK

How forcible are right words.
                    JOB 6:25

8. Verbs of Exceptional Power

THIS is a truly large package of verbs for one assignment. But they are exciting words and will serve you all your life. Should you be human enough to be discouraged with your work from time to time, it may help you to picture to yourself situations where you will enjoy small triumphs by being able to know, to understand, and to use such words as these.

I. The great say that words govern the world. Outstanding leaders are able speakers, whether they are the heads of governments, corporations, or labor unions. Words can also govern the smaller worlds that most of us live in.

(1) Have you ever been in a situation where you were disconcerted and taken aback? Where you were in a quandary, puzzled, and really brought to a mental standstill? How can we explain your situation in a single word?
You were *nonplused*.

(2) In his day Abraham Lincoln was reviled by many. He was subjected to more epithets than Roosevelt and Truman put together. But today he has become a legend and hero. His character and his life receive nothing but praise.
He is *eulogized*.

(3) In the very olden and superstitious days certain rites were performed to cast out evil spirits. They were *exorcised*. Now we use this word in many another fashion. We hope, for instance, to devise plans that will banish war.

The spirit of war must be *exorcised*.

(4) You can, of course, recall more than one occasion in your life when you have been completely absorbed in something of great interest. We will say that it was an exciting novel filled with suspense. You were so intent on your reading that the whole world around you was shut out. You didn't even notice that a friend of yours had entered the room.

You were too *engrossed*.

(5) Here is a habit that probably isn't limited to old age, but it is more apt to be a practice of the old rather than of the young. You have sometimes heard an elderly gentleman grumbling and mumbling and muttering incoherently about something.

He was *maundering*.

(6) The word *spawn* applies to the eggs of fish, especially when they are extruded in masses. But it is often used derisively and contemptuously in other ways. What has a degraded neighborhood often done?

It has *spawned* criminals.

(7) Men of distinction are usually men of energy and drive. They are often moved to seek high position or great power, and they are driven by a strong desire for fame or honor.

They are *actuated* by ambition.

(8) All normal human beings court the esteem of other people. Part of the punishment of an evildoer is that he forfeits the respect of his fellowmen. What happens, for instance, to those in high office who are convicted of graft? What does public opinion do to them? It holds them up to scorn and ridicule.

It *pillories* these agents of crime.

(9) Dictator nations are not usually content merely to win a war. They want not only to conquer and subdue the other people. It is usually their ambition to make the inhabitants of the defeated nation subservient and to reduce them almost to slavery.

They wish to *subjugate* the people.

(10) You are the prime minister of a great country. You want to convince the other nations that you do not desire war. You realize that your statement to this effect must be an emphatic one. So you decide to make a positive declaration of your wish for quiet, order, and security. You speak earnestly and solemnly.

You *asseverate* your peaceful intentions.

(11) She is a snobbish type. She has received an invitation from people who she believes are her social inferiors. Whenever she has met them she has patronized them and treated them with lofty condescension. But she finally decides that it won't hurt her socially to go to the party.

She *deigns* to accept the invitation.

(12) The general has given orders for a dawn attack. But during the night he receives the news that the enemy has vast reinforcements on the way. To attack at the moment would be hazardous. What must he do to his original orders?

He must *countermand* them.

(13) When an enemy invades the cities of another nation, it takes over certain buildings for its own use. What does it do?

It *expropriates* the buildings.

(14) Some people do not believe in a college education. They undervalue it and speak slightingly about it.

They *disparage* it.

(15) You are enraged at someone who has done you a grave injustice. You heap reproof on him. You scold him, rail at him, and chide him severely.

You *berate* him.

(16) They are a small but dangerous group who are intent on getting into power. They know that the only way that they can overthrow the government is by stirring up the masses. They are rabble-rousers.

They *incite* revolution.

II. The pronunciations of these words are not very difficult. You have probably already called them off correctly. Please check yourself against this list. Before you do so, however, why not first review the 16 words and get their meanings fixed in your mind. Then, as you pronounce each word out loud, try to recall its meaning.

(1) NONPLUSED—non plust′

(2) EULOGIZED—yu′lō jized

(3) EXORCISED—eks′or sized

(4) ENGROSSED—en grōst′

(5) MAUNDERING—mawn′dur ing

(6) SPAWNED—spawnd

(7) ACTUATED—ak′choo ate id

(8) PILLORIES—pil′ lō rēz

(9) SUBJUGATE—sub′joo gate

(10) ASSEVERATE—ă sev′ur ate

(11) DEIGNS—danes

(12) COUNTERMAND—kownt ur mand′

(13) EXPROPRIATES—ex prō′pri ates

(14) DISPARAGE—dis păr′ĭj

(15) BERATE—be rate′

(16) INCITE—in site′

III. Now for the definitions.

(1) NONPLUSED: Disconcerted; taken aback; brought to a mental standstill; puzzled; in a quandary.

(2) EULOGIZED: Praised highly; spoken in praise of the life and character of someone.

(3) EXORCISED: Cast out as something evil expelled by prayer.

(4) ENGROSSED: Absorbed; completely occupied.

(5) MAUNDERING: Grumbling; murmuring incoherently; muttering.

(6) SPAWNED: Generated or produced offspring; brought forth abundantly.

(7) ACTUATED: Incited to action; impelled; influenced.

(8) PILLORIES: Holds up to scorn; ridicules; abuses.

(9) SUBJUGATE: Conquer; subdue; make subservient; enslave.

(10) ASSEVERATE: Assert emphatically; affirm positively; state solemnly; declare earnestly and positively.

(11) DEIGNS: Condescends; stoops patronizingly; thinks something worthy of some notice.

(12) COUNTERMAND: Recall by a contrary order; cancel; revoke a previous order or command.

(13) EXPROPRIATES: Takes from a private owner for public use; takes away from an individual for use by the state.

(14) DISPARAGE: Speak slightingly; undervalue. Another word somewhat stronger than *disparage* is DENIGRATE (den'ĭ grate), which means to make an attack on the reputation of someone in order to defame him and blacken his name. We find still another unpleasant word in IMPUGN (im pūn'), which means to challenge or gainsay. When you *impugn* a man's motives you question them.

(15) BERATE: To scold severely; to rail at; to use insolent language; to give vent to noisy reproach.

(16) INCITE: Stir up; instigate; arouse; stimulate. Another word with a similar meaning is IMPEL (im pel'). This means to drive or urge forward; to encourage or excite to action; to push or force forward. Ambition, for instance, will *impel* you to put forth greater effort.

IV. Will you be able now to fit each of the 16 words into its proper sentence? Try anyhow. The exercise is valuable and any mistakes will be a challenge. The initial letters of the words are offered as an aid. The order of the words has been changed.

(1) He disliked the man and didn't even d_____ to give him a glance.

(2) We heard him a_____ his good intentions but his actions belied his words.

(3) Men and women can only work together effectively if they are a_____ by a desire to contribute to the common effort.

(4) The situation had completely reversed itself and forced him to c_____ the orders he had given in the morning.

(5) The angry woman stood with arms akimbo and started to b_____ him like a fishwife.

(6) I tried to understand what he was saying but the old man was m_____ in his beard.

(7) This one objectionable volume has s_____ a progeny of obscene books.

(8) Public opinion will p_____ these agents of crime.

(9) The enemy plans to e_____ the houses of many residents and use them for his own purposes.

(10) The will to war cannot be e_____ by mere resolutions and declarations.

(11) He sat completely e_____ in the problem.

(12) Thomas Paine was both reviled and e_____ in his lifetime.

(13) It may be hard in the end to s_____ and exploit 400 million people.

(14) They were dumbfounded and n_____ for strange women were not in the habit of flying into this airport.

(15) When you i_____ race hatred you do not further brotherhood.

(16) You will discourage him if you continually d_____ his efforts.

Answers: 1—deign; 2—asseverate; 3—actuated; 4—countermand; 5—berate; 6—maundering; 7—spawned; 8—pillory; 9—expropriate; 10—exorcised; 11—engrossed; 12—eulogized; 13—subjugate; 14—nonplused; 15—incite; 16—disparage.

Such words as these will help to freshen up the battered, stale, trite phrases that most of us use over and over until they are almost without meaning. And it is well to keep in mind that movies, radio broadcasts, magazines, newspapers, books, and even advertisements can help you build your vocabulary. Watch or listen for the effective word and add it to your arsenal.

> Words are the soul's ambassadors.
>
> HOWELL

9. Verbs of Deep Emotion

WE ARE APT to become so used to words that we take them for granted. We accept these little mysterious black and white hieroglyphs that appear on a printed page as a matter of course. We forget that each word is alive and filled with black magic. Try and look at all the words that you read with fresh eyes, as though you had never seen them before.

I. Once again the romantic history behind these words will help us. We'll discuss their biographies one by one.

(1) FULMINATE—Here we have an English word based on the Latin term *fulminatus*, from *fulmino* meaning "to lighten and thunder." So when a reformer *fulminates* from the pulpit, he is lightening and thundering against wickedness of some sort. He is issuing a threat against some variety of sin or crime.

(2) ENTHRALL—In this case the first syllable, en-, means "in," and *thrall* is from an Old English word that meant a "serf" or a "slave." This term has weakened with the years, as some do, and now a girl can be "held in thrall," or *enthralled*, by a man or an opera or a beautiful scene. That is, she can be captivated or fascinated or charmed by such things.

(3) HARANGUE—During political campaigns we are subjected to the orators' *harangues*, a curious word taken over in Old French from a Frankish word related to Old High German and Old English *hring*, the "ring" of people who stood around to hear a public address. Nowadays a *harangue* is the tiresome and bombastic oration we sometimes have to sit around and listen to.

(4) ACCLAIM—An English word that is very near to its Latin ancestor *acclamo*, which meant "to cry out." When we *acclaim* a hero we "cry out" and shout our praise and applause. We *acclaim* the champion victor. We hail him noisily as such.

(5) ABOMINATE—To the Greeks and Romans *omens* were signs of things to come, and in this sorry world of ours we often dread the future. It seems *ominous* to us, and this useful word also derives from the Latin term *omen*. When we *abominate* anything we are almost using a Latin phrase, for the word is from *ab*, "away," and *omen*, "omen." We hate and loathe *abominable* things. They are of evil "omen," and we want them to stay "away" from us.

(6) ADULATE—When you *adulate* a person you flatter him in a servile way and praise him in a sickening and extravagant fashion. The Latin term *adulor* gave us our word. It meant "to fawn and cringe before someone" as a dog might do.

(7) EXPOSTULATE—If a friend of yours is doing something that you do not approve of, you *expostulate* with him. You reason earnestly with him against his actions. The Latin parent of our word is *expostulo* which means "to demand earnestly."

(8) OBSESSED—When you are *obsessed* by an idea you are haunted by it. Let's say you are *obsessed* by a desire for money. This would mean that you have a fixed idea on this subject and an unhealthy one. Money is your *obsession*. The Latin word *obsessus* gives us a hint of the meaning since it comes from *obsideo*, which means "to sit before" or "to lay siege to."

II. You now at least have a speaking acquaintance with such of these 8 words as may have been unknown to you before. Perhaps it would be best if you would review them before you take the following test. You will remember from previous tests that you are to select that one of the lettered phrases that you believe to be nearest in meaning to the key word.

(1) FULMINATE (ful'mĭ nate)—A: to fuss. B: to thunder. C: to fumble. D: to bubble.

(2) ENTHRALL (en thrawl')—A: to tremble. B: to grow strong. C: to become great. D: to fascinate.

(3) HARANGUE (hă rang')—A: to exhaust. B: to praise. C: to make a long, pompous speech. D: to find fault with.

(4) ACCLAIM (ă clame')—A: to speak to first. B: to demand as one's own right. C: to criticize. D: to shout applause.

(5) ABOMINATE (ă bom'ĭ nate)—A: to damage. B: to loathe. C: to launch an attack against. D: to overwhelm.

(6) ADULATE (ad'ū late)—A: to mix up. B: to excite. C: to straighten out. D: to flatter in a servile way.

(7) EXPOSTULATE (ex pŏs'chŏŏ late)—A: to shout. B: to exclude. C: to protest earnestly. D: to strike.

(8) OBSESSED (ob sest')—A: harassed by a fixed idea. B: enraged. C: made stubborn. D: beaten.

Answers: 1—B; 2—D; 3—C; 4—D; 5—B; 6—D; 7—C; 8—A.

III. We all have two vocabularies. The first is our "recognition" vocabulary. This really could be called our reading and listening vocabulary. When we see or hear the word we know its meaning.

The second is our working vocabulary, the one that we use when we speak or write. In such a case we have to *recall* the word before we use it. This latter power, of course, is most important.

How many of the foregoing 8 words can you recall? They will be presented in a different order.

1. protest earnestly	ex_____
2. loathe	ab_____
3. make a pompous speech	h_____
4. shout applause	ac_____
5. thunder	f_____
6. flatter	ad_____
7. fascinate	en_____
8. harassed by a fixed idea	o_____

Answers: 1—expostulate; 2—abominate; 3—harangue; 4—acclaim; 5—fulminate, 6—adulate; 7—enthrall; 8—obsessed.

IV. We will turn the words around once again. The trick is to tie the phrases in column 1 to the proper verb in column 2.

1. They shout noisy and sincere applause.	*a.* enthrall
2. They thunder forth in speech and writing.	*b.* fulminate
3. They make a long-winded oration.	*c.* acclaim
4. They are haunted by one idea.	*d.* obsessed
5. They fascinate.	*e.* harangue
6. They loathe.	*f.* adulate
7. They flatter in a servile way.	*g.* expostulate
8. They protest earnestly.	*h.* abominate

Answers: 1—*c*; 2—*b*; 3—*e*; 4—*d*; 5—*a*; 6—*h*: 7—*f*; 8—*g*.

V. The following exercise may be a little difficult if you are still unsure of some of the words. These 8 verbs will be used in different forms, as *abominate, abominates, abominated, abominating*, or even in the noun form, *abomination*. To fill in the spaces with the proper words will test your skill and versatility. Refer back to the other sections if you wish.

(1) He was an avaricious fellow, and he was morbidly _____ with the determination to make money.

(2) The audience went to sleep with boredom while listening to the orator's long _____.

(3) He grew tired of her flattery and her slavelike _____.

(4) The candidate was nominated in the convention by _____.

(5) To the decent citizens of a town vice and crime are an _____.

(6) She would continually _____ with her son about his conduct.

(7) It was awesome to watch the storm _____ in apparent anger.

(8) She was completely _____ by the beauty of the music.

Answers: 1—obsessed; 2—harangue; 3—adulation; 4—acclaim; 5—abomination; 6—expostulate; 7—fulminate; 8—enthralled.

VI. Here are the 8 words you started with. Read them aloud and then refer to Section II and check your pronunciation. *Then* look away from the page and see how many you can recall. As you repeat them, see whether you are reasonably sure of their meanings.

1. enthrall	5. harangue
2. fulminate	6. adulate
3. acclaim	7. expostulate
4. obsessed	8. abominate

There are so many ways of adding to your word power. Your most casual conversation can be a marvelous aid. The words that you have already learned may prove to be helpful substitutes for those few favorite words of yours that you may be overworking.

> Words are the voice of the heart.
> CONFUCIUS

10.   A Miscellany of Verbs

IT IS HARD to overemphasize the importance of the power of words. As a matter of fact it is almost impossible to emphasize this power enough.

You may have a brilliant idea. One that could revolutionize a whole industry. You probably need financial backing for it. But unless you can explain this idea in a way that can convince your potential angel of its value, your idea will be a failure. At the least others will know what word to apply to you.

I. Here is a small group of words that can be made an active part of your vocabulary.

(1) ARRAIGNED—ă raind'

(2) AVOWED—ă vowd'

(3) DESECRATED—des'ĕ krat ed

(4) DISRUPTED—dis rupt'ed

(5) DOMINATE—dom'ĭ nate

(6) EMASCULATED—e mas'kū lāt ed

(7) MULCT—mulkt

(8) SCOURGE—skurj

II. See if these sentences will give you a hint as to the meanings of the words you don't happen to know. They may, however, all be familiar to you.

(1) "Instead of being *arraigned* in public, the child is quietly interviewed in private."—John Gabriel.

(2) "They *avowed* that the object of each plan was to eliminate foreign exchange controls on current account."—Winthrop W. Aldrich.

(3) "They *desecrated* the house of worship."—Thomas E. Dewey.

(4) "We must rehabilitate those countries whose industrial and economic life has been *disrupted* and shattered."—Charles J. Hardy.

(5) "I have been at some pains to set forth the serious preoccupations which *dominate* us."—Winston Churchill.

(6) "We held the line against proposals that would have *emasculated* the bill."—Arthur H. Vandenberg.

(7) "Quacks still confuse, *mulct* and injure the public."—Edward L. Bernays.

(8) "War was considered a calamity sent by God to *scourge* the wicked."—Fulton J. Sheen.

III. These words are not too difficult and you can probably fit each one to its definition without too much trouble. The words will not be in the same order.

1. Deprived of strength; weakened   e_____

2. Broken asunder; torn entirely apart   d_____

3. Acknowledged; openly declared   a_____

4. Called upon to answer a charge   a_____

5. To punish severely   s_____

6. Exercise control over   d_____

7. Diverted from a sacred to a common use   d_____

8. Deprive of something by deceit   m_____

Answers: 1—emasculated; 2—disrupted; 3—avowed; 4—arraigned; 5—scourge; 6—dominate; 7—desecrated; 8—mulct.

IV. The histories of some of these words may be helpful.

AVOWED: From the French *avouer,* "to acknowledge."

DESECRATED: The Latin *de,* "the opposite of," and *sacro,* "to make sacred."

DISRUPTED: The Latin *disruptus,* from *dis,* "apart," and *rumpo,* "to break."

DOMINATE: Latin *dominatus,* "absolute power."

EMASCULATED: The Late Latin *emasculatus,* from *e,* "out," and *masculus,* "male."

MULCT: Latin *mulcto,* "to punish."

When we refer to a dictionary we often only look for the definition of the word. It will be helpful also to look for the derivation. Sometimes this will give a sharper idea to the meaning and will be apt to fix it in your mind. Also you will often find that the word contains a poem within it. If your present dictionary doesn't contain the etymologies I would suggest that you look for the word histories in the next one that you buy.

> A word fitly spoken is like apples
> of gold in pictures of silver.
> PROVERBS 25:11

11. Verbs about Your Fellowmen

MOST OF US go along through life on a minimum of words. The greater part of the English language remains a foreign language to us. This is a damaging and most unnecessary handicap—ignorance is such a nuisance.

There are so few of us who have learned to speak and write well. So why not become one of the millionaires of the language? You will find that your competition will be slight.

I. Here are a few verbs that tie very closely to the habits and doings of those human beings who are your fellowmen. They are warm and they can be valuable. These words will first be given in sentences with more than a broad hint as to their meanings.

(1) "The judge decided to *exculpate* the prisoner." He determined to let him go and free him from all blame.

(2) "I *deprecate* all the remarks that have been made on this subject." I express disapproval of them and regret that they have been made.

(3) "Some people will *carp* and *carp* eternally about the matter." They find fault in an unreasonable way.

(4) "The eminent scientists *scout* the new theory as being unsound and absurd." They scoff at the theory and reject it with disdain.

(5) "The doctors *extol* the merits of this new drug." They praise the drug highly.

(6) "His investments have been fortunate and will *aggrandize* his estate." They will add to the value of the estate.

(7) "It was decided to *cashier* the accountant." It was decided to dismiss the man suddenly in disgrace.

(8) "The general attempted to *extricate* his force from an almost impossible situation." The general tried to set his troops free from a desperate involvement.

(9) "He was a small-time thief who would *filch* from a fruit stand." He was a thief who would steal small things slyly.

(10) "The ambassador was a tactless person who would be bound to *exacerbate* still further our strained diplomatic relations." He aggravated relations and made them more bitter.

(11) "The meeting was called to *consummate* the consolidation of the two companies." The purpose of the meeting was to complete and perfect the joining of the two corporations.

(12) "The older boy would continually *badger* his sister." He would annoy and pester her persistently.

(13) "There is but one thing left and that is to *ferret* out and punish the criminals." The criminals must be hunted out by a keen and persevering search.

II. Of course, if you are going to use these words you must know how to pronounce them. Perhaps, as you read them out loud, some of the strangers will take on a glimmer of meaning. A few are hard, and it may take a bit of doing to get them to stick in your mind. Here they are.

    (1) EXCULPATE—ex'kul pate

    (2) DEPRECATE—dep'rĕ kate

    (3) CARP—carp

    (4) SCOUT—scowt

    (5) EXTOL—ex tole'

    (6) AGGRANDIZE—ă gran'dīze

    (7) CASHIER—cash eer'

    (8) EXTRICATE—ex'trĭ kate

    (9) FILCH—filch

    (10) EXACERBATE—egz ăs'ur bate

    (11) CONSUMMATE—kon'sŭ mate

    (12) BADGER—bă'jur

    (13) FERRET—fer'it

III. Before you try this next test why not run through the pronunciation list again with your mind on the meanings. If any of them are foggy go back to Section I and give yourself a review. Then try to fill in the blank spaces in the sentences below with the proper words. The forms of the words may be slightly changed, but, since it is a hard exercise, the order of the words will be kept the same so that it will be easy for you to refer to the previous sections should you get into trouble.

(1) The father e_____ his son from all complicity in the crime.

(2) I bitterly d_____ your discourteous remarks.

(3) When one does nothing but criticize and c_____ it gets to be extremely tiresome.

(4) I respect your judgment in most things but I s_____ your modern ideas about the upbringing of children.

(5) We who are his followers most naturally e_____ his virtues to the skies.

(6) His sound investments will a_____ the family fortune.

(7) I neglected my job and I can't blame the boss for c_____ me.

(8) My position was untenable and I was most grateful to my friend who e_____ me.

(9) What a cheap thief. He even f_____ money from a poor box.

(10) I was exasperated and e_____ by his persistent criticisms.

(11) He faced failure after failure, but after many long years and with very great effort his success was finally c_____.

(12) It seems to be the habit of good friends to tease and b_____ each other.

(13) She was a determined gossip and in the end would f_____ out all the secrets of her neighborhood.

Answers: 1—exculpated; 2—deprecate; 3—carp; 4—scout; 5—extol; 6—aggrandize; 7—cashiering; 8—extricated; 9—filched; 10—exacerbated; 11—consummated; 12—badger; 13—ferret.

IV. In each blank space write down the word that the sentence reminds you of. The order of the words has been changed.

1. He continually increased his wealth and power. _____

2. I got more and more irritated. _____

3. I'm out of a job now. _____

4. I have to laugh at your silly ideas. _____

5. If anyone can dig out the secret, he can. _____

6. He was a pickpocket. _____

7. He's a born tease. _____

8. I thought he was guilty but he isn't. _____

9. Some dramatic reviewers are destructive and continually find nothing but fault. _____

10. Was I glad to get out of that jam! _____

11. Everybody is a hero worshiper. _____

12. The deal was finally completed. _____

13. I'm sorry about what you said. _____

Answers: 1—aggrandize; 2—exacerbate; 3—cashier; 4—scout; 5—ferret; 6—filch; 7—badger; 8—exculpate; 9—carp; 10—extricate; 11—extol; 12—consummate; 13—deprecate.

V. Here are the 13 words listed in their original order. Do you remember all the pronunciations? As you say them out loud try to recall their meanings.

1. exculpate	7. cashier
2. deprecate	8. extricate
3. carp	9. filch
4. scout	10. exacerbate
5. extol	11. consummate
6. aggrandize	12. badger

13. ferret

This may not have been an easy group to master. Such words as *exacerbate, exculpate, consummate, aggrandize* are in the upper echelons of vocabulary. But they are words of power, just the same, and cannot be omitted from cultured speech. It may be that you won't often use them in your conversation, but you will meet them in your reading and you will be apt to hear them should you listen to world leaders on the radio or television. And being familiar with them when you hear them is of the highest importance.

We must know words to be good citizens. We must be able to understand what our leaders in this country are trying to tell us. There may be a charlatan among them who is using words to deceive us. If we are shrewd in word values we will detect the deception, and we will be better able to know whom it is wise to follow.

> The unaccountable spell that
> lurks in a syllable.   HAWTHORNE

12.   Verbs of Energy

IF YOU have never consciously tried to develop your word power and if you will make this book a beginning, you will discover that you have taken up the most delightful and valuable pastime there is. You will begin to understand that the great men of the world are great because, through command of their vocabulary, they are able to make others see and feel what they feel and see. If you will use this book as a means to this power you will have at your service the greatest force ever put into the hands of man.

I. Words, like people, have personalities. Some verbs are quiet. And some, like most of those that we are about to examine, have energy. We will break the 14 words up into two sections. Here is the way those of the first group are pronounced.

(1) ENGENDER—en jen'der   (4) OBTRUDE—ob trōōd'

(2) HARRY—hăr'ĭ   (5) TRANSFIX—trans fix'

(3) CATAPULT—cat'ă pult   (6) EFFACE—ĕ face'

       (7) APPROPRIATE—ă prō'prĭ ate

II. Set alone and out of its context, the meaning of a word will not be clear. Words have little significance when they stand apart from a phrase. They take on true meaning only when their sleeves are rolled up and when they are put to work in a sentence. So . . .

(1) I'm afraid that your remarks will *engender* ill feeling.

(2) Why do you *harry* and worry him all the time?

(3) In a moment the cannon will *catapult* the circus clown out into the net.

(4) The ugly decorations in her house *obtrude* upon the senses unpleasantly.

(5) She can *transfix* a man with a look.

(6) I tried to *efface* from my mind all memory of the tragedy.

(7) America did not *appropriate* even a square inch of territory for her own use.

III. You may be near enough their meanings now to take a test. Remember, pick that particular one of the lettered words or phrases that you believe to be *nearest in meaning* to the key word.

(1) ENGENDER—A: to confuse. B: to produce or bring into existence. C: to frighten.

(2) HARRY—A: to pester. B: to delay. C: to strike with the fist.

(3) CATAPULT—A: to make an orderly list. B: to build. C: to hurtle through the air.

(4) OBTRUDE—A: to insult. B: to thrust forward or force upon. C: to be stupid.

(5) TRANSFIX—A: to make and hold motionless. B: to repair. C: to change in form and appearance.

(6) EFFACE—A: to stand before. B: to turn about. C: to wipe out.

(7) APPROPRIATE—A: to be polite and thoughtful. B: to take for one's own use. C: to commend or approve.

Answers: 1—B; 2—A; 3—C; 4—B; 5—A; 6—C; 7—B.

IV. Here are 7 more words that belong in our present category. We will first pronounce them.

        (1) ACCENTUATE—ak sen'choŏ ate

        (2) EPITOMIZE—e pit'ŏ mize

        (3) BURGEON—bur'jun

        (4) IMBUE—im bū'

        (5) GALVANIZE—gal'vă nize

        (6) MITIGATE—mit'ĭ gate

        (7) EXCISE—ek'size

V. These sentences will help to make the meaning clearer.

(1) That hat will *accentuate* your blue eyes.

(2) These brief outlines of yours *epitomize* all the things that were said in the longer report.

(3) It is thrilling to see the flowers *burgeon* in the spring.

(4) We try to *imbue* our children with high ideals.

(5) His eloquence will *galvanize* the nation into action.

(6) This drug was designed to *mitigate* pain and thus relieve the sufferer.

(7) We must *excise* the cancer of corruption from the body politic of our city.

VI. Again you are to pick the word or phrase below that you think is *nearest in meaning* to the key word.

(1) ACCENTUATE—A: to emphasize. B: to hurt. C: to hasten.

(2) EPITOMIZE—A: to make longer. B: to summarize. C: to make stronger.

(3) BURGEON—A: to boil. B: to wither. C: to put out buds.

(4) IMBUE—A: to warn. B: to fill. C: to force.

(5) GALVANIZE—A: to stimulate. B: to deceive. C: to weaken.

(6) MITIGATE—A: to increase. B: to soften. C: to explain.

(7) EXCISE—A: to excite. B: to apologize. C: to cut out.

Answers: 1—A; 2—B; 3—C; 4—B; 5—A; 6—B; 7—C.

VII. Have we moved a little too swiftly on these 14 words? It will be easy to back up and consider them at greater length, putting the second 7 ahead of the first.

(1) ACCENTUATE. This really means to "give accent to," "to emphasize or place a stress on." Your walk, for instance, can *accentuate* your age—that is, make you appear older than you really are.

(2) EPITOMIZE. Madame Chiang Kai-shek said one time: "These plans *epitomize* all that we want." That is, the long and detailed plans had been reduced to a brief and adequate summary.

(3) BURGEON. Flowers and trees *burgeon* when they put forth buds. The countryside *burgeons* when it shows signs of life in the spring.

(4) IMBUE. In Latin the word *imbuo* means "to fill" or "to steep." So when we try to *imbue* youth with wisdom we are attempting to instill it in young people and saturate them with it.

(5) GALVANIZE. About 140 years ago the Italian scientist Galvani discovered that electricity would make the muscles of animals twitch. This gave us our word *galvanize*, which now càn mean "arouse to action as if by electric shock." The rabble-rousers can *galvanize* the mob into action.

(6) MITIGATE. When we *mitigate* suffering and hardship we make them less harsh and painful.

(7) EXCISE. The surgeon uses his knife to *excise* (cut out) a tumor; a district attorney tries to *excise* crime from the community.

(8) ENGENDER. Our remarks or our actions can *engender* (produce, bring forth, or give birth to) despair, strife, hope, good will.

(9) HARRY. From an Old English word *hergian*, that meant "to afflict with an army" or "to plunder." It still can be used in that sense but usually it has the milder meaning of "to pester" or "to torment."

(10) CATAPULT. Originally an ancient engine of war that threw rocks, but now, in the case of a collision, for instance, a person can be *catapulted* from a car.

(11) OBTRUDE. This word can apply to a person or a thing. It means that something is thrust or has thrust itself into undue prominence or into some place or company where it is unwelcome. We can *obtrude* on a person's privacy.

(12) TRANSFIX. Literally "to pierce through" or "to impale as with a sharp stake or a sword." But it can also be used as a figure of speech. You can be *transfixed* with fear. That is, you can be held to a spot as though you were impaled there or paralyzed.

(13) EFFACE. "To rub out, erase, or strike out." We can *efface* the letters on a monument or a memory from our mind.

(14) APPROPRIATE. "To take for one's own use," as: "He has a way of *appropriating* anything of mine that he thinks he may need."

VIII. Review the list of words with a thought as to their pronunciations and their meanings:

1. engender	8. accentuate
2. harry	9. epitomize
3. catapult	10. burgeon
4. obtrude	11. imbue
5. transfix	12. galvanize
6. efface	13. mitigate
7. appropriate	14. excise

IX. These are partial definitions. Write in the word that each one calls to mind.

(1) wipe out   _____

(2) instill or fill with   _____

(3) hurtle through the air   _____

(4) emphasize or place a stress on   _____

(5) summarize   _____

(6) take for one's own use   _____

(7) put forth buds or shoots   _____

(8) ease suffering   _____

(9) produce, as hatred   _____

(10) cut out, as a tumor   _____

(11) arouse to action   _____

(12) hold frozen to a spot   _____

(13) pester   _____

(14) thrust oneself in where not wanted   _____

Answers: 1—efface; 2—imbue; 3—catapult; 4—accentuate; 5—
epitomize; 6—appropriate; 7—burgeon; 8—mitigate;
9—engender; 10—excise; 11—galvanize; 12—transfix;
13—harry; 14—obtrude.

X. We will end this chapter with a change of pace. Here are
hints about 5 words that end in "*-ate*." Can you figure out what
the words are? Each dash indicates a letter in the word.

(1) pacify   — — — — — — —ate

(2) use double talk   — — — — — — —ate

(3) imprison   — — — — — — — —ate

(4) reach a climax   — — — — — —ate

(5) charm   — — — — — —ate

XI. If these words are put in sentences it makes their meanings
clearer. The order has been changed.

(1) They threatened to *incarcerate* him unless he stopped spreading his damaging propaganda.

(2) They tried everything to *propitiate* the gods whom they
feared.

(3) Her exquisite voice would *captivate* even a musical dullard.

(4) I believe that his long series of efforts will yet *culminate* in
a triumphant success.

(5) Maybe he didn't tell an outright lie but he certainly did
equivocate.

XII. Now let's define the words in their original order.

(1) PROPITIATE (pro pish'i ate): Pacify; appease; conciliate; win
the favor of.

(2) EQUIVOCATE (ē kwiv'ō kate): Use double talk or ambiguous
language with intent to deceive; to say one thing but
mean another.

(3) INCARCERATE (in kahr'sur rate): Imprison.

(4) CULMINATE (kul'mĭ nate): Reach a climax; reach a final effect;
attain the highest point or degree.

(5) CAPTIVATE (kap'tĭ vate): Charm; fascinate; allure.

Here is one thrilling angle to the work that you are now
doing. With this chapter you have done much more than
merely to familiarize yourself with 19 words. You will
find as you go on with these explorations that you are
revolutionizing your whole life. Those who are masters
in this field will tell you that you will be far richer in
ideas, in imagination—that your thinking will be clearer
and stronger- that your horizons will be wider. It is
not too much to say that other people will begin to show
you the respect such as you yourself now have for those
who write and speak with fluency and skill.

Words are the dress of thoughts.
— CHESTERFIELD

13. Verbs of Violent Criticism

HERE is a group of words that will not be too easy to keep
apart individually in your mind, since they are all synonyms, in a broad sense, and are therefore close in meaning.

Always bear in mind, however, that although synonyms, as we have already said, are *similar* in meaning they are never exactly *identical*. The following verbs will all seem to overlap each other, and they do; but each of them has at least one facet that is different, one meaning that is not precisely the same as those of the other words, one meaning that gives a unique slant to the central idea of bitter criticism that is common to the whole group.

You will notice that these words differ in the circumstances in which they are used and in the objects against which they are directed. You see, if two words ever grow to be *exactly* alike one of them is almost certainly bound to die.

Let's examine them. By so doing we will be able to see the nicety of distinction that divides them, one from the other, in spite of their similarity. This exercise will serve to indicate the beauty and the force of our language and will show you how words can be so chosen as to give sharp definition and extreme accuracy to an idea that you are trying to convey to another person.

I. The 14 words in the following list pack great power, and they will be valuable to you if you can add them to your vocabulary. One, *disparage*, you had in Chapter 8.

1. excoriate	8. stigmatize
2. castigate	9. asperse
3. revile	10. calumniate
4. derogate	11. disparage
5. inveigh	12. malign
6. impugn	13. vituperate
7. traduce	14. vilify

II. Now let's consider their shades of meanings.

(1) EXCORIATE (ex kō'rĭ ate): This is a brutal word. It comes originally from the Latin word *excorio*, which means

"to strip off the skin," and this it still means in English. But, comparatively recently, it began to be used in another sense. We can say that "he would extol his own friends and *excoriate* his opponents." That is, he criticized his opponents severely and denounced them violently. He metaphorically "took the skin off" them. He *excoriated* them with his tongue.

(2) CASTIGATE (kas'tĭ gate): Another brutal word that literally means "to punish with the rod; to chastise, chasten, or discipline." It derives from the Latin word *castigo*, "to make pure." That is, you can be "made pure" of your sins by being beaten. Also this word recently has grown to mean "to rebuke or criticize severely," as "the girl would *castigate* him with angry words."

(3) REVILE (rē vile'): When you *revile* a person you usually do it in speech directly to that person's face. You heap reproach or abuse on him in offensive or scandalous language. You try to make him appear despicable and disgusting to himself. We can say: "He was a violent man who would reward his followers and *revile* his enemies." This word is originally from the Latin *re-*, "again," and *vilis*, "cheap, worthless."

(4) DEROGATE (der'ō gate): The Latin word *derogatus* is from *derogo*, "to propose a law against." So when you *derogate* someone you "take away from" his importance. You disparage him in the eyes of others and detract from his influence as: "The author did everything in his power to *derogate* the President's reputation."

(5) INVEIGH (in vay'): Again the Latin parent makes our English word clear. *Inveho* means "to attack" or "to attack with words." So when you *inveigh* against something you are making a violent verbal attack upon people or upon ideas. Dictators, for example, *inveigh* against those who are for free enterprise.

(6) IMPUGN (im pūn'): You never directly *impugn* a man's personality. Rather, you will *impugn* his motives if you believe them to be insincere. You challenge opinions and doctrines and call them into question. You assail them

with arguments, insinuations, or accusations. *Impugn* takes the color of its Latin ancestor, *impugno*, which meant "to fight against."

(7) TRADUCE (trā duce'): *Traduco*, in Latin, meant "to lead across," then, "to let be seen," then, finally, "to expose to ridicule." In similar fashion our word *traduce* means "to expose to shame through slanderous remarks." You *traduce* a person if you willfully and publicly misrepresent his conduct and character, as: "In his lifetime Lincoln was maligned and *traduced*."

(8) STIGMATIZE (stig'mă tize): In Greek, Latin, and English *stigma* means "a mark," and usually "a mark of disgrace," so when you *stigmatize* a person or a thing you brand the object with a mark of shame; you describe it in scornful terms, as: "He *stigmatizes* this era as an age of infidelity" or "He *stigmatized* the mayor as a charlatan."

(9) ASPERSE (ă spurse'): You never *asperse* persons to their faces. You do your damage behind their backs. The origin of the word is in the Latin *aspergo*, which meant "to sprinkle" or "to strew over." Also "to sully" or "to stain." That is, you sully and spot a man's reputation by "sprinkling" it with scandalous remarks.

(10) CALUMNIATE (kă lum'nĭ ate): We can say, for example, that the jealous always *calumniate* the successful. They accuse their victims falsely and harmfully of a crime or something disreputable. The Latin progenitor *calumnia* meant "a deceitful trick or artifice," so *calumniate* has the idea of deception and secrecy in it.

(11) DISPARAGE (dis păr'ij): This word is generally directed not at the person himself but at what he stands for or what he has done. We *disparage* his achievements—that is, we belittle them. We injure by unjust comparisons with things that are unworthy.

(12) MALIGN (mă line'): Those who *malign* others are apt to have an evil disposition themselves. As a matter of fact the original Latin word *malignus* means "of evil disposition." When we *malign* a person we speak evil things about him

behind his back. We circulate planned and (usually) false attacks upon his character and doings.

(13) VITUPERATE (vĭ tū′per ate): Now we are getting into the area of loud and wordy scoldings, for, in Latin, *vitupero* means "to scold." We will say, "I listened to the prisoner *vituperate* the judge." That is, the prisoner railed at the judge and assailed him with abuse.

(14) VILIFY (vil′ĭ fy): This, usually, is an indirect attack, and the Latin parent, *vilifico*, makes the meaning clear because it is formed of two words: *vilis*, "vile, cheap," and *facio*, "to make." When you *vilify* a person you are attempting to degrade and debase him or his acts and make them appear "vile" to others. You are speaking evil of him and are trying to render him despicable and disgusting, as: "It was his practice to *vilify* his enemies." *Vilification* of another is usually unjustifiable and is generally the product of ill nature.

As has been said, the exact distinctions between these words may be hard to remember. They are here largely for reference. But the more adept you become in using words in their exact senses, the more nearly you will be able to transfer an idea from your mind to the mind of others without loss or blur. And the more power there will be to your speech.

There are several hooks, however, that may help to keep these differences in meanings in mind.

When you *revile*, *vituperate*, or *inveigh* you are speaking, not writing, your criticisms. Some of the other words can be either written or spoken. When you *disparage*, *derogate*, *asperse*, or *calumniate* you are doing it behind your victim's back. When you *vituperate* or *revile* you are telling him what you think of him to his face.

The majority of these words are attacks on an individual's character or reputation. *Inveigh*, however, is a wordy attack that can also be leveled against general opinions or doctrines, as can the words *impugn* and *stigmatize*. And when we *disparage* a person we are not reflecting on his character but on his accomplishments.

It may help you to remember that *excoriate* means "to skin alive" with criticism if you will associate it with the word *score*. When we *score* a board, as you know, we mark it with scratches or gashes. In *castigate* you can almost hear the blows of the rod. *Malign* suggests the evil that lies in the heart of one who *maligns* another. *Vituperate* is a noisy word and will be remindful of loud spoken abuse. *Vilify* and *revile* are suggestive of "vile." *Derogate* rather sounds like dragging down or taking away—and that's what you are doing to your victim's character.

With *stigmatize* you can think of sticking a sign of shame on someone; and *asperse* recalls the word "disperse" or scatter. When we *asperse* a person, you will remember, we "scatter" or sprinkle spots on his character.

You may be able to devise better ways for yourself of remembering these words. We are not going to test you on them. It would be impractical to do that as the line between them is finely drawn. We will have to leave it to you to make these words friends of yours. If you are successful you will find that your reward will be great.

> Words are the most powerful
> drug used by mankind. KIPLING

14. Verbs We Sometimes Neglect

YOU HAVE two main word reservoirs: the one you draw from in understanding people, and the one with which you make others understand you. Keep filling these two and your power will grow apace, for both are invaluable aids to any success you may wish to have.

I. The following 10 usable words will first be presented to you in brief sentences. You will no doubt know the meanings of some of the words. See whether the short sentences will be enough to reveal to you the meanings of the strangers.

(1) He was *bereft* (be reft') of his sanity.

(2) He felt *abased* (ă baste') by the scandal.

(3) The mob *ransacked* (ran'sakt) the store.

(4) The barbarians were *ravishing* (rav'ish ing) the Alexandrian Library.

(5) The *beleaguered* (be lee'gurd) town was starving.

(6) His name was *emblazoned* (em blay'zŭnd) on banners all over the city.

(7) He found that his liberties would now be severely *constricted* (kon strikt'ed).

(8) He felt *constrained* (kon strain'd') to resign.

(9) He is continually *truckling* (truk'ling) to his boss.

(10) He had been *cosseted* (kŏs'it ed) from childhood up.

II. Are you still in doubt about some of these words? Then it may help you to see how they have been used by well-known people.

1. "Had all religious and military themes been taken away from the artists of the past it would have left them sadly *bereft*." —Monroe E. Deutsch.

2. "Mentally he *abased* himself. He had been a traitor to his own better nature."—Don Marquis.

3. "Under their rule your homes would be *ransacked*."—Ellery Marsh Egan.

4. "In those days a ruthless military and air power was *ravishing* all Europe."—Yates Sterling, Jr.

5. "A desperate sortie issued from the gates of the *beleaguered* city."—Stephen Vincent Benét.

6. "Your inspiring words will always be *emblazoned* in my memory."—Douglas MacArthur.

7. "It is a conflict between liberal ways of life and narrowly *constricted* ones."—Francis B. Sayre.

8. "Let us, *constrained* by the love of Christ, seek to make America more truly Christian."—Henry St. George Tucker.

9. "They are always *truckling* to the rich."—Lloyd C. Douglas.

10. "His mood was the opposite of self-pity, a feeling that his life had been too *cosseted* and fur-lined."—John Buchan.

III. Are there a few cloudy meanings left? Then here are the definitions.

(1) BEREFT: Deprived of something beloved and valuable; made destitute by loss.

(2) ABASED: Made humble; brought down; shamed and mortified; lowered in estimation.

(3) RANSACKED: Pillaged; plundered; searched through and looted.

(4) RAVISHING: Seizing by violence; violating.

(5) BELEAGUERED: Encompassed by force; besieged.

(6) EMBLAZONED: Set off in resplendent colors; inscribed as though with heraldic emblems; pictured prominently.

(7) CONSTRICTED: Drawn together or compressed; cramped; bound.

(8) CONSTRAINED: Compelled or urged; obliged; forced to action or inaction.

(9) TRUCKLING: Yielding in a servile, fawning way; currying favor obsequiously.

(10) COSSETED: Treated as a pet; pampered; fondled; treated tenderly.

IV. It is one thing to know words when you see them. It is another matter to recall them when you need them. How many of these words do you remember?

1. b_____   6. e_____

2. a_____   7. c_____

3. r_____   8. c_____

4. r_____   9. t_____

• 5. b_____   10. c_____

Each day you will find your vocabulary growing. And each week you will discover that your expanding vocabulary will enrich your interests in life and in learning. Also business doors and social doors will swing open to you more easily.

After all it is brutally true that there is no excuse for a word bankrupt. Today there is no need to be crippled or embarrassed in this way. The techniques for vocabulary building have been discovered and the texts for accomplishing this are many and cheap.

This was not true in the old days. Teaching methods, then, were primitive. And as to books, they were hard to come by.

Some 1,200 years ago, for instance, an Anglo-Saxon king of Northumbria gave 800 acres of good land for a single book and some 600 years ago a day laborer would have had to work for 15 years to buy a Latin Bible. Today these excuses no longer exist.

FIRST TEST

A Test for You on Your Verbs

YOU ARE one third through the book. The natural hope at this point is that you have developed a greater interest in words and a deeper curiosity about them and their meanings.

You will now receive a quick sampling test made up of a miscellany of verbs selected from each of the preceding chapters. Let's see how well you can recall them.

I. Here are the first 10:

berate	condone	embroil	rescind	expiate
languish	vitiate	repudiate	foist	flaunt

Now write down that one of the 10 words which best fits each of the following synonyms or synonymous phrases.

1. forgive   _____

2. palm off   _____

3. disclaim or disavow   _____

4. manifest weariness or tender emotion _____

5. display ostentatiously   _____

6. impair or destroy   _____

7. to atone for, as by suffering   ———

8. abrogate or repeal   ———

9. to involve in strife   ———

10. scold   ———

Answers: 1—condone; 2—foist; 3—repudiate; 4—languish; 5—
flaunt; 6—vitiate; 7—expiate; 8—rescind; 9—embroil;
10—berate.

II. Do you remember how to use these 10 words in sentences?

(1) Sordid and sensational books tend to ——— the public taste.

(2) When lovers are separated they are apt to ———

(3) Before we know it these angry words will ——— us in a fight.

(4) Don't let him ——— any spurious coins on you.

(5) They heatedly ——— all connection with the subversive groups.

(6) The town council plans to ——— the law at their next meeting.

(7) It is vulgar to ——— your wealth in public.

(8) Whenever she became angry she would ——— her husband in violent terms.

(9) The sinner must often ——— his sins by years of suffering.

(10) I cannot ——— his habit of lying.

Answers: 1—vitiate; 2—languish; 3—embroil; 4—foist; 5—repudiate; 6—rescind; 7—flaunt; 8—berate; 9—expiate; 10—condone.

III. We will take up another group of 10 verbs for review. The numbered key words appear in the first row. Can you pair each one with its proper synonym or synonymous phrase?

1. nullify	*a.* express disapproval of
2. malign	*b.* harden or toughen
3. deprecate	*c.* to call in question
4. lacerate	*d.* annul or make void
5. jeopardize	*e.* to hail with shouts and applause
6. inure	*f.* to satisfy to the utmost
7. satiate	*g.* to lead astray by deception
8. inveigle	*h.* imperil
9. impugn	*i.* to slander
10. acclaim	*j.* to tear the flesh

Answers: 1—*d;* 2—*i;* 3—*a;* 4—*j;* 5—*h;* 6—*b;* 7—*f;* 8—*g;* 9—*c;* 10—*e.*

IV. Now fit the words into these sentences.

(1) In a collision there is always danger that flying glass will _____ your face.

(2) The whole city turned out to _____ its hero.

(3) I _____ your selfish attitude.

(4) He'll never _____ me into buying his worthless property.

(5) Your excesses will _____ all the benefits that you derived from your vacation.

(6) His enemies went to great extremes in their attempts to _____ his reputation.

(7) A person has to _____ himself to the hardships of life.

(8) If you invest too much of your money in that hazardous venture you will _____ your financial position.

(9) I doubt his honesty and I _____ his motives.

(10) There are enough good plays this season to _____ the most avid theatergoer.

Answers: 1—lacerate; 2—acclaim; 3—deprecate; 4—inveigle;
5—nullify; 6—malign; 7—inure; 8—jeopardize; 9—
impugn; 10—satiate.

V. This third and final list of words will complete your test on the
verbs that you have been studying. There will be three choices
after each key word. In each case check the one, A, B, or C, that
you think is *nearest in meaning* to the key word.

(1) ASPERSE—A: to scatter. B: to slander. C: to be profane.

(2) EFFECTUATE—A: to assume an unnatural manner. B: to
bring about or cause. C: to exchange.

(3) COERCE—A: to persuade by soft words. B: to grow angry.
C: to force.

(4) SUBVERT—A: to overthrow. B: to deceive. C: to support.

(5) EXPOSTULATE—A: to remonstrate. B: to explode in rage.
C: to put off or delay.

(6) CONFUTE—A: to embarrass. B: to prove to be wrong. C: to
deny a request.

(7) BADGER—A: to cheat. B: to entertain. C: to torment by
teasing.

(8) OBTRUDE—A: to force oneself in where not wanted. B: to
block or obstruct. C: to be stubborn.

(9) CARP—A: to find fault unreasonably. B: to be generally
irritable. C: to be selfish and grasping.

(10) EFFACE—A: to cheat. B: to hide. C: to wipe out.

Answers: 1—B; 2—B; 3—C; 4—A; 5—A; 6—B; 7—C; 8—A;
9—A; 10—C.

You have been tested on 30 verbs that have been selected
in such a way as to give you an accurate knowledge as to
your total progress. If you got 25 of the meanings correct
you may rank yourself as *excellent.* Twenty would still be
good. If you are below this I would suggest that you apply
yourself a little harder to the future exercises and that you
review your verbs when you get the time.

SECOND INTERMISSION

What about Slang?

NOW THAT we are building a vocabulary it might be apt and timely to determine whether slang should be a part of the project. What about this slang business anyway? Is it wise to use it? Or wicked? Or what?

Of course, if a scholar were to say that slang is at all times a vulgar and coarse instrument of speech, and that it should be left sharply alone, young people would be quite correct in calling him stuffy. And if, on the other hand, he were to recommend to youth that they use slang words freely, he would have their parents about his ears—and with good reason.

In a question of this kind some acceptable middle ground can usually be discovered. Let's try.

Now, of course, all down through the ages the high-brows have wagged their gray heads sadly and mumbled and grumbled in their beards over slang. But sometimes the very words they so passionately railed against, up and left the East Side and the gas-house districts where they were born and moved right into the most exclusive Mayfair circles.

For instance, when Benjamin Franklin came home to America in 1789 after a nine-year stay in France, his ears were shocked by the cheap new "slang" words that had crept into use during his absence. He couldn't believe that literate people were using such ugly upstart words as *deputize, nice, raise,* and *oppose;* or such tawdry inventions as to *advocate,* to *progress,* to *deed,* to *notice,* to *locate.* He urged the great Noah Webster to help him put down this ruinous rebellion before the language should be destroyed!

Again, the dictionary maker, Samuel Johnson, in his day fulminated against the then new, brash slang words *fun, banter, coax, budge, fib, glee, jeopardy, smolder,* and *chaperon.* What was going to happen to the young folks, he asked, if they were to adopt such barbarisms?

Around the middle of the nineteenth century, grammarians were appalled by a host of fresh slang incursions. Vicious verbs like to *endorse,* to *itemize,* and to *affiliate* had been introduced into the business vocabulary, and there were other such demoralizing terms as *predicate, collide, resurrect,* and *Americanize.* And now we, of today, use them happily.

In 1787 Thomas Jefferson was reviled for using the sordid word *belittle.* John Quincy Adams faced a devastating purist barrage when he dared use *antagonize,* and George Washington shocked the civilized world with the barbarian word *derange.*

Way back in 1599 the dramatist, John Marston, devised three reprehensible terms, *strenuous, spurious,* and *clumsy,* and so invited the wrath of the poet Ben Jonson, who attacked these new coinages as being uncouth and vulgar.

So we had better be careful when we get too exercised about slang. Sometimes it goes social fast. It was only in 1929 that the *Encyclopaedia Britannica* listed these words as slang: *bootlegger, speakeasy, fake, fizzle, bilk, hobo, racketeer.* Already the first five have moved up from "slang" to the more respectable level of "colloquial." While *hobo* and *racketeer* are no longer entered either as "slang" or "colloquial," but have become full-fledged words in their own right and very proper socially.

Slang, you see, is often poetry. It is frequently a fresh figure of speech. Witness such colorful inventions as

bellhop	lipstick	stardom
boiled shirt	newsprint	stickup
gunmoll	preview	straphanger
highjack	soft-pedal	streamline

Slang usually grows from the bottom up. It's the pepper, salt, and spice of language, but, like these condiments, it must be used sparingly and with some care and taste. Slang words are the green shoots that come up and often crowd out the dry verbiage of dead phrases. Even Woodrow Wilson, the purist, used "that is going some," "to hog it all," "to gumshoe," and "to get a move on." And it was the philosopher and stylist, Ralph Waldo Emerson, who said: "The language of the street is always strong. What can describe the folly and emptiness of scolding but the word 'jawing'? How laconic and brisk it is by the side of a page of the *North American Review*."

But with all this, it's just as well to be careful of slang. *Swell* is a swell word if you don't work it too hard. But if you are going to say "a *swell* time," "a *swell* guy," "a *swell* house," "a *swell* party," "a *swell* trip," you will develop lazy speech habits and you are on your way to the language poorhouse. You can wear a single word so thin and smooth with much handling that, like a coin, it will lose its seal and superscription and be without value.

So much of slang is short-lived and fragile. A new slang word stales quickly, and it's well to be the first to put it aside. And always remember that slang is largely local and is apt to be known only to those who are in on the secret.

THIRD WEEK

The use of the right word is
more important than the right
argument.   JOSEPH CONRAD

15. Nouns of Unusual Power

WE ARE now ready for nouns, and a noun, as you know,
is a word used as the name for a thing, quality, or action.
Nouns are the building blocks of our language, and we
are going to expose you to a quick challenge without
giving you any time to warm up. The power that even
one noun can pack is a continuing miracle. The single
term *liar* or the poison-label word *crook* can lose a friend.
Three unfortunate nouns, "Rum, Romanism, and Rebellion," once lost a Presidential election.

I. These 8 nouns have measurable charges of dynamite in them
and can be used at times with almost explosive force.

(1) If you are subjected to *derision,* you are
    a. insulted.
    b. complimented.
    c. completely indifferent.

(2) A *harridan* is
    a. a cripple.
    b. a hag.
    c. a disagreeable old man.

93

(3) If one is given to *debauchery*, he is
   a. of high character.
   b. good humored.
   c. grossly intemperate.

(4) Some people are noted for *intransigence*. They are
   a. easy to get along with.
   b. uncompromisingly hostile.
   c. corrupt.

(5) The orator's speech was filled with *invective*. It was full of
   a. railing abuse.
   b. flowery phrases.
   c. disgusting conceit.

(6) There are those who practice *austerity*. They are
   a. self-restrained.
   b. wasteful.
   c. dissipated.

(7) The *voracity* of some people is boundless. They are
   a. extremely enthusiastic.
   b. overtalkative.
   c. greedy.

(8) A *wastrel* is
   a. a crook.
   b. a spendthrift.
   c. a miser.

Answers: 1—*a*; 2—*b*; 3—*c*; 4—*b*; 5—*a*; 6—*a*; 7—*c*; 8—*b*.

II. Now that you have had some guidance from Section I, try to match the descriptions in the second column below with the key words in the first column.

(1) DERISION (dē rizh'un)   *a.* a violent accusation

(2) HARRIDAN (hăr'ĭ dan)   *b.* a hag

(3) DEBAUCHERY (dē bawtch'er ĭ)   *c.* self-restraint

(4) INTRANSIGENCE (in tran'sĭ jence)   *d.* refusal to compromise

(5) INVECTIVE (in vek′tiv)   *e.* a spendthrift

(6) AUSTERITY (aws těr′ĭ tĭ)   *f.* moral corruption

(7) VORACITY (vō ras′ĭ tĭ)   *g.* greed

(8) WASTREL (wăst′rŭl)   *h.* scorn

Answers: 1—*h;* 2—*b;* 3—*f;* 4—*d;* 5—*a;* 6—*c;* 7—*g;* 8—*e.*

III. These definitions, sentences, and word histories will clear up any doubts that you may still have about the meanings of these 8 powerful nouns.

(1) DERISION: from the Latin *derideo,* "to laugh loudly." Contemptuous laughter; scornful or mocking ridicule, as "There was a look of *derision* on the face of the head waiter."—Henry J. Powers.

(2) HARRIDAN: from Old French *haridelle,* "a disreputable old woman." A hag; a vixenish old woman, as "That old *harridan* aunt of yours has been talking melodrama."—Helen C. White.

(3) DEBAUCHERY: from the French *debaucher,* "to lure from work." Sensuality; moral corruption; intemperance; licentiousness, as "Why do you yourselves bray before them in their dance of *debauchery?*"—Thomas Mann.

(4) INTRANSIGENCE: from the Latin *in-,* "not," and *transigo,* "settle a dispute." Irreconcilability; refusal to agree or compromise, as *"Intransigence* and rebellion is the characteristic of those people."—Madame Chiang Kai-shek.

(5) INVECTIVE: originally from the Latin *inveho,* "to attack with words." A violent accusation; railing abuse; bitter condemnation, as "Victor Hugo excoriated Napoleon III with magnificent *invective.*"—Orville Prescott.

(6) AUSTERITY: originally from the Latin *austerus,* "dry; harsh in taste." Severe simplicity; gravity or rigor of conduct toward others; absence of luxury or ease, as "We can smile now at the *austerity* of the Scotch Calvinists."—John Buchan.

(7) VORACITY: the Latin *vorax*, from *voro*, "to devour." Greediness; gluttony; rapacity, as "Our tax bill is not sufficient to meet the *voracity* of an extravagant administration."—George W. Maxey.

(8) WASTREL: derived from the English word *waste*. A spendthrift; a waster; a profligate, as "Will you be the *wastrels* of a glorious patrimony?"—Irving T. McDonald.

This chapter and this book, as a whole, will give you a chance to increase the word supply on your mental shelves. It is important that you discard outmoded and shabby terms and replace them with new and shining words. For the words that you use proclaim you to the world and disclose unmistakably your taste, temperament, ideas, education, and degree of culture. So choose your words with the same discrimination that you would use in choosing your friends.

Our words have wings.
ELIOT

16. Nouns of Personal Characteristics

THERE IS probably nothing more difficult to attain, and there is certainly nothing more important to acquire, than the ability to transfer an idea from your mind to the mind of another with complete clarity and without loss of power. This skill is necessary to salesmanship, to teaching, to conversation, to every department of life.

You may have a million-dollar idea, but it will be worthless to you if you can't convince others of its value. And words, the right words, the words of power, are the only instruments you have to accomplish this. There are no others.

Great leaders have all developed the power of expression to the highest degree. By the magic of words they make millions think as *they* think, feel as *they* feel. Unless you have this skill you will be bitterly handicapped all your life. But with it you can come near to getting almost anything you want.

I. In this chapter you will deal with nouns that have to do with your fellow men.

(1) He is a man who you considered was your friend. You have performed a gracious and generous service for him. He has never so much as acknowledged your kindness and when you met him he didn't even mention the matter and gave you no word of thanks. What is he?

He is an *ingrate*.

(2) You have another friend of a different type. He had a profitable piece of business offered to him. But he happened to know that you were in financial straits and so he was unselfish enough to refuse the business and turn it over to you. What is such an act of renunciation and self-denial called?

It is an act of *abnegation*.

(3) There are unprincipled politicians who seek to gain position and power by pandering to the prejudices of the people. They will set labor against capital, the poor against the rich, or they will even incite class hatred if it will help them to power. What is our word for them?

They are *demagogues*.

(4) When war sweeps over a territory it brings many horrors with it. There is often spoliation, robbery, plundering, the taking of property by force. The countryside is ravaged. There is a noun for such acts of violence.

Such acts are called *rapine*.

(5) When a totalitarian nation conquers a country it sometimes reduces the inhabitants to the level of slaves and serfs. There is another name for slaves.

They are sometimes called *helots*.

(6) There was that desperate time in England when she was un-armed and Hitler was threatening to cross the Channel. It

was then that Winston Churchill made his speech of "blood and sweat and tears" in an effort to arouse and incite the British to action. This type of speech has a name.

It is called an *exhortation*.

(7) There are those who have a contempt for danger and are bold to the point of recklessness. They are rash and venturesome.

This characteristic is called *temerity*.

(8) There are times when almost any human being can bitterly resent the actions of another. He is then apt to be filled with the spirit of enmity, hostility, and ill will.

He is filled with *animosity*.

(9) When Benito Mussolini used to address the multitudes from a balcony in Rome he indulged in a lot of pretentious bluster and bragging. Such vainglorious boasting is often called *braggadocio*. There is still another mouth-filling word for it.

It can be spoken of as *rodomontade*.

(10) In strikes malicious damage is sometimes done to a plant to secure compliance with the demands of labor. Also, in another field, damage is done secretly by enemy agents in an attempt to slow down the war effort of a nation. What are those who do this damage called?

They are *saboteurs*.

II. There may be some pronunciation difficulties connected with these words. It is suggested that you first go over the 10 words that you have just had with care. Fix in your mind the meanings of those that are new to you. Then read the list below out loud and try to recall each meaning as you do so.

> (1) INGRATE—in'grate
> (2) ABNEGATION—ab nĕ gay'shun
> (3) DEMAGOGUES—dem'ă gogs
> (4) RAPINE—rap'in
> (5) HELOTS—hel'ots
> (6) EXHORTATION—egs or tay'shun

(7) TEMERITY—tĕ mĕr'ĭ tĭ

(8) ANIMOSITY—an ĭ mŏs'ĭ tĭ

(9) RODOMONTADE—rod o mon tāde'

(10) SABOTEURS—să bō turs'

III. Are you well enough acquainted with these words to connect each one with its proper descriptive phrase?

1. ingrate	*a.* plundering
2. abnegation	*b.* venturesome boldness
3. demagogues	*c.* those who do malicious damage
4. rapine	*d.* vainglorious boasting
5. helots	*e.* one who is not thankful
6. exhortation	*f.* ill will
7. temerity	*g.* rabble-rousers
8. animosity	*h.* slaves
9. rodomontade	*i.* a speech designed to incite action
10. saboteurs	*j.* renunciation and self-denial

Answers: 1—*e;* 2—*j;* 3—*g;* 4—*a;* 5—*h;* 6—*i;* 7—*b;* 8—*f;* 9—*d;* 10—*c.*

IV. You will become better acquainted with these words if you see them in normal sentences that are quoted from modern writers. Watch for the meanings.

(1) "Aaron Burr was a traitor and an *ingrate*."—Donald G. Cooley.

(2) "Behind those ill-guarded doors what triumphs, what *abnegations*, what partings pass and are forgotten."—Samuel Hopkins Adams.

(3) "When *demagogues* set out systematically to ruin corporations, who gets hurt?"—M. S. Rukeyser.

(4) "Until one was hardened to those tales of bloodshed and *rapine* one simply could not believe them."—George N. Shuster.

(5) "They are wholly unaware of the mad arrogance of desiring those immigrant stocks to remain inarticulate *helots*."—Ludwig Lewisohn.

(6) "The Sermon on the Mount is a breath-taking *exhortation*."
    —George Bernard Shaw.

(7) "I had the *temerity* to make this estimate some weeks ago."
    —George H. Houston.

(8) "Despite the outward signs of peace between the two groups
    some subsurface *animosity* exists."—M. S. Rukeyser.

(9) "He addressed himself to his guest with a torrent of
    rodomontade."—W. Somerset Maugham.

(10) "We must destroy the insidious *saboteurs* of democracy."—
     Westbrook Pegler.

V. These words will now be tested from another angle. Each statement made about a word will be true or false. It is yours to tell
which is which.

(1) Those who have *temerity* could never dare to
    be explorers.   True   False

(2) *Saboteurs* are destroyers.   True   False

(3) *Helots* are rulers.   True   False

(4) *Demagogues* are sincere.   True   False

(5) A man filled with *animosity* has usually been
    stirred by hatred.   True   False

(6) Those who practice *abnegation* are selfish.   True   False

(7) Anyone who makes an *exhortation* is trying to
    arouse or incite by an appeal or admonition.   True   False

(8) Those who indulge in *rodomontade* are
    braggarts.   True   False

(9) An *ingrate* is generous.   True   False

(10) The ones who commit *rapine* are savage.   True   False

Answers: 1—False; 2—True; 3—False; 4—False; 5—True; 6—
             False; 7—True; 8—True; 9—False; 10—True.

One great purpose that this book has is to encourage the
interest of the reader in words. Truly the way to learn
words is to get excited about them and to develop a prying
curiosity concerning them. Money poverty often can't
be helped. But there is no excuse for poverty of language.
A shabby vocabulary is an inexcusable disgrace.

> Every word was once a poem.
>
> EMERSON

17. Nouns of Emotion

TWO professors, Curoe and Witted, of Hunter College in
New York, made a pronouncement that seems to sustain
all of the claims that have gone before in this book.
"Vocabulary enrichment," say they, "is the open road to
putting students in possession of the means to more
discriminating, more selective, thinking, and this is because
we think with words. Words lead to concepts," they continue. "Concepts are the basis of judgments and judgments in turn are the stuff of reasoning."

Wherever we turn in the world of scholarship and of
education there is a general agreement as to the supreme
importance of vocabulary building.

I. The nouns that follow have all been chosen because of their
emotional content.

    (1) MALIGNITY—mă lig′nĭ tĭ

    (2) CHAGRIN—chă grin′

    (3) TRAVAIL—trav′ale

    (4) TREPIDATION—trep ĭ day′shun

    (5) REVULSION—rē vŭl′shun

    (6) UMBRAGE—um′brij

(7) RECRIMINATION—rē krim ĭ nay′shun

(8) FRUSTRATION—frŭs tray′shun

(9) NOSTALGIA—nos tal′juh

(10) ALTERCATION—awl tur kay′shun

(1) He has suffered indignities at the hands of a certain person. The friendship that he had felt has turned to bitter hatred and he actually wishes harm to this particular individual. His heart is filled with *malignity*.

(2) His club had asked him to give a talk on archaeology. This was his pet topic and he was looking forward to the occasion. But he was an amateur speaker, and when he stood on his feet he was tongue-tied with stagefright and his failure filled him with *chagrin*.

(3) There is the *travail* of childbirth that women experience. But there is sometimes a mental suffering that can be as great or greater than that. A woman, for instance, had lost her husband and her spirit was in *travail*.

(4) Perhaps air travel is your *bête noir*. You have never been up, but a business emergency demands that you take a plane flight. You are worried about it and you look forward to the trip with *trepidation*.

(5) He had believed in the honesty of his town's government. For this reason he read the startling revelations of local graft with a feeling of *revulsion*.

(6) It was a club he particularly wanted to get into, but he was blackballed. He attributed his turn-down to social snobbery. No wonder that the rejected candidate took *umbrage*.

(7) He faced the accusations of his enemies for a long while with patience, but finally he felt forced to resort to *recrimination*.

(8) The fact that his purpose was a worthy one made the failure the more bitter. He tried in every way to gain his ends,

but the handicaps were many and could not be overcome. It all left him with a feeling of bitter and hopeless *frustration*.

(9) He was a long way from home and from friends and familiar scenes and as the loneliness of night came on he was filled with *nostalgia*.

(10) In spite of his earnest attempts to smooth things over, feelings started to rise high, personalities crept into the discussion, and the first thing he knew he found himself in the middle of an *altercation*.

II. Are you ready for this next test? Certainly some of the meanings of even the unfamiliar words must have dawned on you. Try to match the words in the first column with the ideas in the second column. These are only *ideas* and not necessarily synonyms, but the hints that they give should be sufficient in most cases. When you are through you had better check yourself against Section I, as some of the choices are rather finespun.

1. malignity	*a.* humiliation
2. chagrin	*b.* hate
3. travail	*c.* disgust
4. trepidation	*d.* homesickness
5. revulsion	*e.* agony
6. umbrage	*f.* fear
7. recrimination	*g.* accusation
8. frustration	*h.* bafflement
9. nostalgia	*i.* resentment
10. altercation	*j.* quarrel

Answers: 1—*b;* 2—*a;* 3—*e;* 4—*f;* 5—*c;* 6—*i;* 7—*g;* 8—*h;* 9—*d;* 10—*j.*

III. If you missed a few it will help you to hold a rehearsal on Sections I and II before you tackle the next test. When you feel confident about the meanings, try fitting the correct word in each of the following sentences. The order has been changed.

1. I take ———— at your insulting remarks.

2. Discussions on the subjects of politics and religion so often end in an _____.

3. I faced the danger with natural _____.

4. His hatred for the man had grown until it was destructive in its force and could only be called _____.

5. At one time she had loved him, but his recent and most offensive actions had caused a _____ in her feelings.

6. Time after time he was on the point of success, but time after time something beyond his control would block him and he was left with a sense of hopeless _____.

7. When your accuser persists in his verbal attacks you are apt to resort to _____.

8. The loss of his son was a bitter one and left him in _____ of spirit.

9. He was embarrassed and humiliated and filled with _____ at making such a stupid remark.

10. I have a sort of _____ for the little town I was born in.

Answers: 1—umbrage; 2—altercation; 3—trepidation; 4—malignity; 5—revulsion; 6—frustration; 7—recrimination; 8—travail; 9—chagrin; 10—nostalgia.

IV. See if you can check the correct one of the three choices that follow each of these 10 words.

(1) *Malignity* is a feeling of (a) hopelessness, (b) shame, (c) hatred.

(2) *Trepidation* is the absence of (a) hope, (b) courage, (c) fear.

(3) Those who suffer from *nostalgia* are (a) ignorant, (b) humble, (c) homesick.

(4) An *altercation* is (a) a fist fight, (b) a bitter argument, (c) a sudden change in feeling.

(5) If you take *umbrage* at anything you (a) resent it, (b) regret it, (c) are afraid of it.

(6) *Chagrin* gives one a feeling of (a) dislike, (b) anger, (c) shame.

(7) *Travail* has to do with (a) agony, (b) fright, (c) rage.

(8) If you suffer from *frustration* you feel (a) thwarted, (b) embarrassed, (c) timid.

(9) *Recrimination* is (a) a lie, (b) a counteraccusation, (c) a feeling of disgust.

(10) Those who suffer a *revulsion* experience (a) great pain, (b) great humiliation, (c) violent change in feeling.

Answers: 1—(c); 2—(b); 3—(c); 4—(b); 5—(a); 6—(c); 7—(a); 8—(a); 9—(b); 10—(c).

V. We can make another move to establish these words and their meanings in your mind. All but two of them are originally from the Latin and the history of each one holds a colorful story. These ancient Latin words are, to us, like fossils, but they once were clothed with flesh.

(1) MALIGNITY: Almost identical in meaning and spelling with its Latin ancestor, *malignitas*, which meant ill nature and spite. A person filled with *malignity* is dangerous since he wishes to injure others.

(2) CHAGRIN: A word of Turkish and French origin that suggests a feeling of humiliation, defeat, and regret, as "I am filled with *chagrin* at my failure."

(3) TRAVAIL: This again comes through the French with many changes of spelling from the Late Latin *trepalium*, "an instrument of torture." Here we have the meaning of suffering. A woman is "in *travail*" when she is suffering the pains of childbirth. Your spirit can be in *travail*, too, when you are suffering mentally.

(4) TREPIDATION: A state of mingled excitement, uncertainty, and alarm, which is suggested by its Latin parent *trepido*, "to tremble," as: "He faced the crisis with real *trepidation*."

(5) REVULSION: A sudden violent change of feeling; a "pulling away" from something, usually in disgust. This is hinted at by the Latin progenitor, *revulto*, "to pull back."

(6) UMBRAGE: When you take *umbrage* at somebody's actions or remarks it means that you are offended and have a sense of injury or resentment; you have a feeling of being obscured or overshadowed by another. As a matter of fact our word traces to the Latin *umbra* which meant "shade." This same root gives us "umbrella."

(7) RECRIMINATION: From the Latin *recriminatus* which divides into *re-*, "back," and *crimino*, "to accuse." And so when we are indulging in *recrimination* we are answering a charge with a countercharge and are resorting to abusive argument.

(8) FRUSTRATION: Again the Latin *frustratus*, originally from *frustra*, "in vain." So when you are *frustrated* or are experiencing a feeling of *frustration* you have a sense of failure and defeat in whatever you are trying to do. Your efforts are "in vain."

(9) NOSTALGIA: A combination of two Greek words, *nostos*, "return home," and *algos*, "pain." If you suffer from *nostalgia* you may be said to have a "return home pain"; you are homesick.

(10) ALTERCATION: In Latin *altercatus* meant "a wrangling"; our English word means a noisy and angry dispute.

There are other nouns of great strength that fall naturally into this emotional group. *Odium, venom,* and *acerbity* are three such. A heart filled with *odium* is filled with hatred and disgust. If a person's remarks are touched with *venom* they imply a malicious and spiteful spirit. And if someone speaks with *acerbity* it means that his manner of speaking is sharp and harsh.

At this point it will be helpful if you will go back to Section I, read the words out loud, and try to recall the meaning of each.

It is sometimes hard to go over your work a second time. But your ability to accomplish anything depends on one

thing, and one thing only. It depends upon the strength of
your desire. It would be too bad to forget the words that
you have just learned, for words that you don't remember
are not yet yours.

> What a man cannot clearly state
> he does not know.   *British*

18.   Nouns That Stand for Human Traits

IN MODERN schools of the more forward-looking type,
languages are taught by the inductive method. In the
olden days language-teaching began with grammar. Words
and their meanings were memorized. Conjugations and
declensions were learned by rote and then promptly forgotten.

Nowadays the new words are shown first in their context, in sentences where they make sense, and their meanings are come upon by the student naturally and gradually after his curiosity has been aroused. The grammar
part is introduced later on and in its turn when the need
for it is apparent.

In this book the latter method is followed. With this in
mind we suggest that it may be best when you see a new
word not to run right to the dictionary. First concentrate
on the word in question for a few seconds. Let it make an
impression on you. If you do this you will be surprised
how often you will meet this same word again in your
reading, and you will be interested to see how its meaning
will gradually dawn on you. And, oddly enough, by
following this method the meaning will be more apt to
stay in your mind.

I. Perhaps the most interesting nouns are those that have to do
with human traits. We will follow out the inductive method,
and we will first meet some of these words in sentences.

(1) BIGOTRY (big'ŏ trĭ)

It is well enough to be a reformer but his *bigotry* is objectionable.

His *bigotry* in the field of religion was hard to tolerate.

We can't help but admire a sincere belief in a cause, but *bigotry* breeds opposition.

(Here we can guess that *bigotry* is probably an obstinate and intolerant attachment.)

(2) TENACITY (tĕ nas'ĭ tĭ)

In spite of continued failures he kept on trying with a *tenacity* that was beyond belief.

She was bound that she was going to be an actress and her *tenacity* was admirable.

Tenacity can be said to be one of the touchstones of success.

(Quite evidently in this word there is the element of stubborn persistence, of holding fast to a plan.)

(3) CHICANERY (shĭ cane'ă rĭ)

He gained his fortune through *chicanery* and fraud.

The *chicanery* of the so-called "tax expert" got him in trouble with the government.

I would rather lose a legal case than resort to *chicanery*.

(Obviously, this is a term that has something to do with trickery.)

(4) ADULATION (ad ū lay'shun)

The *adulation* they gave to the dictator was insincere and slightly sickening.

He received an *adulation* for his success that transcended the merits of the case.

I am human enough to like true praise but I am not complimented by *adulacion*.

(You can imagine that *adulation* is a servile and exaggerated type of praise.)

(5) COMPUNCTION (kom punk'shun)

He had a serious mental make-up and could commit a crime without the slightest *compunction*.

We'll have to teach these troops to kill without *compunction*.

His sin was slight but the *compunction* that he felt was pathetic.

(The matter of conscience and a sense of guilt are obviously a part of the word.)

II. You had best review the 5 words in Section I as you are going to be examined on them at the end of this chapter. Now that you are warmed up we will move more swiftly through the next 9 words. Let your mind dwell on each one of them for they will be part of the test.

(1) His *opulence* (op'ū lence) put him in a position where he could give liberally to charity.

(2) The *mendacity* (men dăs'ĭ tĭ) of the man made it impossible to trust a thing he said.

(3) After this *surfeit* (sur'fit) of food and drink my thirst and appetite were gone.

(4) He was rich beyond the dreams of *avarice* (av'ă rĭs).

(5) He was a generous man, noted throughout the countryside for his *munificence* (mū nif'ĭ sense).

Of course, you don't know the full meanings of these words if they are strange to you, but you must have an inkling that *opulence* has something to do with wealth, *mendacity* with lying, *surfeit* with aplenty and too much, *avarice* with a greed for wealth, *munificence* with generosity. Four more human words will follow.

(6) I have an *antipathy* (an tip'ă thĭ) for liars.

(7) In spite of all his defiance and *bravado* (bră vah'dō) he was a coward at heart.

(8) They were enjoying the *felicity* (fĕ lĭs'ĭ tĭ) of young love.

(9) He was an *ascetic* (ă set'ik) who regarded the pleasures of the world as vile and of no account.

Again the guesses shouldn't be too hard. We certainly have a dislike for liars; *bravado* might easily be a bluff at bravery; *felicity* could be bliss; and an *ascetic* sounds as though he would live a rather austere and self-denying life.

III. The 14 words you have just had are listed below in a staggered order. You are to pick that one of the three words that you think *most nearly* expresses the meaning of the main word.

(1) CHICANERY—A: foolishness. B: low trickery. C: hatred.

(2) AVARICE—A: envy. B: generosity. C: greed.

(3) BIGOTRY—A: pride. B: morbid dislike. C: unreasoning attachment to one's opinions.

(4) BRAVADO—A: servile praise. B: state of well-founded happiness. C: pretense of bravery.

(5) TENACITY—A: persistence in holding fast. B: prejudice. C: sympathy.

(6) ASCETIC—A: an artist. B: a self-denying person. C: an ambitious person.

(7) OPULENCE—A: maudlin praise. B: generosity. C: wealth.

(8) MUNIFICENCE—A: luxuriance. B: liberality in giving. C: flattery.

(9) COMPUNCTION—A: stubborn adherence to ideas. B: ambition. C: sense of guilt.

(10) SURFEIT—A: intense dislike. B: oppressive fullness. C: fraud.

(11) FELICITY—A: affection. B: blissful happiness. C: gratification beyond desire.

(12) ADULATION—A: hatred. B: boasting. C: excessive praise.

(13) MENDACITY—A: threat of danger. B: lying. C: joy.

(14) ANTIPATHY—A: aversion or dislike. B: forgiveness. C: toughness.

Answers: 1—B; 2—C; 3—C; 4—C; 5—A; 6—B; 7—C; 8—B; 9—C; 10—B; 11—B; 12—C; 13—B; 14—A.

IV. You are about to face a drill that may be a little on the hard side, so don't be at all discouraged if you end up with a few misses. The following phrases give broad hints as to the 14 words you have just covered. Write in the word that you think best fits each sentence.

1. He had eaten too much and had reached a state of
_____

2. He had a greed for gain and was burning with _____.

3. He was most charitable and was known for his _____.

4. He was a coward but put on a front of _____.

5. His admiration grew into a foolish _____.

6. To gain his dishonest ends he resorted to _____.

7. His stubborn and intolerant beliefs could only be called
_____.

8. He retired from worldly pleasure and became an _____.

9. During his honeymoon he lived in a state of _____.

10. His moral attitude toward gambling was one of deep
_____.

11. You can't trust his word so great is his _____.

12. His success is due to hard work, long days, and stubborn
_____.

13. He lives in fantastic comfort and Babylonian _____.

14. He robs the poor without mercy or _____.

Answers: 1—surfeit; 2—avarice; 3—munificence; 4—bravado;
5—adulation; 6—chicanery; 7—bigotry; 8—ascetic;
9—felicity; 10—antipathy; 11—mendacity; 12—
tenacity; 13—opulence; 14—compunction.

V. Even if you fail in a large part of this final test the practice
will enrich your vocabulary and will help to clinch the meanings
of these words in your mind. Ten of these words have adjective
forms. How many can you write in correctly?

    1. bigotry   _____

    2. tenacity   _____

    3. adulation   _____

        4. opulence   _____

        5. mendacity   _____

        6. avarice   _____

        7. munificence   _____

        8. antipathy   _____

        9. felicity   _____

       10. ascetic   _____

Answers: 1—bigoted; 2—tenacious; 3—adulatory; 4—opulent;
        5—mendacious; 6—avaricious; 7—munificent; 8—
        antipathetic; 9—felicitous; 10—ascetical.

You have learned the words in this chapter in about the
fashion that you learn them in everyday life. You have met
them first in sentences and gradually the meanings of the
unfamiliar ones dawned on you. And with every chapter,
whether you realize it or not, your power over words is
growing.

> So long as the language lives the
> nation lives too.   *Czech Proverb*

19. Nouns of Pleasant Meaning

UNFORTUNATELY, in this harsh world the preponder-
ance of words of power appears too often to be on the side
of the disagreeable. *Cruelty*, considered only as a word,
seems to have more sheer force behind it than *kindness*,
and the word *torture* more impact than the word *gentle-
ness*. In this chapter, we will consider forceful words of
agreeable meanings.

I. We will begin by listing 9 of them with their pronunciations.

(1) PARAGON—par'a gon

(2) VINDICATION—vin dĭ kay'shun

(3) GUSTO—gŭs'tō

(4) ACCOLADE—ak'ō lade

(5) VERACITY—vuh ras'ĭ tĭ

(6) PROFUNDITY—prō fun'dĭ tĭ

(7) EXUBERANCE—egz ŭ'bur ense

(8) ÉCLAT—ā klah'

(9) AFFLUENCE—ăf'flew ense

II. The sentences that follow will give you an introduction to these words but only slight hints as to their meanings.

1. She was a *paragon* of wifely virtues.

2. His long trial ended in his *vindication*.

3. The youth tackled the job with great *gusto*.

4. The Olympic distance runner received an *accolade* as he broke the tape, a winner.

5. You can always trust the *veracity* of his remarks.

6. We are forced to respect the *profundity* of his thoughts.

7. Part of her charm is the *exuberance* of her spirits.

8. The wedding was celebrated with great *éclat*.

9. Only a family of *affluence* could afford to live in that neighborhood.

III. Write in each blank space in the second column that one of the 9 words you think best fits the descriptive phrase. You may find it necessary to refer to Section I, although please note that the order has been changed.

1. great riches   _____

2. freedom from all guilt   _____

3. truthfulness _____

4. a model of perfection _____

5. intellectual depth _____

6. a salutation in recognition of achievement _____

7. superabundance _____

8. hearty enjoyment _____

9. brilliance and splendor _____

Answers: 1—affluence; 2—vindication; 3—veracity; 4—paragon; 5—profundity; 6—accolade; 7—exuberance; 8—gusto; 9—éclat.

IV. If you can do this next test with fair accuracy it will prove that these words are now a part of your growing vocabulary.

(1) He finished his piano recital with great *éclat*. His performance was (a) mediocre (b) noisy (c) brilliant.

(2) The critics claimed that his writings lacked *profundity*. This meant that they considered his work (a) shallow (b) dull (c) learned.

(3) The understudy to the star at last had a chance to take the lead in the show and she faced the occasion with *exuberance*. She took over the part with (a) fear (b) thoughtfulness (c) overflowing energy.

(4) His trial resulted in *vindication*. He was (a) let go free (b) imprisoned (c) criticized.

(5) Among all the men of his coterie he stood out as a *paragon* of excellence. He was (a) a bad example (b) a puzzle (c) a model of perfection.

(6) His play deserved an *accolade*. It earned (a) an especial award (b) an unfavorable criticism (c) an indifferent reception.

(7) He was in a position of *affluence*. He was (a) poor (b) rich (c) weak.

(8) She undertook her new job with *gusto*. She assumed it with (a) grave doubts (b) distaste (c) keen enjoyment and relish.

(9) His *veracity* even as a boy was well known. He was (a) lying (b) beloved (c) truthful.

Answers: 1—(c); 2—(a); 3—(c); 4—(a); 5—(c); 6—(a); 7—(b); 8—(c); 9—(c).

If you have kept on with this book to this point it is obvious that you really wish to build your vocabulary power. To do this there is only one important secret, and that is to have a burning curiosity about the world that you live in. If you have this, your vocabulary will grow apace. Don't just try to memorize words. They will slip away from you if that's all you do. Develop new interests and you'll be sure to remember what you are interested in and all the words that go with it. And if you will study to whet your intellectual curiosity in the world around you, it will not only enrich your vocabulary, it will revolutionize your whole life.

The power of words that you will gain by these practices is a power that is known to every dictator. The first act of the tyrant is to take over the empire of words. He confiscates the press and radio. He dictates the "right" books to read. He burns the "wrong" ones, and, with freedom of speech gone, you are his slave.

> Language is the armory of the
> human mind.   COLERIDGE

20. Nouns That Carry Insults

AS WE well know, people can be unpleasant. And so can words. There are fighting words like *liar* and *cheat*. There are poison-label words such as *kike, wop, chink*, and others without end. A right word can make a friend. A wrong word can earn an enemy.

I. The 15 words that follow are of the unfriendly type. We will take them up in three sections. Here are the pronunciations of the first group:

> (1) MARTINET—mar tǐ net'
>
> (2) BOOR—bo͞or
>
> (3) SADIST—sad'ist
>
> (4) PARIAH—pah'rǐ uh *or* pah rǐ'uh
>
> (5) RENEGADE—ren'ǐ gade

(1) He's the bossy type of person, likes to give orders and run other people's lives. His favorite job would be top sergeant in the army. He's a *martinet*.

(2) He just doesn't fit in a social gathering. He is clumsy, rude, and atrocious in his manners. He is a *boor*.

(3) This chap has a cruel side. It is possible that he doesn't realize it, but, nevertheless, he gets a strange pleasure out of hurting other people. He is a *sadist*.

(4) As we know there are all kinds of castes in India that go from the top Brahmans down to the so-called "untouchables." In between comes a middle servant class, which, of course, is not too acceptable socially. The name of the class is applied in our country to the social outcast. He is called a *pariah*.

(5) There are always people who will be disloyal and desert a cause, or who even will desert their own country in its time of need. Such a person is known as a *renegade*.

Let's see if you have a fair idea of these 5 words. Each phrase below is descriptive of one of them. Try to write in the one that you think fits.

1. he wants to run everything   _____

2. he has bad manners   _____

3. he likes to make others suffer   _____

4. a degraded class anywhere   _____

5. a person who deserts his faith   _____

Answers: 1—martinet; 2—boor; 3—sadist; 4—pariah; 5—renegade.

II. At this point we come to another group.

> (1) PHILISTINE—fĭ lis'tĭn
>
> (2) MALEFACTOR—mal'ĭ fak tur
>
> (3) CHAUVINIST—show'vin ist
>
> (4) MISANTHROPE—mis'an thrope
>
> (5) LAGGARD—lag'urd

(1) There was once an ancient and warlike race who lived in Philistia. You have read about them in your Bible. They were looked down upon as untutored barbarians, and so, in our day, a person who is ignorant, narrow-minded, and who is commonplace in his tastes and ideas is sometimes called a *Philistine*.

(2) In Latin the word *malefactor* meant an evildoer, and in English the same borrowed word means the same thing. A President of the United States once spoke of the "*malefactors* of great wealth*." We speak of one who commits a crime as a *malefactor*.

(3) Even after Napoleon lost the battle of Waterloo there was one officer in his army, Nicholas Chauvin by name, who still kept his faith in the Little Corporal. His fanatical admiration for his general and his unreasoning patriotism gave us a word for the rabid nationalist of today. He is known as a *chauvinist*.

(4) He has little faith in human nature and harbors a real distaste for his fellowman. He is a *misanthrope*.

(5) There is a type of person who is always falling behind, always slow, always late. He is known as a *laggard*.

Match the words with the phrases.

1. a passionate patriot   _____

2. a materialistic and commonplace person   _____

3. a doer of wicked deeds   _____

4. one who is always tardy   _____

5. a person who dislikes the human race   _____

Answers: 1—chauvinist; 2—Philistine; 3—malefactor; 4—laggard; 5—misanthrope.

III. Now for the last group.

> (1) MOUNTEBANK—mount'ĕ bank
>
> (2) IGNORAMUS—ig nō răm'us
>
> (3) TERMAGANT—tur'muh gant
>
> (4) SYCOPHANT—sik'ō fant
>
> (5) MASOCHIST—mas'ō kist

(1) The world, as we know, is full of charlatans who make false pretenses and sell fake wares. In Italy the word for them is *montambanco*, which literally means "to mount a bench." At fairs or other public gatherings they "mount a platform" or wagon and call attention to their goods and phony cures. A person of this type, whatever his line, is known as a *mountebank*.

(2) In Latin the word *ignoramus* means "we do not know." We have adopted this word, spelling, meaning, and all. We call a stupid and ignorant person an *ignoramus*.

(3) There was a Moslem god called Trivigan who was a quarrelsome fellow. His name came down to us through Old French, the spelling was changed, and this word in its new form is now used as a name for an ill-tempered, scolding woman. We call her a *termagant*.

(4) There is a type of man who lives on others as much as he can and who tries to get ahead by servile flattery. He is known as a *sycophant*.

(5) Some strange people actually enjoy being dominated and even abused by others, or they can get a morbid pleasure out of self-torture. Such a one is identified as a *masochist*.

Can you recall them?

1. he doesn't seem to know anything   _____

2. she scolds and nags   _____

3. he peddles quack medicines   _____

4. the East Indian religious fanatic who holds his
   arm up until it withers   _____

5. he gets along by flattering the boss   _____

Answers: 1—ignoramus; 2—termagant; 3—mountebank; 4—masochist; 5—sycophant.

IV. You are now asked to fill each blank space with that one of the 15 words that best fits the sentence.

(1) The _____ believes that his nation is always right in whatever it does.

(2) There is many a _____ in this world who actually enjoys making others suffer.

(3) I have met stupid people in my day, but never such an _____ as he is.

(4) Perhaps only a psychiatrist could explain how a _____ can get pleasure out of self-inflicted punishment.

(5) He is an apostate and a _____ who has deserted his faith.

(6) His orders were the bossy, insistent, disciplinary ones so characteristic of a _____.

(7) He is a _____ and an outcast, totally unacceptable to those of his social level.

(8) His life had made him bitter and cynical about the human race and had turned him into a sour _____.

(9) If anybody ever earned his way by repulsive and repellent flattery, that _____ did.

(10) His writing was trite, mediocre, and commonplace, the product of a _____.

(11) He was always prompt, always on time for his appointments, never a _____.

(12) They claim that the wife of Socrates was a violent, quarrelsome, scolding woman, a veritable _____.

(13) Nobody but a faker and _____ could peddle such worthless remedies.

(14) You'll meet a taxi driver who is a courteous and polished gentleman and a so-called "gentleman" who is a rude and uncivil _____.

(15) The crooks are not limited to the criminal class. Many a _____ can be found among politicians.

Answers:　1—chauvinist; 2—sadist; 3—ignoramus; 4—masochist; 5—renegade; 6—martinet; 7—pariah; 8—misanthrope; 9—sycophant; 10—Philistine; 11—laggard; 12—termagant; 13—mountebank; 14—boor; 15—malefactor.

Never let yourself feel that the task of acquiring a really superb vocabulary is beyond you. Let me tell you a true story that illustrates what can be done if you make up your mind to it.

A few years ago a young man of my acquaintance received a scholarship for the University of Basle in Switzerland. All the lectures were to be in the German language of which he knew not one single word. Within the six months of spring and summer he gained such a complete mastery of German that he was able to take and to understand accurately a most abstruse course in the subject of philology. So it *can* be done.

Words are the body of thought.
CARLYLE

21. Nouns That Are Spoken

OF COURSE it goes without saying that many of the words you have come upon in this book are already acquaintances of yours. But you will be the first to admit that you will not have the courage to use them as long as they remain *mere* acquaintances. You must be comfortable with them. Know how to pronounce them. And you must know how they can be properly set in sentences. It is time to make them your first-name friends.

I. The 6 nouns in this chapter deal mostly with the subject of spoken language. Here is how these words are pronounced.

(1) BRAGGADOCIO—brag ă dō'shĭ ō

(2) ENCOMIUM—en kō'mĭ um

(3) GIBBERISH—jib'ur ish

(4) DIATRIBE—dī'a tribe

(5) JEREMIAD—jer ĕ my'ad

(6) EXPLETIVE—ex'plĭ tiv

II. And this is how the 6 nouns may be used in appropriate sentences.

(1) We grew tired of his fantastic vanity and *braggadocio*.

(2) Never have I listened to such an eloquent *encomium* or to one that was more deserved.

(3) I have heard monkeys talk *gibberish*, but what he said made just as little sense.

(4) The critical reception of the play was mixed, scornful *diatribes* almost drowning out the ecstatic reviews.

(5) He prolonged his doleful complaints about our times into a lengthy *jeremiad*.

(6) He turned to fling an unprintable *expletive* over his shoulder.

III. I am sure that you have recognized most, if not all, of these nouns, but the interesting histories of these words will clarify them.

(1) BRAGGADOCIO: The English poet, Edmund Spenser, wrote a narrative poem called *The Faerie Queene*. In it was a vain boaster called Braggadocio. Now when we hear *braggadocio* we are listening to empty and pretentious bragging. *Gasconade* is a synonym for *braggadocio* and also means extravagant boasting. Gascony is a province in France, and the native Gascon by habit is a noisy braggart.

(2) ENCOMIUM: In Greek the word *enkomion* had to do with a celebration or revel. Now it has to do with high praise. If you have earned an *encomium* from someone you have received a discriminating and formal expression of praise.

(3) GIBBERISH is senseless chatter and nonsense talk.

(4) DIATRIBE in Greek, with the same spelling as our English, meant "wearing away." Now it means a discourse full of bitter abuse. The one who receives it is "worn away" by criticism. The words *invective*, *malediction*, and *imprecation* are very close in meaning to *diatribe*. They, too, have to do with violent attacks, abusive language, and the latter two can almost be placed in the field of curses.

(5) JEREMIAD: This is a lamentation or a doleful and dismal complaint. The word is based on the name of the prophet *Jeremiah* and writer of the book of Lamentations in the Bible.

(6) EXPLETIVE: An oath; an exclamation, and usually a profane one.

IV. Which of the above words would these sentences suggest?

1. What you say doesn't make any sense to me.   _____

2. He seems to think that this wicked world is lost.   _____

3. What a wonderful opinion that man has of himself.   _____

4. I just don't happen to like profanity.   _____

5. I wouldn't be human if I weren't pleased by praise.   _____

6. I am sickened of his long-winded abuse.   _____

Answers: 1—gibberish; 2—jeremiad; 3—braggadocio; 4—expletive; 5—encomium; 6—diatribe.

Are two or three of these words new to you? At the least this is a short exercise and it won't take long to make the new terms your own.

THIRD INTERMISSION

Word Magic

ONE completely fascinating thing about words is the magic that surrounds them and the superstitions that they are all bound up with.

One thing is certain, however. A modern like you is not superstitious about words. Are you sure?

Let's say you are taking off in a plane for the East or West Coast. It's midwinter and the weather is bad. Just yesterday there had been a terrible accident on this same flight—a crash against the mountains where all the passengers were killed.

I will challenge you at such a time to turn to your seatmate and say: "I have flown thousands of miles but I've never had a plane accident in my life."

Possibly you'll take my dare if such an occasion arises, but I'll make a small bet that you'll knock wood if there happens to be any around!

This superstition about the power of words comes out of the mists of the ages. In ancient Egypt, these thousands of years ago, the skill of writing and reading was kept a secret of the temple. Word magic gave the priests a hold over the common people. In the Dark Ages the art of communication retreated into the monasteries and was again tied up with the mysterious rites of religion.

This strange slant on language persisted in the England of not too long ago. In the days of Queen Elizabeth few could read or write. Most of the young girls who applied for a marriage license had to sign the papers with a cross. The ability to write and read was looked upon askance, and was thought to have something to do with the works of the devil. And even if you could so much as spell a word you were thought to be dealing in black magic.

This old idea is preserved in our language today.

When a woman is sick she is said by some to have had a "spell." And we all know of the political "spellbinders" who cast a "spell" over their listeners.

We, who are sophisticated, think we can smile at these childish things. But we had better not smile too broadly. We still believe in word magic.

For instance, when a man is discussing his will, how often do you hear him say, "After I am dead" or "When I die"? He's more apt to say, "If anything happens to me," or "If I should get hit by a truck," or "If I'm not around."

People don't die, nor are they often even dead. It is the "late" Mr. Brown. "The deceased." He "passed away" last Tuesday. I "lost" my father. "He met with a fatal accident." Boys aren't "killed" in battle. They "fall" in battle. They aren't "drowned." They are "lost" at sea. They "meet their end." The undertaker is a "mortician." His place of business is a "funeral parlor." The hearse is an "ambulance." And even the word *cemetery* in its original Greek sense meant a "sleeping place."

The nice words and phrases that we use as symbols for unpleasant or fearful things are, as we know, called *euphemisms*, from the Greek words *eu*, "well," and *phemi*, "speak."

You would be surprised at how many euphemisms there are in our language. These euphemisms are used on the assumption that names can alter things. And even in modern days we feel that these evasions will appease the evil spirits.

We share these primitive fears with other tribes of the world. The natives of Madagascar are reluctant to speak of lightning. They have too many frightening thunderstorms there to take a chance. The Boziba native never mentions earthquakes, and rain is not spoken of by its right name in Samoa; while the word *fire* is never said out loud in China in such places where there is a risk of fire.

Speak of the devil and he will surely appear.

These evasions even apply to the gentler side of life. In the matter of sex we go into full verbal flight.

Around a hundred years ago it was an open insult to mention the word *shirt* before ladies, so the term *smock* was invented. But in the course of time even *smock* got befouled and the word *shift* was substituted for *smock*. But over the years *shift* became vulgar, and in Ireland, if you can believe it, in a Dublin theater as recently as 1907, when the word *shift* was said out loud by an actor in one of Synge's plays, the audience broke up in wild disorder.

Of course we are no longer as fussy as Dublin about "smock" or "shift" or "shirt," but even today no real lady *ever* wears a shirt. We cover her with the French *chemise* although this sometimes nylon article may not be very effective as far as actual modesty is concerned.

In these days, as a matter of fact, milady doesn't own much underwear of any kind. At least by that name. Our modern girl wears "underthings" or "undies," or as they used to say in long past days, "indescribables," "irrepressibles," "ineffables," "unutterables," "unmentionables." Never *underwear*. The articles are the same, but, by some sort of modern voodoo, names change them and make them decent.

The advertising experts have taken advantage of this necromancy, for they have discovered that the right words *can* alter things, at least in the minds of their customers, and they practice their magic on us every day.

For example you are not asked to buy a product in a package of a large size. You are sold the "economy size." No dealer tries to sell you a secondhand car. There aren't any of them anymore. They are "reconditioned." Steamship lines no longer sell third-class or steerage tickets. They are always "tourist class." A piece of furniture becomes irresistible when it is called a "snuggle sofa."

Clothing is never cheap. It is "underpriced." There are no old men where clothing is concerned. It is made for "men" and "young men," and women's dresses are designed not for the fat figure but for the "classical" figure.

One time an experiment was tried. Two counters were arranged with men's hats of identical make displayed on each. On one counter a sign was set with the word *Tyrolean* on it. The other counter had no sign. Three times as many men purchased the gray hats called "Tyrolean" than those which were unnamed.

Another similar experiment was conducted. In the fashion described above, two lots of plain beige stockings, all of them the same brand, were placed on two tables, one nameless, the other bearing the display sign "Gala." Ten times as many of the "Gala" ones were sold. And doggy shades in hosiery such as Spaniel and Collie sell ten to twenty times more than anonymous shades. Women seem more susceptible to word magic than men!

The euphemisms that follow are truly amusing.

We don't go into a *saloon* anymore to get a drink. Oh, no! The late prohibition era killed that one! We now go into a "cocktail lounge," a "café," a "tavern," a "taproom," or, at worst, a "bar."

People are no longer "fired" or even "discharged." Their "resignations are accepted," that is if they are important folks. And when they have quit, they are "at liberty" or possibly "on a leave of absence." They are rarely "out of work."

Even the acts of dictators have gotten more gentle. They don't kill anybody. They merely "liquidate" them.

The most innocent words can get dirtied up. In the days of long ago the phrase "that rose stinks" meant that its odor was pleasant. "You stink" was a compliment. The word *stink* degenerated, however, and had to be replaced by *smell*, but *smell* deteriorated in turn and *odor* took over. Now even the word *odor* without an adjective is offensive and we are forced to say "what a delightful odor." "Body odor" has changed to "B. O." and "bad breath" to "halitosis."

In spite of Shakespeare, you see, a rose by any other name will *not* smell as sweet! You will never suspect the number of these evasions, circumlocutions, and euphemisms that there are in our language unless you become curious about them and watch for them. And all of this has to do with the eternally fascinating mystery of words.

FOURTH WEEK

And a word spoken in due season, how good is it!

PROVERBS 15:23

22. Nouns We Sometimes Neglect

THERE IS a price tag to everything. Even a vocabulary is not given to us for free. It must be bought with time and work—but with so little work and so infinitely little time, when we compare our small efforts with those of masters.

Thomas A. Edison, for instance, stuck continuously at one job for 5 days without going to bed, and he kept on at another experiment for 48 hours without a shift of attention. Victor Hugo locked his clothes in his chest to finish his novel, *Notre-Dame de Paris*. Noah Webster took 30 years to complete his dictionary.

Alexandre Dumas wrote 18 hours a day for 40 years. Sir Harry Lauder, the Scottish comedian, tried out his superb song, "Roamin' in the Gloamin' " 10,000 times to perfect it for the stage. Maurice Ravel worked 12 hours a day for two years composing a piano concerto, and Paderewski practiced 8 hours a day as a matter of routine.

So let's not give lack of time as an excuse if anything important is at stake. And a better knowledge of words *is* important. As John Ruskin once said: "If I had a son or daughter possessed of one accomplishment it should be that of speech."

Learning the 23 words in this chapter will be no easy task. But you are getting more skilled now in the work and

it may not be out of reason to cover this in one evening.
If it so happens that you can't, don't concern yourself.
There are no deadlines to press you. And, truly, these
words will serve you all your life. You are going to receive
them this time right off and in full, with their pronunciations, their meanings, and with sentences in which they
have been used.

I. These three words identify certain troublesome people.

(1) The JINGO (jing'go). Watch out for him. He'll get you into
war if he can. He's a chauvinist who is always demanding
warlike policies in foreign affairs, as: "In these days there
are *jingoes* who demand worldwide war."—Dean Acheson.

(2) The CURMUDGEON (kur muj'un). He's a miserly type who
hates to give a waiter a tip. He's churlish, ill mannered,
and generally ornery, as: "Mr. Ickes seems to think that a
curmudgeon and a reformer are one and the same thing."—
Luther Huston.

(3) The HELLIONS (hel'yunz). These are folks who are given to
deviltry and bad deeds in general, as: "Our men are determined that his *hellions* will never again crash their lines."—
Roane Waring.

II. The next 10 words have to do with the characteristics, emotions, and actions of human beings.

(1) POMPOSITY (pom pos'i ti). An unpleasant attitude, this, of
pride and self-importance. *Pompous* individuals have an
affected dignity and bearing, as: "Her air of *pomposity*
was tactless and offensive."—Pearl S. Buck.

(2) BILLINGSGATE (bil'ingz gate). This is the name for the
vulgar and abusive language that coarse people use when
they are quarreling, as: "She poured out a flood of *billingsgate* that would better fit the tongue of an angry fishwife."
—Malcolm Babbitt.

(3) FORTITUDE (for'ti tude). People with this trait have the
strength of mind to meet pain, peril, and adversity. They

are filled with resolute courage, as: "We must learn again the patience and *fortitude* that armed our ancestors."— William O. Douglas.

(4) INCREDULITY (in krĕ dū'lĭ tĭ). When a person regards something with *incredulity* it means that he is filled with doubt and unbelief. He's skeptical about the matter. To him it is *incredulous*, as: "She gave a sniff of *incredulity* as she listened to the story."—Edith Wharton.

(5) CONTRITION (kon trish'un). Sincere sorrow for wrong doing, as: "*Contrition* of heart should be accompanied by an act of faith."—Henry M. Wriston.

(6) ALACRITY (ă lak'rĭ tĭ). Here we have the word for cheerful willingness and promptitude. If you do anything with *alacrity*, you do it at once and with eager and lively action, as: "He took his place with *alacrity*, his face beaming with interest."—Pearl S. Buck.

(7) DECREPITUDE (dē krep'ĭ tude). Just a state of enfeeblement through infirmity or old age, as: "The next day he started out in a state of abject *decrepitude*."—John Buchan.

(8) BANALITY (bă nal'ĭ tĭ). The quality of being commonplace, flat, and trite. A trivial and stale remark is called a *banality*, as: "His expression of gratification was not a mere *banality*."—Lord Cecil.

(9) IMMOLATION (im ō lay'shun). Sacrifice; offering up as victims, as: "When republics encounter setbacks those in power are marked for *immolation*."—George W. Maxey.

(10) ANIMUS (an'ĭ mus). Watch out for a man who is filled with *animus*. His heart is full of active dislike, as: "His feeling was not one of mild dislike; there was deep and violent *animus* in his heart."—Owen D. Young.

III. The following 10 nouns are more general in their meanings.

(1) BASTION (bas'chun). A fortification, but this word can also be used in the form of a figure of speech, as: "They are storming the *bastions* of democracy."—Frank Knox.

(2) LEVIATHAN (le vī'ă than: *th* as in *thin*). An enormous sea animal, hence, something unusually huge, of colossal size or importance, as: "His eyes rested on the huge pile of manuscript and it seemed impossible that a publisher could be found who would publish this *leviathan*."—Thomas Wolfe.

(3) WELTER (wel'tur). Actually a rolling motion, but eventually this word came to mean a commotion, confusion, or turmoil, as: "Deeply hidden in the *welter* of casual news about warfare, the morale of these struggling people was not understood."—C. T. Feng.

(4) MAGNITUDE (mag'nĭ tude). Any time that you speak of the *magnitude* of a thing you are talking of great size, of vastness and immensity, as: "It should be possible to finance the program without increasing the *magnitude* of current treasury deficits."—Harold G. Moulton.

(5) DEMOLITION (dem ō lish'un). This means destruction. It is the act of reducing something to a shapeless mass. Such a thing has been *demolished*, as: "Entire populations will be menaced by instruments of *demolition*."—Alexander P. de Seversky.

(6) INFINITUDE (in fin'ĭ tude). The *infinitude* of time or space means space or time without limit or end. There are no boundaries in the word, as: "On a day like this one has the feeling of being able to see into *infinitude*."—Bodo Wuth.

(7) EFFICACY (ef'fĭ kă sĭ). When you *effect* a change you bring it about. *Efficacy* is the power to produce the intended result, as: "We will make the burglar doubt the *efficacy* of burglary. Then the world will become safe for good people."—Rebecca West.

(8) CATHARSIS (kă thahr'sis). Here we have the purification of the emotions. A *catharsis* is a cleansing outlet, a purging of the soul of sordid ideas, as: "The beauty in this talent has little commerce with earthly things, but like great tragedy, effects a *catharsis* in its lovers and worshipers."—Ludwig Lewisohn.

(9) FRANKENSTEIN (frank'in stine). A student described in fiction as having made a monster to which he gave a kind of life power that it finally used to kill its maker. Hence, a person or agency that is destroyed by something that it created. Something that ruins its maker, as: "They soon found themselves powerless to control the *Frankenstein* monster thus called into being."—H. W. Prentis, Jr.

(10) LIMBO (lim'bō). An indefinite border region, neither heaven nor hell, where the souls of unbaptized infants and those who lived before the Christian era are said to dwell. A place of oblivion, as: "I have faith that war will be relegated to the *limbo* of things forgotten."—Cordell Hull.

IV. Here is the list of the words you have just had and in the order that they were presented to you. How many of their meanings can you recall? Fifteen would be extremely good.

1. jingo	12. immolation
2. curmudgeon	13. animus
3. hellions	14. bastion
4. pomposity	15. leviathan
5. billingsgate	16. welter
6. fortitude	17. magnitude
7. incredulity	18. demolition
8. contrition	19. infinitude
9. alacrity	20. efficacy
10. decrepitude	21. catharsis
11. banality	22. Frankenstein
23. limbo	

V. Now you will be faced with 23 words or phrases that describe these words. Can you write in the proper word in each case? The order is changed.

1. great size   m_____

2. a pretentious bearing   p_____

3. a warmonger   j_____

4. an enormous sea animal   l_____

5. destruction   d_____

6. vulgar, vituperative language   b_____

7. a mean, stingy person   c_____

8. firm endurance and great courage   f_____

9. indisposition to believe   i_____

10. deep and sincere penitence   c_____

11. confusion and turmoil   w_____

12. people given to mischief and deviltry   h_____

13. time and space without limit   i_____

14. prompt and cheerful willingness   a_____

15. offering up as victims   i_____

16. active hatred   a_____

17. infirmity   d_____

18. a commonplace remark   b_____

19. power and efficiency   e_____

20. a cleansing of the soul of sordid ideas   c_____

21. something that ruins its maker   F_____

22. a fortification   b_____

23. a place of oblivion   l_____

Answers: 1—magnitude; 2—pomposity; 3—jingo; 4—leviathan; 5—demolition; 6—billingsgate; 7—curmudgeon; 8—fortitude; 9—incredulity; 10—contrition; 11—welter; 12—hellions; 13—infinitude; 14—alacrity; 15—immolation; 16—animus; 17—decrepitude; 18—banality; 19—efficacy; 20—catharsis; 21—Frankenstein; 22—bastion; 23—limbo.

Please don't have any sense of failure if your record hasn't been too good with these words. Some of them are in the upper levels of vocabulary. A workout of this kind is a challenge. It strengthens the muscles of the mind and sharpens the memory. Make a list of the words and meanings that elude you and review it from time to time.

> Whose words all ears took captive. SHAKESPEARE

23. Nouns of Force and Pressure

NO WORDS are as "common" as they seem. We often use familiar words with a certain surety and confidence. Yet if we were asked to delineate their boundaries we might be puzzled. As someone has well said: "What incorrect, imperfect, inaccurate, primitive, fuzzy, and woolly ideas we have about the meanings of the simplest words."

In this chapter some of the words are simple, some on the higher levels. But a lack of knowledge of any one of them would represent a slight handicap.

I. We will first meet 10 of them in definitive sentences which will give a glimmer of their meanings.

1. A treaty, where it is not imposed under *duress* (du′res *or* dū res′), rests on moral obligations.

2. He felt that the *stringency* (strin′jen sĭ) of the discipline in this school killed the initiative of the pupils.

3. He met the emergency with an *audacity* (aw das′ĭ tĭ) that put his life in danger.

4. We agreed not to remain longer than the military *exigency* (ex′ĭ jen sĭ) required.

5. The antipreparedness *zealots* (zel′uts) were defeated and the draft bill was passed.

6. He was in a high *dudgeon* (dudj'un) over the injustice.

7. I know with what *assiduity* (as ĭ dū'ĭ tĭ) the propaganda factories turn out fictitious stories.

8. His support gave great *impetus* (im'pĕ tus) to the cause.

9. Their minds and hearts are warped by passion and *rancor* (rang'kur).

10. In this emergency we must act with greater *dispatch* (dis patch').

II. After you have carefully analyzed the foregoing sentences and have gotten at least a rough idea of the meanings of the words, try to match each one with its definition. They are not in their previous order.

1. risky boldness; reckless daring   _____

2. bitter and vindictive malice   _____

3. momentum; force   _____

4. strictness or severity   _____

5. those who engage warmly in any cause; immoderate partisans   _____

6. constrained by force or fear; compulsion   _____

7. the state of being urgent; a critical period   _____

8. anger   _____

9. prompt performance; speed   _____

10. persistent and continuous application and effort   _____

Answers: 1—audacity; 2—rancor; 3—impetus; 4—stringency; 5—zealots; 6—duress; 7—exigency; 8—dudgeon; 9—dispatch; 10—assiduity.

III. One more turn will help to sharpen the meanings for you. Other forms of the words than the noun form will sometimes be used.

1. *Zealots* are people who
   a. are filled with doubts.
   b. show an excess of enthusiasm for a cause.
   c. are driven by fear.

2. A man in a *dudgeon* will be apt to say:
   a. I hate you.
   b. I will do it for you willingly.
   c. I don't dare to do it.

3. You should act with *dispatch*
   a. when you have plenty of time.
   b. on a hot day.
   c. when you are late for an appointment.

4. The *audacious* man is
   a. filled with courage.
   b. slow to act.
   c. timid.

5. When a man under *duress* is asked how he feels his natural reply would be:
   a. I'm looking forward to great success.
   b. I wish I weren't being pressed so hard.
   c. I'll delay as long as I wish.

6. If a matter is *exigent,*
   a. you dismiss it from your mind.
   b. you handle it at your leisure.
   c. you give it immediate attention.

7. A man filled with *rancor* might say:
   a. I'm looking forward to the occasion.
   b. I will destroy him if I can.
   c. I love my neighbor.

8. Anything that receives an *impetus*
   a. is held back.
   b. is helped along.
   c. is utterly defeated.

9. When a town has *stringent* traffic laws,
   a. you can park anywhere.
   b. the police are apt to be careless.
   c. you had better watch out.

10. When the *assiduous* man is asked how he is going to handle a hard job he says:

    a. just watch me work!

    b. there's nothing to it.

    c. I'm tired before I begin.

Answers: 1—*b;* 2—*a;* 3—*c;* 4—*a;* 5—*b;* 6—*c;* 7—*b;* 8—*b;* 9—*c;*
            10—*a.*

There are those who believe that wide reading alone will build their vocabularies. They are wrong. Wide reading, however, *will* add importantly to a person's word supply if it is tied in to the type of work that you are now doing.

You would be surprised at the number of difficult words that we come upon even in our newspaper reading. Here, for instance, are a few that have been selected from that least likely of all places, the sports pages of a metropolitan daily: *misfeasance; banal; gargantuan; encomium; cognoscenti.* When you meet words such as these you are apt either to skip over them or to assign wrong meanings to them which may stay with you for the rest of your life. If, however, you conscientiously study this book you will no longer be content to pass strange words by without checking on their true meanings. Then you will be astonished at the speed with which your vocabulary will grow.

> Words are the pegs to hang ideas
>   on.   BEECHER

24. Nouns of Shame and Shameful Acts

A FEW of the nouns in this chapter are very close to each other in their meanings. The little facets that differentiate them are so slight that it will take a bit of practice to learn them, but once again we will be introduced to the infinitely fine shadings of our language.

I. In the present case it may be best to start right off with the pronunciations and definitions.

> (1) TURPITUDE—tur'pĭ tude
> (2) DUPLICITY—dū plis'ĭ tĭ
> (3) DERELICTIONS—der ĭ lik'shuns
> (4) OPPROBRIUM—op prō'brĭ um
> (5) CALUMNY—cal'um nĭ
> (6) CONTUMELY—kon'tū mē lĭ
> (7) SCURRILITIES—skŭ ril'ĭ teez
> (8) BLASPHEMY—blas'fĕ mĭ
> (9) RAPACITY—ră pas'ĭ tĭ

(1) TURPITUDE: Directly from the Latin *turpitudo*, and in both languages the word means inherent baseness, vileness, and depravity.

(2) DUPLICITY: Again based on the Latin word *duplex* which meant "double," then "double-faced" or "two-faced," and thus, trickery, deceit, the act of pretending one thing and doing another. Three other words come close to *duplicity* in meanings. *Perfidy* (pur'fĭ dĭ) is a strong term that means treachery, falseness to a trust. A *subterfuge* (sub'tur fūj) is a tricky means that you use to evade an issue or to avoid criticism. And an *imposture* (im pos'tūr) is a fraudulent act, an attempt to deceive by false pretenses.

(3) DERELICTION: Latin *derelictio*, "a deserting," hence a failure in duty; neglect or willful omission, as of an obligation or a responsibility.

(4) OPPROBRIUM: A Latin word that we have taken over bodily with the original meaning: reproach mingled with contempt and disdain. And this introduces us to a whole group of powerful synonyms—*obloquy* (ob'luh kwĭ) meaning public reproach, abuse, blame; *objurgations* (ob jŏŏr gay'shuns), severe rebukes and scoldings; *odium* (ō'dĭ um), the state of being offensive or disgusting; *ignominy* (ig'no min ĭ), signifying disgrace and dishonor; and *stigma* (stig'muh), a mark of infamy and shame.

(5) CALUMNY: The Latin word was *calumnia*, and it had the same meaning as our English word: false, malicious, and injurious accusations; slander.

(6) CONTUMELY: Our word and the Latin term *contumelia* both mean insulting rudeness in speech and manners; scornful insolence.

(7) SCURRILITIES: Indecencies; low and vile abusiveness or vulgar railing. The clowns and jesters of ancient Rome were a vulgar crew and their coarse buffoonery was called *scurrilitas*.

(8) BLASPHEMY: Any irreverent act or utterance; evil or profane speaking of God or sacred things. Greek *blasphēmos*, "evil speaking."

(9) RAPACITY: The act of seizing that which is coveted; grasping greed. This word has its source in the Latin *rapax*, which meant "seizing to oneself."

II. You are going to be tested on these 9 key words, so it would be best to read them off again, to practice their pronunciations, and to recall their meanings. These words are not too easy, but they are still the proper part of an accomplished vocabulary.

1. turpitude	5. calumny
2. duplicity	6. contumely
3. dereliction	7. scurrilities
4. opprobrium	8. blasphemy
9. rapacity	

III. The sentences that follow are settings for these words. To fill each one of the blank spaces with the right word will be extremely difficult, and for that reason the initial letters are given as guides. If you are not sure, refer to the definitions in Section I. You will notice that the order has been changed.

1. I am bored and sickened with the s———— of the modern stage.

2. The mayor took so many vacations that he was bitterly criticized for his d————.

3. He would say one thing to my face and another behind my back. His d_____ knew no bounds.

4. It was a lie as black, a c_____ as foul as ever issued from the throat of man.

5. Some people get depraved as they go through life, but his t_____ was born in him.

6. They heaped c_____ on Negroes, Jews, and Catholics alike.

7. The r_____ of the usurer is now punished by law.

8. He is a religious zealot who regards every differing faith as b_____.

9. Some nations have been contemptuously criticized for their ruthless ambitions toward empire, but America has never been subjected to that o_____.

Answers: 1—scurrilities;   2—dereliction;   3—duplicity;   4— calumny,   5—turpitude,   6—contumely,   7—rapacity, 8—blasphemy; 9—opprobrium.

IV. See how well you can recall these words. Write the proper one after each synonym or synonymous phrase.

1. irreverence _____

2. scornful insolence _____

3. greed _____

4. failure in duty _____

5. slander _____

6. inborn wickedness _____

7. deceit _____

8. vile abusiveness _____

9. reproach mingled with contempt _____

Answers: 1—blasphemy; 2—contumely; 3—rapacity; 4—dereliction; 5—calumny; 6—turpitude; 7—duplicity; 8—
scurrilities; 9—opprobrium.

This chapter may need a review when you have the time,
not so much to keep the words themselves in mind as to
keep their *differences* clear.

> Hold fast the form of sound
> words.   II TIMOTHY 1:13

25. Nouns We Often Forget

WHETHER we like it or not there is class distinction in
speech. If someone asks you for a match and you say,
"I ain't got none," the communication is perfect. We
know that you have no matches, but you have fallen far
down the social scale in our eyes. You have told us that
your friends are of the lower level, that your early education has been neglected, and that you have done nothing
to improve it.

The "working vocabulary" that a young American uses
in speech or writing is not more than a few hundred words.
His "recognition" or "reading vocabulary" adds up to
some thousands. Beyond this his native language is as
obscure as Greek.

If your grammar is well groomed, and if you are rich in
words, you will have an entrée into business or into
society that cannot be easily won in any other way. So
please consider the time spent with this book more than
worthwhile.

We are apt to be lazy in the matter of words. We often
use the same stale ones over and over again, when so
many fresh ones are at hand. Here, for instance, are 13
that we are wont to neglect.

I. We will warm you up with the first 5 and then take the last 8 in another group.

(1) If you had ambitious plans to get ahead in business and your boss put a *quietus* (kwī ē′tus) on them, you would be

    a. encouraged.
    b. disheartened.
    c. indifferent.

(2) If you asked a question of an acquaintance of yours and he answered you with *acrimony* (ak′rĭ mō nĭ), would you

    a. be resentful?
    b. thank him?
    c. tell him he is correct?

(3) When you have reached an *impasse* (im′pass) in a discussion,

    a. you have agreed on the general principles.
    b. you are at least approaching a compromise.
    c. you are in a deadlock.

(4) If you described some animal as a *monstrosity* (mŏn strŏs′ĭ tĭ), you would mean that it was

    a. large.
    b. savage.
    c. unnaturally distorted and malformed.

(5) Should you treat a situation with *levity* (lev′ĭ tĭ), you are regarding it with

    a. grave seriousness.
    b. frivolous gaiety.
    c. indifference.

Answers: 1—*b;* 2—*a;* 3—*c;* 4—*c;* 5—*b.*

II. You may not yet have a full and clear understanding of all these words, but it will still be good practice to try to fit each one to the proper definition.

1. a silencing   _____

2. bitterness of speech   _____

3. a way or condition that seems blocked   _____

4. a thing unnaturally distorted   _____

5. lack of seriousness   _____

Answers: 1—quietus; 2—acrimony; 3—impasse; 4—monstros-
            ity; 5—levity.

III. The 5 words are grouped again below with their order
changed and two of them are repeated with different descriptive
phrases just to confuse you!

1. a way or condition that seems impassable   _____

2. bitterness of temper   _____

3. a thing like a monster   _____

4. lack of seriousness   _____

5. the act of quieting   _____

6. trifling thoughtlessness   _____

7. sharpness of language   _____

Answers: 1—impasse; 2—acrimony; 3—monstrosity; 4—levity;
            5—quietus; 6—levity; 7—acrimony.

IV. Can you fill out a sentence with these words?

   1. Let us not treat this serious situation with _____.

   2. I thought that that particular piece of hideous furniture she
had was a _____.

   3. The parties to the treaty had reached an _____ and a
solution to the dilemma seemed hopeless.

   4. He began to resent the _____ of her tongue.

   5. The boss put a _____ on his employee's ambitious plans.

Answers: 1—levity; 2—monstrosity; 3—impasse; 4—acrimony;
         5—quietus.

V. Let's list the next 8 words with their pronunciations and use
them in sentences.

> (1) BATHOS—bay'thoss
>
> (2) RUCK—ruck
>
> (3) ENORMITY—e norm'ĭ tĭ
>
> (4) STOIC—stō'ik
>
> (5) MALEVOLENCE—mă lev'ō lense
>
> (6) CANT—cant
>
> (7) CUPIDITY—cū pid'ĭ tĭ
>
> (8) AFFRONT—ă front'

1. The play began as high romance but ended on a note of
maudlin *bathos*.

2. Ambitious young people struggle to get out of the *ruck* of
mankind.

3. Not until the crime had been actually committed did I
realize the *enormity* of it.

4. He was as impassive as a *stoic* when he met his end.

5. He witnessed the brutal *malevolence* of the barbarians.

6. His words sounded eloquent, but at heart they were empty
cant.

7. He was poor but humble and had no *cupidity* in his heart.

8. I considered his remark insulting and I was incensed at the
affront.

VI. Several of these are somewhat unusual words and it may be
hard for you to check the choices presented below, but it is perhaps the best way to reach an understanding of their meanings.

1. If a story closes on a note of *bathos*, it ends with

    a. an insincere expression of sadness.
    b. a note of uplift.
    c. bitter tragedy.

2. If you are trying to free yourself from the common *ruck*,

    a. you are cheapening yourself.
    b. you are snobbish.
    c. you are ambitious and are struggling to stand out from the common herd.

3. If you are appalled at the *enormity* of an offense, you are shocked at its

    a. suddenness.
    b. wickedness.
    c. stupidity.

4. When you say that a man is a *stoic* in the face of pain,

    a. you are referring to his cowardice.
    b. you are commenting on his calmness and his apparent indifference to suffering.
    c. you are thinking of his physical strength.

5. People who are filled with *malevolence* are

    a. merciful and kindly.
    b. unusually generous with their money.
    c. spiteful and of evil disposition.

6. The whole spiritual atmosphere of today is saturated with *cant*. It is filled with

    a. radiant hope.
    b. insincere talk.
    c. boundless faith.

7. His riches excited the *cupidity* of many people.

    a. He was admired.
    b. He was criticized.
    c. He was envied.

8. When a man gives you an *affront,*

    a. you thank him for it.
    b. you refuse it.
    c. you are insulted by it.

Answers: 1—*a;* 2—*c;* 3—*b;* 4—*b;* 5—*c;* 6—*b;* 7—*c;* 8—*c.*

VII. At this point we will bring in the definitions of the 13 words that you have just covered. Better pronounce them out loud for practice.

(1) QUIETUS: Eventually from the Latin *quies,* "quiet," hence a complete silencing of something; a check on activity.

(2) ACRIMONY: Again we turn to the Latin *acrimonia,* "sharpness," for our word; hence, sharpness of speech, writing, or manner.

(3) IMPASSE: A French loan word meaning a "dead end"; a condition that cannot be resolved or gotten around; a complete block.

(4) MONSTROSITY: A thing unnaturally distorted; a malformation; an abnormal form. Originally from the Latin *monstruosus* which meant "strange," "singular," "incredible."

(5) LEVITY: Lack of mental gravity; trifling thoughtlessness; frivolous gaiety; light-mindedness. The germ of the idea is in the Latin term *levitas,* "trifling."

(6) BATHOS: A ridiculous descent from the sublime and lofty to the commonplace. This matter of "going to the depths" is inferred in the Greek parent word *bathos,* which meant "deep."

(7) RUCK: The common herd; the crowd of ordinary people who are out of the running. It is related to the Norwegian word *ruka,* "crowd."

(8) ENORMITY: Great wickedness; atrocity; depravity; enormous and monstrous sin. Latin *enormis,* "unusual."

(9) STOIC: Xeno, the Greek philosopher, founded a school of *Stoics* who believed the duty of a wise man is in calm and unperturbed submission to the divine will. With us our adopted word means a person who is indifferent to pleasure or pain; one who is entirely self-controlled and represses all feeling.

(10) MALEVOLENCE: Ultimately the Latin *malevolens*, from *male*, "evil," and *velle*, "wish." And so *malevolence* is the character of having "evil wishes" concerning others; malicious spitefulness; ill will; a wish to injure.

(11) CANT: Insincere statements about religion and morals; phrases of empty piety having no real meaning. This comes from the Latin *cantus*, "song," and refers to the singsong chant of beggars asking alms.

(12) CUPIDITY: We find it in Latin as *cupiditas*, from *cupio*, "desire"; but our English word took on the stronger meaning of morbid desire; avarice; an inordinate craving for wealth; greed.

(13) AFFRONT: An open insult and indignity; an act of intentional disrespect; rude treatment. *Affront* traces to the Latin phrase *ad frons*, "to the front" and suggests that an *affront* is given right to your face.

VIII. A review should be helpful at this point. Set down, if you can, the correct one of these 13 words after each synonym or synonymous phrase:

1. a person who represses his feelings   ————

2. a horrid crime   ————

3. insincere talk   ————

4. an anticlimax   ————

5. malicious hostility   ————

6. greed   ————

7. an insult   ————

8. sharpness of manner   ————

9. lack of proper seriousness   ———

10. a complete blockage   ———

11. a quieting   ———

12. an abnormal form   ———

13. the common herd   ———

Answers: 1—stoic; 2—enormity; 3—cant; 4—bathos; 5—malevolence; 6—cupidity; 7—affront; 8—acrimony; 9—levity; 10—impasse; 11—quietus; 12—monstrosity; 13—ruck.

Once you make these words your very own you will be surprised how often you will meet them in your daily reading. And don't think that those who use them—that those who can always pick the right word for the right occasion—were born with this ability. They probably even had no natural aptitude. They were just smart enough to know that a poor vocabulary is a cruel and unnecessary handicap and they found that it was so easy to overcome it.

> How strong an influence in well-placed words!   CHAPMAN

26. Nouns of Sorrow and Suffering

THERE IS a beauty and there are riches in the English language that almost transcend the imagination. And they can be had for not much more than the asking. So why not become a millionaire in the field of words?

Many people wish to succeed, but they have never thought out precisely what they want to succeed in. They haven't picked out a definite goal. So why not make up your mind that words are now your goal?

We Americans are fortunate. We are heirs to the greatest
of all languages. A foreigner has to go by slow, childlike
steps to learn the elementary simples of a speech that we
already know. What a challenge that should be to us.

There is an English word for almost every occasion in
life. Are humans troubled? Each shade of suffering and
sorrow has a term to describe it. Here are a few sample
colors from the palette of our language.

I. In each line that follows are exactly two words of similar
meanings, a key word that we will study and one other. Try to
locate them.

1. (a) suffering (b) tribulation (c) stupidity (d) stubbornness
   (e) selfishness

2. (a) determination (b) despair (c) stupor (d) ignorance
   (e) stupefaction

3. (a) mayhem (b) curses (c) unconsciousness (d) death
   (e) injury

4. (a) destruction (b) perdition (c) weakness (d) dullness
   (e) failure

5. (a) dirt (b) fear (c) squalor (d) nonsense (e) humility

6. (a) miserliness (b) confusion (c) turbulence (d) hopelessness
   (e) wickedness

7. (a) poverty (b) penury (c) stinginess (d) starvation (e) hate

8. (a) presentiment (b) sickness (c) greed (d) foreboding (e) filth

9. (a) shame (b) wickedness (c) danger (d) ignorance (e) extremity

10. (a) failure (b) throes (c) rage (d) agony (e) sickness

Answers: 1—a:b; 2—c:e; 3—a:e; 4—a:b; 5—a:c; 6—b:c; 7—a:b;
            8—a:d; 9—c:e; 10—b:d.

II. This may have proved to be a brain twister, and if you failed
on several of the pairs you will have had plenty of company. But

we are past the halfway mark in this book and you are better prepared for such a hard test than you would have been at the beginning. If we put these words in sentences it will help to clarify their meanings. Before you read them perhaps you had better review your mistakes, if any, in Section I.

(1) In this time of our *tribulation* you have shown compassion, which is the mark of a good neighbor.

(2) The sudden shock left him in a state of complete *stupefaction*.

(3) The author, who is abroad, probably hasn't seen the *mayhem* committed by Hollywood on his book.

(4) All I can say is that that boy is going on the way to *perdition*.

(5) The millions of people who have come out of the *squalor* of our slums will never return to it.

(6) She captures in her writing the fever and *turbulence* of men's emotions.

(7) So much of India is still a land of *penury* and woe.

(8) They had a faint, far-off *presentiment* of impending disaster.

(9) It was in the days when England was in her most dire *extremity*.

(10) Our nation is in the *throes* of war.

III. If some words were strangers to you, their meanings are now more sharp. But a few of these terms overlap and it will be necessary to define them in order that they may become your possessions.

(1) TRIBULATION (trib ū lay′shun)—A condition of affliction and distress; suffering; also that which causes it.

(2) STUPEFACTION (stū pĕ fak′shun)—A stunned and overwhelmed state; a deadened and blunted condition; a dazed and senseless state.

(3) MAYHEM (may′hem)—A willful disfiguring of the body; a maiming; by extension, any injury to a person or thing that lessens its use.

(4) PERDITION (pur dish'un)—Future misery or eternal death as the condition of the wicked; hell; utter loss and destruction; ruin.

(5) SQUALOR (skwŏl'ur)—The filth of shiftless poverty; misery and neglected dirt.

(6) TURBULENCE (tur'bū lense)—The state or condition of being violently disturbed, restless, or confused.

(7) PENURY (pen'ū rĭ)—Extreme poverty or want; indigence; destitution.

(8) PRESENTIMENT (prĭ zen'tĭ ment)—A foreboding; a prophetic sense of coming misfortune.

(9) EXTREMITY (ex trem'ĭ tĭ)—Desperate distress or need; extreme peril.

(10) THROES (thrōze)—Agony; anguish; violent pangs or pains.

IV. You can see that there are some rather nice distinctions between these words. *Tribulation, extremity,* and *throes* all imply suffering in varying degrees. *Tribulation* is suffering in a broader sense and usually covers a longer period of time than the others. We can speak of a life of *tribulation* or of the *tribulation* (the sufferings and oppression) of the Jewish race through history. *Extremity* is the highest point in distress and often implies extreme peril and possible disaster or death. With *throes* we have the sense of anguish and agony comparable to the pains of childbirth to which the word often refers.

Squalor and *penury* are also close in meaning. *Penury,* however, applies only to extreme poverty and destitution. *Squalor,* as you have seen, identifies the sordid misery and filth that results from shiftless poverty. So each of these words deserves a niche in our vocabulary.

V. Can you recall the words?

1. a dazed condition   s_____

2. bodily mutilation   m_____

3. a vague sense of coming danger   pr_____

4. utter destruction   pe_____

5. the filth of poverty   s_____

6. desperate distress and peril   ex_____

7. a disturbed state of confusion   tu_____

8. violent pangs and pains   th_____

9. a condition of affliction and distress   tr_____

10. extreme poverty   p_____

Answers: 1—stupefaction; 2—mayhem; 3—presentiment; 4—
perdition; 5—squalor; 6—extremity; 7—turbulence;
8—throes; 9—tribulation; 10—penury.

You are gradually gaining power over words and you are adding words of power to your vocabulary. And all this can lead to a great reward. Successful men differ widely in their talents, but one skill they all have in common and that is a supreme mastery in the field of words.

Words are the signs of ideas.
SAMUEL JOHNSON

27. Nouns of Negation and Destruction

THE AVERAGE articulate person who mixes with people and who leads a normally active life will say 30,000 or more words a day. You, yourself, would be surprised at your own word output if you ever counted it.

These words you speak are revealing *you* to *us*, your listeners. We are judging your personality, your character, your ability, your level of intelligence. As soon as you speak we are beginning to pigeonhole you. So this word study you are doing can be of high personal importance to you.

Remember, the word *dumb* was once used only to mean someone who couldn't talk. But people gradually formed their own opinion about people who couldn't talk, and as a result our word *dumb* grew to mean "stupid." Those who have gained a command over language usually have a command over men.

I. Now we come upon another group of words of almost savage power and destructive force.

(1) HOLOCAUST (hol'ō cost)—In ancient days the Greeks made sacrificial offerings of animals that were burnt whole or wholly consumed. Their word for this rite was *holokaustos* (*holos*, "whole," and *kaustos*, "burnt") which entered English as *holocaust* and first meant wide destruction by fire and sword as in war. It still means that, but more generally it refers to a fire disaster, especially one in which humans are burned, or it can even mean any wholesale destruction.

(2) CARNAGE (car'nij)—Here is a similar word that means an extensive and bloody slaughter, a wholesale massacre, without the involvement of fire. This term came to us through Italian and French from the Latin *carnalis*, from *caro*, "flesh." Several other English words derive from this Latin source. A man, for instance, with *carnal* desires has gross and "fleshly" appetites. And there are varieties of the *carnation* that are "flesh-colored."

(3) DEPREDATIONS (dep rĕ day'shuns)—The Latin source, *depredatus*, splits up into *de*, "thoroughly," and *præda*, "prey," hence it is easy to understand why the English word means "acts of plundering and ravaging."

(4) USURPATION (ū sur pay'shun)—The original source of this word is found in the Latin *usurpo*, "to appropriate unlawfully." Our English noun refers to the act of seizing or holding without right or legal authority; unlawful seizure of power or position.

(5) TRAVESTY (trav'es tĭ)—A fairly simple word with a rather complicated but logical history. In French the word *travesti* means "disguised." This originally was made up

of the Latin parts *trans*, "over," and *vestio*, "to clothe." With us *travesty* has come to signify a burlesque or caricature; a parody; an absurd distortion—that is, a serious subject is "dressed over" so as to render it ridiculous.

(6) CANARD (kă nahrd')—A French word that means a "duck" or "drake," but can also, in a colloquial French phrase, mean "a hoax." This is the sense in which we have taken it over in English. Our word *canard* refers to a fabricated, sensational story; a hoax; an absurd piece of gossip invented to deceive the public.

(7) FIASCO (fee as'kō)—An Italian word for a bottle of wine, but a bottle of wine can break and that may be why, when we borrowed the word, we used it to refer to a crash, a complete and humiliating failure, especially of a play or any pretentious venture.

(8) ANATHEMA (ă nath'ĕ muh)—Straight from the Greek with the same spelling and the same meaning, "a curse." In the church, *anathema* is the greater excommunication pronounced by ecclesiastical authority upon worst offenders only; with laymen the word can mean anything forbidden by social usage; any object of loathing.

(9) TRUCULENCE (truk'ū lense)—Savageness of character or behavior or aspect. Latin *truculentus*, "fierce."

(10) NEMESIS (nem'ĕ sis)—We end the list with the name of the Greek goddess of vengeance. In English the word *nemesis* means a return for evil done; retribution; downfall brought about by just punishment, or someone or something that inflicts retribution.

II. The meanings of two or three of these words may yet be a little fuzzy and woolly in your mind. If you will try to put them into sentences they will become more clear.

1. Twenty years ago collective bargaining was the businessman's a————.

2. Once the fire started the high wind turned it into a h————.

3. A base c_____ was circulated which particularly enraged him.

4. You wish to be a success but laziness may be your n_____.

5. The play was a tragic f_____.

6. The general realized that no military purpose could justify further c_____.

7. After the revolution the d_____ went on unchecked.

8. He had an offensive t_____ of manner.

9. There are those who claim that there has been a federal u_____ of the powers of the states.

10. The court's decision was a t_____ on justice.

Answers: 1—anathema; 2—holocaust; 3—canard; 4—nemesis; 5—fiasco; 6—carnage; 7—depredations; 8—truculence; 9—usurpation; 10—travesty.

III. Do you think you can remember these words now? Which word does each of the following sentences bring to mind?

1. What a silly story that was to spread around. _____

2. The play folded after two days. _____

3. There was a disastrous fire today. _____

4. He got his just deserts. _____

5. During the revolution in Cuba the stores were all plundered. _____

6. A bloody slaughter took place. _____

7. The dictator seized power. _____

8. He is a rude and ruthless man. _____

9. It was an amusing takeoff. _____

10. I loathe liars. _____

Answers: 1—canard; 2—fiasco; 3—holocaust; 4—nemesis; 5—depredations; 6—carnage; 7—usurpation; 8—truculence; 9—travesty; 10—anathema.

IV. It will be good practice to say the words out loud and to think of their meanings at the same time.

1. holocaust	6. canard
2. carnage	7. fiasco
3. depredations	8. anathema
4. usurpation	9. truculence
5. travesty	10. nemesis

Don't think that you are learning a lot of obscure words. Even many small abridged dictionaries have all the words that appear in this chapter. But, on the other hand, you won't find these expressive and dynamic terms in a mediocre vocabulary.

We rule men with words.
NAPOLEON

28. Nouns We Should Remember

YOU SHOULD easily learn the words in most of these chapters in one evening. But in the present one you will be faced with a heavier project. Possibly by now, at the end of your fourth week, you will be ready for it. If not, it may be best to review this chapter once or twice at a later period when you have leisure.

It will be encouraging to keep in mind that you are gaining a rich vocabulary, and a rich vocabulary is a magic key that can open up a new world of understanding, of competent thinking, of increased power.

There will be 22 words in all, and we will deal with them in four groups.

I. The first group of 5 words will bear watching, as they all delineate doers of evil, and their meanings are easily confused.

(1) The MISCREANT (mis′krē unt) who is a villain in all ways.

(2) The PANDERER (pan′dur ur) who ministers to the base desires of others, usually to gain his own ends.

(3) The LIBERTINE (lib′ur teen) who gives free rein to his appetites.

(4) The CHARLATAN (shahr′luh tun) who is an impostor and quack.

(5) The APOSTATE (ă pos′tate) who deserts his faith or religion.

II. We are now considering rather fine distinctions in the way of meanings. We can gain a better grasp of these words if they appear in sentences.

1. His fate may serve other *miscreants* with the reminder that base and depraved people are punished and that the wages of sin is death.

2. Such politicians are *panderers* who climbed to power by appealing to the basest passions of the masses.

3. The licentiousness of the stage and the immorality of the court circles formed an era that was a heyday for the *libertine*.

4. This conscienceless *charlatan* made a fortune out of a fake cure-all.

5. They ranked him as a renegade and an *apostate* from the Democratic Party.

III. Will this brief introduction enable you to recall the words? Try anyhow to place the proper word after each phrase. Refer to the previous section if you need to.

1. an evildoer

   m_____

2. one who furthers the illicit acts of others for his
   own profit

   p_____

3. one who does not restrain his appetite

   l_____

4. a faker

   c_____

5. a deserter from a cause, religion, or party

   a_____

Answers: 1—miscreant; 2—panderer; 3—libertine; 4—charlatan; 5—apostate.

IV. Here are statements about these 5 words that you are to
mark "true" or "false."

1. A *miscreant* is one who deserts his religion.   True   False

2. A *panderer* caters to the low desires of others.   True   False

3. The *libertine* indulges his own carnal appetites.   True   False

4. A *charlatan* goes back on his faith.   True   False

5. An *apostate* is a thief.   True   False

Answers: 1—False; 2—True; 3—True; 4—False; 5—False.

V. In this section we will introduce 5 more words of widely
different meanings.

> (1) PLETHORA—pleth'o ruh
>
> (2) RETRIBUTION—ret ri bū'shun
>
> (3) ASPERITY—as pĕr'ĭ tĭ
>
> (4) ATTRITION—at trish'un
>
> (5) OCCULT—ŏ kult'

VI. Don't be afraid of these words if you haven't met them
before. Once acquainted with them you will come upon them
again and again. We suggest that you first concentrate on the
following questions and try to answer them in your own mind.

(1) When there is a *plethora* of wheat in the country have the crops been too small or too large?

(2) If a man has done wrong and has received *retribution* for his act, what has happened to him?

(3) If someone should speak to you with a touch of *asperity* in his voice, is he in a temper?

(4) The newspaper says that victory was gained by the *attrition* of the enemy's forces. What other word or words could you use in place of *attrition?*

(5) A person is said to have *occult* powers. What would these be?

VII. The sentences that follow will give you a clue to the answers to the above questions, although when you have finished you may still be in doubt about one or two.

1. The low returns paid to owners of government securities were due to a *plethora* of gold.

2. When you do an undeserved injury to someone you are inviting *retribution*.

3. His temper was rising and there was a touch of *asperity* in his voice.

4. Our constant sinking of their submarines led to the progressive *attrition* of their naval power.

5. She had weird and ghostly powers and was said to possess a knowledge of the *occult*.

VIII. Can you make a proper pairing of words and definitions? The order is changed.

1. A gradual wearing away; wearing down, as of resources, by continual slight impairment   a_____

2. Something that is mysterious and supernatural   o_____

3. Hastiness or sharpness of temper; severity; irritability; acrimony   a_____

4. Superabundance; excess; excessive supply; oversupply   p_____

5. Punishment for wrong deeds; requital for evil; deserved punishment; return for evil done   r_____

Answers: 1—attrition; 2—occult; 3—asperity; 4—plethora; 5—retribution.

IX. The next assignment will take a little thought. Each phrase is the approximate *opposite* in meaning to what one of the above words? Again the order of the words is different.

     1. too little   _____

     2. soft speech   _____

     3. the natural and normal   _____

     4. absence of all punishment   _____

     5. no wear and tear   _____

Answers: 1—plethora; 2—asperity; 3—occult; 4—retribution; 5—attrition.

X. Now we will take up 6 new nouns with their pronunciations.

         (1) PITTANCE—pit′unse

         (2) INTRICACIES—in′trĭ kă seez

         (3) EFFULGENCE—ĕ fŭl′jense

         (4) DEFECTION—de fek′shun

         (5) PANDEMONIUM—pan de mō′nĭ um

         (6) COLOSSUS—ko lŏs′us

XI. You are to be questioned on these words:

1. When a person receives a *pittance* for his work is he being well paid or poorly paid?

2. When a subject is full of *intricacies* is it simple or complicated?

3. If we speak of the *effulgence* of the stars are we saying that they are bright or dull?

4. When there is *defection* from a political party what is happening?

5. Should there be *pandemonium* in a public square is the place noisy or quiet?

6. When we speak of a bridge as a *colossus* do we mean that it is large or small?

XII. The meanings of some of the unfamiliar words have probably begun to reveal themselves. They will be clearer yet if the words are seen in sentences.

1. If they receive any compensation whatsoever it should be no more than a *pittance*.

2. He was deep in the *intricacies* of his income tax figures.

3. The shop windows glowed with brightness. Nothing I have ever seen could compare with their *effulgence*.

4. There was great unrest among the men and even *defection* from their ranks.

5. His name was proposed at the convention and the place was immediately a *pandemonium*.

6. Russia is the new *colossus* that bestrides the continent of Europe.

XIII. Fit the word to the definition. If necessary, reread Section XII for help.

1. Desertion; abandonment of allegiance or duty   _____

2. Complexities; complications; perplexing and
    involved states; difficult details   _____

3. Radiance; splendor; beaming brightness;
    diffusion of light   _____

4. Any place remarkable for disorder and uproar;
    a fiendish and riotous confusion   _____

5. A meagre allowance or dole; a very small
   portion; a small payment   _____

6. Anything of gigantic size   _____

Answers: 1—defection; 2—intricacies; 3—effulgence; 4—pan-
           demonium; 5—pittance; 6—colossus.

XIV. Can you recall the words?

      1. a very small payment   _____

      2. complications   _____

      3. beaming brightness   _____

      4. desertion   _____

      5. a wild uproar   _____

      6. gigantic size   _____

Answers: 1—pittance; 2—intricacies; 3—effulgence; 4—defec-
           tion; 5—pandemonium; 6—colossus.

XV. Now we come to the final group of 6 nouns to be considered
in this chapter.

      (1) TORPOR—tor′pur

      (2) EFFRONTERY—ĕ frunt′ur rĭ

      (3) LACKEY—lak′ĭ

      (4) LOUT—lowt

      (5) MAELSTROM—male′strum

      (6) AVIDITY—ă vid′ĭ tĭ

XVI. If these are in sentences the meanings will begin to take
shape.

1. The shock had left her in an almost deathlike *torpor*.

2. He had the *effrontery* to tell me what I could and could
not do.

3. He serves his boss without dignity, like a *lackey* and a slave.

4. He is crude, clownish, stupid, a full-fledged *lout*.

5. He was caught in the *maelstrom* of passions.

6. They were starved and they wolfed the food with startling *avidity*.

XVII. Here are the definitions.

(1) TORPOR: suspended animation or vitality; apathy; sluggish-
    ness; stupor.

(2) EFFRONTERY: shameless boldness; impudence.   '

(3) LACKEY: a footman; hence, a servile attendant; a menial; a
    clownish follower.

(4) LOUT: an awkward, ill-mannered, ungainly fellow; an ill-bred
    country bumpkin.

(5) MAELSTROM: a great and tumultuous whirlpool; hence, any
    widespreading influence or restless movement that is
    violent.

(6) AVIDITY: greed; eager desire.

XVIII. After each of the 6 words are three choices. Pick the word
or phrase, A, B, or C, that you think is nearest in meaning to the
key word.

(1) TORPOR—A: sadness. B: stupor. C: an insulting manner.

(2) EFFRONTERY—A: pride. B: awkwardness. C: shameless
    boldness.

(3) LACKEY—A: a servile attendant. B: a lazy person. C: a fool.

(4) LOUT—A: a greedy person. B: a vain person. C: an ill-
    mannered person.

(5) MAELSTROM—A: restlessness. B: tumultuous whirlpool.
    C: widespreading.

(6) AVIDITY—A: overbearing pride. B: eager desire. C: laziness.

Answers: 1—B; 2—C; 3—A; 4—C; 5—B.

XIX. Can you recall the words?

1. a slavish follower ———————
2. sluggishness ———————
3. greed ———————
4. a stupid boor ———————
5. like a whirlpool ———————
6. impudence ———————

Answers: 1—lackey; 2—torpor; 3—avidity; 4—lout; 5—maelstrom; 6—effrontery.

XX. The story behind a word, the romantic history that tells us where it came from, almost always throws a new light on the meaning. We will take up the derivations of 19 of the words we have just covered. Three histories are omitted because they are not interesting.

MISCREANTS: From the Old French word *mescreant* which meant "unbelieving." It was originally a religious term visited upon unbelievers or non-Christians who, in the eyes of that day, were vile people. Hence our modern meaning of "evildoers."

PANDERER: A *panderer* is a "go-between in illicit love affairs." The word comes from Pandarus, the name of a Greek in Homer's *Iliad* who obtained the girl, Chryseis, for the pleasure of the king of Troy. Now a *panderer* is more generally "a person who ministers to the base appetites of others for his own benefit or profit."

LIBERTINE: In Latin the parent term *libertinus* meant a "freedman." With us a *libertine* is "one who takes advantage of his freedom and has no moral restraints."

CHARLATAN: A quack must be a fast talker to sell his fake medicines. So *quack* is a clipped form of the Dutch term *quacksalver*,
one who "quacks" like a duck to peddle his wares; and *charlatan*
comes through French from the Italian *ciarla*, "babble." So the
basis of fakery seems to be "fast talking."

APOSTATE: From a Greek word that means "stand away from."
And one who deserts his faith can be said to "stand away"
from it.

PLETHORA: Its Greek ancestor *plethos*, "fullness," suggests our
meaning of "superabundance."

RETRIBUTION: In Latin *retribuo* means "to pay back." Our English
word means "to pay back" an injury that has been done to us.

ASPERITY: Right from the Latin *asperitas*, "harshness."

ATTRITION: Our meaning of "wearing away" is direct from the
Latin *attritus*, "rubbed away."

OCCULT: The Latin word *occultus*, "hidden," gives us our meaning
of mysterious and supernatural powers, "something hidden."

INTRICACIES: The Latin *intricatus*, "entangled."

EFFULGENCE: From the Latin *effulgeo*, "to shine forth."

DEFECTION: Identical in meaning with the Latin term *defectio*,
"a desertion."

PANDEMONIUM: According to the poet Milton *Pandemonium*
(literally "all demons") was the palace of Satan in Hell. We use
it as a word to describe wild disorder.

COLOSSUS: The Colossus of Rhodes was a huge bronze statue that
stood astride the ancient harbor some 2400 years ago. We use
the word to describe anything of awe-inspiring size.

TORPOR: Taken directly from the Latin and meaning "dullness"
and "sluggishness" in both languages.

EFFRONTERY: From a Latin combination meaning "out front."
Hence, *effrontery* is impudence right in "front" of your face.

MAELSTROM: This is the name of a famous whirlpool off the Norwegian coast, and hence means with us "a violent and restless movement and confusion."

AVIDITY: The English meaning of "greed" or "eager desire" is identical with the Latin word *aviditas*.

You have come to the end of the working part of this chapter, but I want to tack on an addendum of terms that could hardly be omitted from a book of power words. Please don't try to learn them now or you will find yourself overburdened. Merely read them over as a matter of interest. We will take them up and discuss them briefly and informally, and you can review them at your leisure. Here they are:

There are many *exactions* that go with an important job—that is, many requirements and pressing demands.

Obduracy is obstinacy, stubbornness.

Profanation is the act of abusing or dishonoring things that are considered sacred.

Provocation is an act or cause that stirs anger, as: "It is true that I struck him but he gave me great *provocation*."

And *strictures* are severe criticisms. We can say: "They resented the *strictures* that he laid upon their actions."

You may possibly feel that the words you have had in this chapter belong more aptly in the world of books. But these words and the other terms that appear in this volume are not merely the literary tools of professional writers.

The study of words in general is a practical business. All the affairs of life are carried on by words. All of our thinking is done with words. All the knowledge of the past has been passed on to us in the medium of words. Beyond this, a mastery of words is not only the best single indication of intelligence but it is also the most accurate prediction of success in many fields. A man who commands words can usually get a job even if he can't keep it. And a girl who is a really good conversationalist is rarely lacking in dates.

SECOND TEST

A Test for You on Your Nouns

LET'S SEE how well you have done with your nouns. Like the verbs these sample nouns have been chosen in such a fashion that the results will show you what your progress has been.

I. We will take them in groups of 10. Here is the first group.

1. tenacity
2. adulation
3. compunction
4. mendacity
5. antipathy

6. efficacy
7. truculence
8. martinet
9. levity
10. nostalgia

II. I will describe each of these words in the first column below. Write down in each case the word that you think most nearly fits the description. The order is changed.

1. lightness of humor   _____

2. lying   _____

3. extravagant praise   _____

4. dogged persistence   _____

5. savage behavior   _____

6. homesickness   _____

7. a feeling of dislike   _____

8. power and efficiency   _____

9. remorseful feelings   _____

10. a strict disciplinarian   _____

Answers: 1—levity; 2—mendacity; 3—adulation; 4—tenacity; 5—truculence; 6—nostalgia; 7—antipathy; 8—efficacy; 9—compunction; 10—martinet.

III. Please fit these 10 words into these sentences.

(1) Never fear. He will carry the plan through. He is a man with great _____.

(2) Some people enjoy musical comedies but I have an _____ for them.

(3) He will succeed. He is a hard worker and has an extraordinary _____ of purpose.

(4) He deserved a reprimand but it was cruel to attack him with such _____.

(5) There were periods of great loneliness in this far-off land when she was swept by waves of _____.

(6) To him this great statesman was almost a god and he looked up to him with _____.

(7) This subject is too serious and too important to treat with _____.

(8) He is a lazy worker and I have not the slightest _____ about discharging him.

(9) He is notorious for his _____ and no one can trust him.

(10) The teacher was severe and strict—a true _____.

Answers: 1—efficacy;   2—antipathy;   3—tenacity;   4—truculence;   5—nostalgia;   6—adulation;   7—levity;   8—
compunction;   9—mendacity;   10—martinet.

IV. Now to test you similarly on a second group of 10 nouns.

1. malefactor	6. affluence
2. laggard	7. assiduity
3. termagant	8. dudgeon
4. masochist	9. derelictions
5. lout	10. rapacity

V. I am going to ask you to write in the correct word after each
descriptive sentence.

(1) He finds pleasure in being abused or dominated.

He is a _____.

(2) He is a doer of evil.

He is a _____.

(3) She is a common scold.

She is a _____.

(4) He is a stupid oaf.

He is a _____.

(5) He is always falling behind.

He is a _____.

(6) A man is in a high temper.

He is in a _____.

(7) A man is known for his close and continuous effort.

This quality is called _____.

(8) A man neglects his duties.

He has committed _____.

(9) A man is greedy and grasping for gain.

He is noted for his _____.

(10) A man has great wealth.

He is a man of _____.

Answers: 1—masochist; 2—malefactor; 3—termagant; 4—lout;
5—laggard; 6—dudgeon; 7—assiduity; 8—derelic-
tions; 9—rapacity; 10—affluence.

VI. We will finish with a similar test on another list of 10 nouns.

1. acrimony	6. canard
2. mayhem	7. accolade
3. umbrage	8. miscreant
4. presentiment	9. plethora
5. holocaust	10. turpitude

VII. On this occasion you will be met with another type of test. A
statement will be made about each word and you are to tell
whether it is true or false.

(1) *Acrimony* has to do with kindness.   True   False

(2) *Mayhem* is an offense causing a disabling
mutilation of the body.   True   False

(3) *Umbrage* is resentment.   True   False

(4) *Presentiment* is a prophetic sense of danger.   True   False

(5) A *holocaust* is a feast of celebration.   True   False

(6) A *canard* is a made-up sensational story.   True   False

(7) An *accolade* is a false accusation.   True   False

(8) A *miscreant* is a rascal.   True   False

(9) A *plethora* is an oversupply.   True   False

(10) *Turpitude* is inherent wickedness.   True   False

Answers: 1—False; 2—True; 3—True; 4—True; 5—False; 6—
True; 7—False; 8—True; 9—True; 10—True.

VIII. Let's place the 10 nouns in sentences.

1. He was worried because he had a _____ of disaster.

2. He denied the scandalous _____ that they were spreading about him.

3. He went to jail for the crime of _____ since his victim was too badly injured even to return to his job.

4. He took _____ at the insult.

5. He's a _____ who is always up to some kind of villainous mischief.

6. The ground is drenched as we have certainly had a _____ of rain this year.

7. She was severe and sarcastic and her tongue was acid with _____.

8. The building was gutted by a fiery _____.

9. They gave an _____ to the winning athlete.

10. He was a congenital sinner whose life was filled with _____.

Answers: 1—presentiment; 2—canard; 3—mayhem; 4—umbrage; 5—miscreant; 6—plethora; 7—acrimony; 8—holocaust; 9—accolade; 10—turpitude.

These 30 nouns are difficult ones and 22 correct answers would be excellent; 18 very good.

FOURTH INTERMISSION

A Word Miscellany

IN ONE WAY this isn't a true intermission. It's a test. But it should be an amusing one and may be a relief from the ones you have been facing.

A few of the words in this intermission are difficult. But quite a number are of the simple, sensible, commonplace type that you use in your everyday conversation. You, of course, know their meanings.

Do you? Let's see.

What do you mean when you say that that lovely blonde has *limpid* eyes? Are they clear or watery or calm and unruffled or what?

That was a *lurid* crime, wasn't it? And what a *livid* scar the victim had on his face. Well, what kind of crime is a *lurid* crime, and what is the color of a *livid* scar? Or is it several colors? Or hasn't *livid* anything to do with color? And further, if the criminal got off *scot-free* is he any freer than free? What does the funny word *scot* mean anyhow?

Speaking of crime, there are lots of different kinds of sin in this world of ours. Some sins, for instance, are *venal;* others, *venial.* One of them is pretty bad. Which one?

While we are on unpleasant subjects, precisely what type of an accident is a *grisly* accident? And if the man who broke his leg had a *grizzly* beard would his beard be gray or dishevelled or bristly or something else?

Have you ever used the quaint words *wherefore* and *wherefor*? Possibly not, but they are common in the Bible, Chaucer, and elsewhere in literature. Are they identical in meaning? Would you write "*Wherefore* art thou, Romeo?" or "*Wherefor*"? Or wouldn't you care! And you might find it interesting also to look up *therefore* and *therefor*.

When you call your cellar *dank*, do you mean that it is dark or damp or neither? Or is it just cold? And when we say that a man is *lank*, do we mean that he is tall or thin or weak or wiry or any combination of these four? Or is the meaning something entirely different?

Sometimes an author will write of the *pristine* beauty of the snow. What kind of beauty would he be describing? At other times a writer's style will *cloy* your taste. What happens when your taste is *cloyed*? And what, may I ask, is a *crass* remark?

Just to make it all harder, where are the *antipodes*? Or aren't they anywhere? Or should we say where *is* the *antipodes*? And what is an *archipelago*? And, for the highbrow readers, if *choreography* is the art of dancing, what is *chorography*? And then there is *cartography*, if you care to worry about it.

There may be a few of these queries that have puzzled you. Shall I give you the answers?

Limpid eyes or a *limpid* brook are both crystal clear. That's all.

Lurid originally meant the unearthly type of red and yellow flames seen through smoke or mist. Then it came to be used in connection with any event that is harshly vivid or terrible, often marked by violent passion or crime, or the description of such an event. As for a *livid* scar, this is one that has been discolored, as after a blow, and it may be black and blue or ashy gray.

Scot-free means without any penalty. A *scot* used to be a fine in Old English law.

A *venal* act is the act of a person who is willing to sacrifice his honor or principle for payment or profit. A *venial* sin is one that can be forgiven.

The word *grisly* comes from an Old English term that meant "horrible," and that's just what it means today. A *grizzly* beard is black streaked with white or gray.

Shakespeare wrote "*Wherefore* art thou, Romeo?" since *wherefore* means for what reason? for what end? for what object?; while the rare word *wherefor* means "for which," as: "I bought a car *wherefor* I paid a handsome sum."

The matters of the *dank* celler and the *lank* man are easily settled. The *dank* celler is disagreeably damp and the *lank* man is thin and that's all.

The rest of the answers can be swiftly given.

Pristine snow is the first fall of snow, unsullied and untouched, for *pristine* means "virgin pure." When your reading taste is *cloyed* it is surfeited, satiated by a literary style that is overrich and sickly sweet, while a *crass* remark is one that is unrefined and stupid.

The *antipodes* is the place or region on the opposite side of the earth from where you are. The singular is *antipode*. While *archipelago* applies to any large body of water studded with islands, or to the islands themselves. There are several *archipelagos* in the South Pacific. *Chorography*, roughly, is the art of mapping or describing of regions or districts, and *cartography* is the art or business of making maps themselves.

You may have done well on this test. But, curiously, whenever it has been tried out on scholars, they usually got the hard words but were often stumped by the simple ones. Few of us have ever bothered to look them up.

That matter of being willing to "bother," incidentally, can often be the difference between success and failure. It frequently spells laziness, and after all we will have to confess that most of us are a little lazy at heart.

This willingness to make an effort to accomplish things is more important than you may think in the history of success. That was proved one time in a dramatic way in an investigation that was made by the Chicago Sales Executive Club. They wanted to find out the prime reason why salesmen are fired—and found that more employees were let go for *lack of effort* than for drunkenness, crookedness, gambling, and stupidity combined.

Sometimes I wonder whether handicaps aren't actually a help in overcoming this human laziness, whether some people don't succeed *because* of their handicaps rather than *in spite* of them. There was the great British statesman William Pitt who bullied Parliament with his crutches; and Robert Louis Stevenson, dying of consumption, who won immortality; Charles Darwin who devised his theory of evolution in the scattered half-hours that his blinded eyes permitted him to work; the sick hunchback Alexander Pope and his brilliant satires; the stone-deaf Beethoven and his miraculous "Ninth Symphony."

It could easily be that these great men were driven to fame by their frustrations. We, who have no such handicaps, will have to think up other ways to overcome our inertia. We should commit ourselves by telling our friends what we are planning to do in this vocabulary-building business, so that we will be ashamed not to keep on with it. We should continually lure ourselves with thoughts of the rewards we are going to win with our efforts. We should use every device and crutch that we can. The trick is, therefore, to take for granted that you're lazy and then plan to outsmart yourself!

FIFTH WEEK

Language is the immediate gift
of God.   NOAH WEBSTER

29. Workday Adjectives and Adverbs

THIS opening chapter of your fifth week will be divided
into two parts. In the first half we will discuss 16 very
useful adjectives. The second half will be given over to 11
adverbs.

The English word *adjective* comes from the Latin term
adjectivus, which meant "added to." That is, an adjective
is "added to" a noun to describe or limit it.

If we were sitting in the classroom of our old grammar
school we would hear the teacher say: "An adjective is a
word used to qualify the application of a noun or a nominal
phrase, as: *this* book; *sweet* sounds; *beautiful* flowers; a *red*
brick house."

English, of course, has a vast wealth in adjectives, and
adjectives give color to our language.

Now we all tend to be a little careless, and our careless-
ness creeps into our vocabularies. We are apt to say "a big
statue," "a big room," "a big occasion," when we could so
easily say "a colossal statue," "a spacious room," "a momentous occasion." We are apt to use the words that lie
nearest and come easiest. But if our words are worn and
dull, people will come to unfair, or at the least, unin-
formed judgments about us and think that we are dull.

We all have hidden powers within us, and the words that
you are learning will release them.

I. Here are some adjectives that we may easily forget to use. We will give them in two groups. The first 8 terms touch, directly or indirectly, upon human beings and they will be presented to you in sentences from modern authors. Watch for the meanings.

(1) "At all times his writing is devoid of *didactic* dullness."— Bruce Barton.

(2) "Though their eyes were fixed on me, I caught a *surreptitious* glance passing from one to another."—W. Somerset Maugham.

(3) "His oration was *banal* and boresome."—Ralph Starr Jordan.

(4) "Our usually placid chauffeur suddenly went *berserk*."— Leland Stowe.

(5) "His ability to silence these *bombastic* and verbose men is unequalled."—Edward R. Murrow.

(6) "Those who set the policies are the *culpable* officials."— James E. Murray.

(7) "The Congressmen were showered with *denunciatory* editorials."—William Green.

(8) "The Old Guard leaders of former years considered some of the enlightened doctrines of government *heretical* from the established political point of view."—James A. Farley.

II. Now for their pronunciations.

    (1) DIDACTIC—dī dak′tik

    (2) SURREPTITIOUS—sur rep tish′us

    (3) BANAL—bay′nal *or* bă nal′

    (4) BERSERK—bur′surk

    (5) BOMBASTIC—bom bas′tik

    (6) CULPABLE—kul′pă b′l

    (7) DENUNCIATORY—de nun′sĭ ă tō rĭ

    (8) HERETICAL—hĕ ret′ĭ kul

III. Would a rereading of Section I put you in a position to place the proper word after each of the following descriptive words or phrases?

1. deserving of blame or censure _____

2. secret or stealthy _____

3. resembling a furious, frenzied fighter _____

4. accusing or censuring _____

5. speaking in extravagant or ranting phrases _____

6. having to do with beliefs contrary to the fundamental doctrines of a church, school, or profession _____

7. commonplace, ordinary, and dull _____

8. teacherlike _____

Answers: 1—culpable; 2—surreptitious; 3—berserk; 4—denunciatory; 5—bombastic; 6—heretical; 7—banal; 8—didactic.

IV. Each key word will be given with three choices following. The correct choice will not necessarily be an *exact* synonym, but it will be *nearest of the three* in meaning to the key word.

(1) DENUNCIATORY: A: vainglorious. B: accusing. C: sly.

(2) HERETICAL: A: absurd. B: bombastic. C: revolutionary.

(3) CULPABLE: A: blameworthy. B: uninteresting. C: easily fooled.

(4) SURREPTITIOUS: A: stealthy. B: proud. C: talkative.

(5) BANAL: A: guilty. B: absurd. C: commonplace.

(6) BOMBASTIC: A: trite. B: loudmouthed. C: criminal.

(7) DIDACTIC: A: proud. B: instructive. C: wild-eyed.

(8) BERSERK: A: complaining. B: banning. C: half-crazy.

Answers: 1—B; 2—C; 3—A; 4—A; 5—C; 6—B; 7—B; 8—C.

V. The next 8 words are a miscellany of adjectives.

(1) He has a brow that gives him a rather lowering and scowling
look. At the least it overhangs and is projecting.
He has a *beetling* brow.

(2) After the drouth the rains have come in a plenteous and
abundant fashion. There is ample water.
There is a *copious* water supply.

(3) Sometimes it becomes very urgent and most necessary to
do certain things. They are obligatory.
It is *imperative* to do them.

(4) Occasionally there are memories, for example, so vivid that
they cannot be wiped out or obliterated. They are incapable of being erased from your mind.
They are *ineffaceable*.

(5) This world holds things so valuable that they are above
price. They are actually priceless.
They are of *inestimable* value.

(6) Once in a while an extraordinary event occurs, so novel
that it is beyond all previous experience. No former
example of it exists.
It is *unprecedented*.

(7) Sometimes a person will make a statement that is so plain
and clear that it is impossible to misunderstand or mis-
interpret it.
This is an *unequivocal* statement.

(8) There is another kind of statement that is absolute, positive,
unconditional, explicit, and without qualification. Sometimes it is bluntly put.
This is a *categorical* statement.

VI. Try to recall the meanings of the words as you repeat the
pronunciations.

(1) BEETLING—bē't'ling

(2) COPIOUS—kō' pĭ us

(3) IMPERATIVE—im pĕr'ă tiv

(4) INEFFACEABLE—in ef face'ă b'l

(5) INESTIMABLE—in es'tĭ mă b'l

(6) UNPRECEDENTED—un pres'ĭ dent ed

(7) UNEQUIVOCAL—un ĕ kwiv'ă kul

(8) CATEGORICAL—kat ĕ gor'ĭ kul

VII. It will help to clarify the meanings if we see the words in normal sentences.

1. "His *beetling* gorilla eyebrow ridge was a mark of the older males only."—Raymond W. Murray.

2. "They welcomed the broad and *copious* flow of the latest weapons of all kinds."—Winston Churchill.

3. "It seemed *imperative* to reassure the American people that their government was telling them the truth."—Elmer Davis.

4. "There is an *ineffaceable* picture of him in my mind."—Peter W. Rainier.

5. "We enjoy the *inestimable* privilege of free speech."—Burton Rascoe.

6. "The *unprecedented* opportunity exists for the American nations to cooperate to make the spirit of peace a practical living fact."—Franklin Delano Roosevelt.

7. "The achievement of an orderly, *unequivocal*, and workable body of laws must be part of the higher civilization toward which we are striving."—Thomas C. Desmond.

8. "Let me make the *categorical* statement that the main purpose of our administration is to train them to stand securely on their own feet."—Malcolm MacDonald.

Our words tell an eloquent story of our intelligence and of our education. It is, perhaps, wise to have them speak well of us.

Have you done reasonably well with the adjectives? Then we will move on to the adverbs.

An adverb, as you know, is that part of speech used to modify a verb, adjective, or other adverb. Adverbs denote a way or manner in which an action takes place, or the relations of place, time, manner, quality, and number.

Adverbs are close physical cousins to adjectives. Of the 16 adjectives that we have just had there are 3 that have no adverbial form. These are *denunciatory*, *berserk*, and *beetling*. By various forms of respelling all the remaining 13 can be changed into adverbs, and each one will end in "-ly."

Because of the close relationship of adjectives and adverbs and also because adverbs are not usually so strong as the other three parts of speech we have been discussing, they will not be presented again in the remainder of this book.

VIII. We will discuss here 11 adverbs. They will be given first in modern sentences.

(1) John Hay Whitney speaking: "We believe the showing of these works of art will demonstrate *incontrovertibly* the community of our material interests."

What do you think *incontrovertibly* means? _____

(2) T. V. Soong: "Through us the fate of the East is *inextricably* bound to that of the West."

Inextricably means _____

(3) Walter Adams: "These animated maps of world conquest are as *meticulously* truthful as historians can make them."

Meticulously means _____

(4) Margaret Mead: "To be reared in one culture in our society makes one *irrevocably* partake of that culture."

Irrevocably means _____

(5) Walter Lippmann: "They are *irretrievably* and inexpiably implicated in the crimes of the regime."
Irretrievably means ———

(6) Arthur Krock: "The galleries were in an uproar and were *vociferously* in favor of his nomination."
Vociferously means ———

(7) Bertram M. Myers: "He presented his reasoning *fallaciously* and in a fanatical fashion."
Fallaciously means ———

(8) Anne O'Hare McCormick: "His communiqués were deprecated as unsoldierly because they were presented *flamboyantly*."
Flamboyantly means ———

(9) Dorothy Thompson: "One group is *virulently* attacking the government policy."
Virulently means ———

(10) Nelson P. Mead: "Before 1914 the American people were *abysmally* ignorant concerning international relations."
Abysmally means ———

(11) John Haynes Holmes: "There was something about the grave of the Unknown Soldier in Washington that was *ineffably* beautiful."
Ineffably means ———

IX. These are the things that people say to you in the newspapers each day or each month. How well did you do toward understanding them? Here are the definitions of the words you have just had.

(1) INCONTROVERTIBLY (in kon trō vur′tĭ blĭ): Indisputably; in a manner impossible to disprove.

(2) INEXTRICABLY (in ex′trĭ ka blĭ): In a way that cannot possibly be separated or set free; in a manner from which it is impossible to escape.

(3) METICULOUSLY (mĕ tik′ū lus lĭ): Excessively carefully; finically; scrupulously; paying great attention to all small details.

(4) IRREVOCABLY (ĭr rev'ŏ kuh blĭ): Unalterably; in a way that cannot be changed.

(5) IRRETRIEVABLY (ĭr rĕ treev'ă blĭ): In a way that cannot be repaired or made good; irreparable; incurable in a way that cannot be recalled or changed.

(6) VOCIFEROUSLY (vō sif'ur us lĭ): In a noisy and clamorous way.

(7) FALLACIOUSLY (fă lay'shus lĭ): In a misleading way; deceptively; delusively; illogically.

(8) FLAMBOYANTLY (flam boy'ant lĭ): Extravagantly; with pompous, high-sounding phrases.

(9) VIRULENTLY (vĭr'ū lent lĭ): Maliciously; venomously; bitterly.

(10) ABYSMALLY (ă biz'mal lĭ): Deeply, in a moral and intellectual sense; unfathomably; bottomlessly; unendingly; profoundly.

(11) INEFFABLY (in ef'a blĭ): In a way that is too lofty to be expressed in mere words.

I am tempted to add three more workaday words to this miscellany: *scathing*, *satiric*, and *ribald*. A *scathing* criticism or remark is one that burns and sears. Writing that is *satiric* holds something or someone up to ridicule with cruel wit, while *ribald* remarks are offensive, vulgar, or coarsely mocking.

If you will study to have a word for every situation, and for every expression that you wish to convey to others, it will give you a type of courage that you may never have had before.

> Good words are worth much and
> cost little.   HERBERT

30.   Adjectives That Suggest Unpleasant Ideas

WORDS can connote bad and good. There are words that express ill will, evil, and danger; words that threaten, and words that repel.

I. We will record a few adjectives of this type and we will introduce them to you in a series of 12 sentences. After each sentence you will find three lettered choices. Check a, b, or c according to which definition you think comes nearest in meaning to the underscored word.

(1) His *blatant* speeches against democracy offend our ears. (a) loudmouthed. (b) foolish. (c) boastful.

(2) Pressure groups are *iniquitous* because they undermine national unity. (a) bitter. (b) gloomy. (c) wicked.

(3) He has tried hard to convince me but I will not be taken in by his *specious* reasoning. (a) vain. (b) plausible. (c) cheap and coarse.

(4) He said that John was his favorite son, a most cruel and *invidious* distinction to make. (a) offensively unfair. (b) tricky. (c) superficial.

(5) His fists were getting bloody, for by now it had developed into a *sanguinary* fight. (a) bloody. (b) noisy. (c) angry.

(6) He was one of the most cantankerous and *disputatious* men I have ever known. (a) given to lying. (b) fond of arguing. (c) given to fisticuffs.

(7) We motored along the dizzy heights and up and down the *tortuous* roads of Guatemala. (a) painful. (b) sharply winding. (c) frightening.

(8) He has been for years one of the most *mordant* critics of the Russian regime. (a) frenzied. (b) sarcastic. (c) noisy.

(9) We tried every manner of training but he kept on being just the same old *refractory* horse. (a) broken. (b) sensitive. (c) unruly.

(10) International politics are cursed with the *pernicious* habit of name-calling. (a) harmful. (b) angry. (c) stubborn.

(11) Now at last he would be able to leave the *noisome* tenements of the slums. (a) clamorous. (b) disgusting. (c) broken down.

(12) We plan to take over this *moribund* business and bring it back to success. (a) gloomy. (b) dying. (c) complicated.

Answers: 1—(a); 2—(c); 3—(b); 4—(a); 5—(a); 6—(b); 7—(b); 8—(b); 9—(c); 10—(a); 11—(b); 12—(b).

II. Here are the pronunciations of the words you have just seen.

      (1) BLATANT—blay'tant

      (2) INIQUITOUS—in ik'wĭ tus

      (3) SPECIOUS—spē'shus

      (4) INVIDIOUS—in vid'ĭ us

      (5) SANGUINARY—sang'gwĭ ner ĭ

      (6) DISPUTATIOUS—dis pū tay'shus

      (7) TORTUOUS—tor'chū us

      (8) MORDANT—mor'dant

      (9) REFRACTORY—re frak'tŏ rĭ

      (10) PERNICIOUS—pur nish'us

      (11) NOISOME—noy'sum

      (12) MORIBUND—mor'ĭ bund

III. It is possible that the meanings of some of these words may still be vague. It would be simple enough to give you the definitions. It is much better, however, if you will try to figure them out for yourself. By following this method you will remember them far longer and far more easily than if you were merely to read and to memorize the dictionary definitions themselves.

Now we will take the first 6 words that you have had and present them to you in a single paragraph.

> My ears were deafened and outraged by his *blatant* address and his *iniquitous* proposals. His phrases were cleverly worded, but I hoped and prayed that his audience would not be deceived by his *specious* reasoning. At least some people started to heckle him. He was a *disputatious* type and argued with them. Finally he overstepped himself and made an *invidious* comparison between our institutions and those of Russia. Fists were shaken at him, and I became afraid that the meeting might break up in a *sanguinary* riot.

IV. Let's test now whether this has helped you along in your understanding of these words. Below you will find 6 descriptive phrases. Which one of the 6 words in this section does each phrase remind you of?

1. noisy   _____

2. wicked   _____

3. plausible   _____

4. unfairly discriminating   _____

5. bloody   _____

6. argumentative   _____

Answers: 1—blatant; 2—iniquitous; 3—specious; 4—invidious; 5—sanguinary; 6—disputatious.

V. We will now follow the same procedure with the second group of 6 words. Again they are worked into a single paragraph.

> Now we were really in the wilds, cutting a *tortuous* path through the tangled jungle, wading knee-deep through *noisome* swamps, breathing the steaming *pernicious* air, fetid with *moribund* and decaying undergrowth. Our native guides were getting *refractory*, and my com-

panion was trying to hold them in hand, first with cajolery and flattery, then, finally with the whip of a *mordant* tongue.

VI. Did you come near enough to the meanings of the 6 words in the previous paragraph to be able to pair them off with the following descriptive words?

7. winding   _____

8. nauseating   _____

9. harmful   _____

10. dying   _____

11. unruly   _____

12. biting and sarcastic   _____

Answers: 7—tortuous; 8—noisome; 9—pernicious; 10—moribund; 11—refractory; 12—mordant.

VII. Do some of the words still have fuzzy edges for you? Their meanings will be set down more fully.

(1) BLATANT: Here is a word that was coined by the English poet Edmund Spenser from the Latin term *blatio*, "to babble." With us *blatant* means "noisy" or "offensively loudmouthed."

(2) INIQUITOUS: The Latin parent of our English word is *iniquitas*, from *in-*, "not," and *æquus*, "equal." If you do "not" get an "equal" share of something, you are not apt to be having a fair deal. So *iniquitous* came to mean "grossly unjust; wicked; sinful." We speak of *iniquitous* deeds.

(3) SPECIOUS: In Latin *speciosus* means "good looking," but good-looking things are sometimes deceptive. So in English *specious* grew to mean, "appearing right, reasonable, and desirable, but not being so; apparently fair at first sight." A *specious* type of reasoning is designed to take you in and fool you.

(4) INVIDIOUS: "Unjustly and irritatingly discriminating; giving offense because unfair; tending to excite ill will and envy." (Latin: *invidiosus*, envious.)

(5) SANGUINARY: Again we turn to the Latin *sanguinarius*, from *sanguis*, "blood." A *sanguinary* battle is one attended by much bloodshed. Our English word *sanguine*, meaning "confident and hopeful," comes from the same source. In olden days it was thought that a buoyant and hopeful disposition was due to a plentiful supply of active blood.

(6) DISPUTATIOUS: This word applies to someone who is fond of arguing; who loves to carry on a dispute. It comes from the Latin *disputo*, meaning "to argue."

(7) TORTUOUS: In Latin *tortuosus* means "full of twists and turns and windings," and that's exactly what our English word signifies. The Latin root *tort-* gave birth to a host of English words. "*Tort*ure," for instance, implies that the victim's legs and arms have been "twisted." "*Tortoises*" are so named because they have "twisted" feet. When a thug *extorts* money, he literally "twists" it out of a victim, and when you make a re*tort* to another's remark you "turn" his words back on him. When we speak of a *tortuous* road we mean one that is "twisting" and "turning" in several directions; winding about in irregular "turns" or bends. To call it an *anfractuous* road would be even more emphatic.

(8) MORDANT: In Latin *mordeo* means "to bite," so a *mordant* critic is one who is "biting" and sarcastic, caustic, and cutting.

(9) REFRACTORY: Straight from the Latin *refractarius*, and with the same meaning of "stubborn, resistant, and contentious." The Latin word *refractarius* itself came from *refringo* which meant "to break in pieces." The root *fract-* has contributed "*fracture*" to our language; and "*infraction*," which is a "breaking" of a law or rule; and a *fraction* in mathematics, which is a "broken" part of a number and not a whole number. A man who is *re-*

fractory, then, is apt to "break" away from control. He is unruly, ungovernable, resistant, and obstinate.

(10) PERNICIOUS: Once more the Latin and English words are almost the same in spelling and are identical in their significance. *Pernicious* in English and *perniciosus* in Latin both mean "causing harm; working mischief or evil; having the power of destroying or injuring."

There are other words in our language that are almost synonyms of *pernicious*. INSIDIOUS (in sid'ĭ us), for example, means "doing harm, but doing harm and working ill by slow and stealthy means; treacherous; sly; intended to ensnare." We can say that gambling is an *insidious* habit. SINISTER (sin'is tur) is another sister word to *pernicious*. In this case harm is predicted. *Sinister* means "boding disaster" and therefore "adverse or harmful; disastrous; ominous; evil, perverse, and malevolent," as "He turned to him with a *sinister* look that was filled with hatred."

(11) NOISOME: An odd word made up of -*noy*, the second syllable of *annoy*, and -*some*, an Old English termination that indicates a quality or characteristic. If you were to say, for instance, that some object was "loathsome," you would mean that this object had the characteristic of something that you would loathe. So a *noisome* thing "annoys" you profoundly. It is "very offensive, particularly to the sense of smell; nauseating; disgusting." You can speak of "the *noisome* odors of the stockyards."

12) MORIBUND: A clipped form of the Latin word *moribundus*, "dying"; at its last gasp; in a dying condition. When we speak of a *moribund* civilization we mean one that is dying.

You have probably noticed in this chapter that the derivation of a word can often help to give you a more precise idea of its meaning. You have, for example, just finished reading about the Latin derivations of *pernicious*, *insidious*, and *sinister*. All these words mean "harmful," but if we go into their word histories a little more deeply we will discover the fine discriminations that divide them.

Anything that is *pernicious*, as you will remember, has the power of destroying or injuring. The Latin word that it comes from (*perniciosus*, "causing harm") is formed from two other words, *per*, "through" and *neco*, "kill," which indicates the violence of the word.

Insidious is a word of harm, too, but with a different slant. *Insidiae* (meaning "ambush") is its Latin ancestor, and hence *insidious* means harm that is accomplished by stealth.

The third word, *sinister*, can also mean harmful and disastrous, but it usually refers to harm that threatens in the future. This "future" implication originated in an ancient superstition. In Latin the word *sinister* meant "left," which is one of its meanings in English. But in the days of the Greeks and the Romans an omen seen on the "left" boded ill.

It is not always true that derivations can throw light on meanings, but frequently they are very helpful.

> Words are the only things that
> last forever.   HAZLITT

31. A Group of Useful Adjectives

THERE ARE words of high value in this chapter that will be useful to you in many departments of your life. Some of them you can employ in your everyday conversation or letter writing. Others will be more properly a part of your reading vocabulary, as some of them might be too unusual to use in the ordinary talk of the day with friends. Whatever uses you make of these adjectives, please try to get these meanings clearly in your mind. This will set you above the vast majority who have only the fuzziest ideas of words and their meanings.

I. We will cover 12 adjectives in this chapter. The first 6 are included in the following paragraph:

He is really an *exemplary* character, of good manners and good taste, although I will say he goes around with a *motley* crew. He is *adamant* on the subject of morals and will not be swayed from the straight path. His principles are *immutable*. In his reading he is *omnivorous* and covers all subjects. As a matter of fact he regards reading as a *mandatory* part of a cultured life.

II. Go over these words again, if you will, and then try to fit each of them to the following definitions. The order is not the same.

1. unyielding   _____

2. obligatory   _____

3. setting an example   _____

4. fond of all kinds   _____

5. made up of individual units   _____

6. never changing   _____

Answers: 1—adamant; 2—mandatory; 3—exemplary; 4—omnivorous; 5—motley; 6—immutable.

III. Now for the second group of 6. You will at least get a hint as to the meanings from this paragraph.

He felt keenly that the loss of religion and the absence of ethical standards were *portentous* signs of the times. Atheism was *rife*. He longed to awaken the people but he knew that they were indifferent and *comatose*. He was a crusader at heart, and he had a plan that was touched with imagination, but he felt that the moment was not *propitious*, that the obstacles were *insuperable*, and that the situation for the time, at least, was *irremediable*.

IV. Now match the words to the definitions.

1. not able to be overcome   _____

2. widespread _____

3. favorable _____

4. solemn and ominous _____

5. abnormally sleepy and lethargic _____

6. that cannot be remedied _____

Answers: 1—insuperable; 2—rife; 3—propitious; 4—portentous; 5—comatose; 6—irremediable.

V. Below is a list of the 12 words with their pronunciations.

     (1) EXEMPLARY—egz em'plă rĭ

     (2) MOTLEY—mot'lĭ

     (3) ADAMANT—ad'ă mant

     (4) IMMUTABLE—im mū'tă b'l

     (5) OMNIVOROUS—om niv'ō rus

     (6) MANDATORY—man'dă tō rĭ

     (7) PORTENTOUS—por ten'tus

     (8) RIFE—rife

     (9) COMATOSE—kom'ă tose

    (10) PROPITIOUS—prō pish'us

    (11) INSUPERABLE—in sū'pur ă b'l

    (12) IRREMEDIABLE—ir rĕ mē'dĭ ă b'l

VI. You will come very close to the accurate meanings if the words are set in individual sentences.

1. His conduct was *exemplary* in the handling of a very difficult situation.

2. He was walled in with a crowd of *motley* people.

3. We found her still angry, still unwilling to act, still *adamant*.

4. The laws of economics are *immutable* and unchangeable.

5. He reads widely, for he has, truly, an *omnivorous* taste for literature.

6. The attendance at chapel should be made *mandatory*.

7. With all these rumors of war, the times are *portentous*.

8. The stories of midnight revels were *rife* when I first went there.

9. It should be the duty of the president to awaken to life that *comatose* department.

10. He wanted to ask me something, but he didn't feel that the occasion was *propitious*.

11. The Atlantic Ocean may no longer be an *insuperable* barrier to the military invasion of this hemisphere.

12. Britain's plight then seemed *irremediable*.

VII. Which of the 12 words do the following sentences suggest?

(1) To us he seemed like Rip Van Winkle. _____

(2) He's never changed one of his ideas since childhood. _____

(3) The gossip is all over the countryside. _____

(4) The future looks dark to me. _____

(5) The situation is so involved that I doubt if anybody could remedy it. _____

(6) He reads everything from the pulps to the slicks. _____

(7) He's as stubborn as a mule. _____

(8) When the boss gives an order it really is a command. _____

(9) It was the most mixed up and miscellaneous crowd I have ever seen. _____

(10) That's the type of problem that you can't surmount. _____

(11) What a lovely time to have held the wedding. ———————

(12) That's a life I would like to imitate. ———————

Answers: 1—comatose; 2—immutable; 3—rife; 4—portentous; 5—irremediable; 6—omnivorous; 7—adamant; 8—mandatory; 9—motley; 10—insuperable; 11—propitious; 12—exemplary.

VIII. If you had a perfect score you are an exceptional person. Even 7 or 8 correct answers would be good. But, as we have said before, your greatest benefit will come from the *effort* to discover the meanings. Now please read the definitions.

(1) EXEMPLARY: Worthy to serve as a pattern or type; fit to be imitated; setting an example; hence, commendable.

(2) MOTLEY: Of different colors; made up of miscellaneous units (a *motley* crowd); clothed in varicolored garments (a *motley* clown).

(3) ADAMANT: Impenetrably hard; unyielding. From the Greek *adamas*, "not tamed."

(4) IMMUTABLE: Unchangeable; invariable; permanent; incapable of change.

(5) OMNIVOROUS: From the Latin *omnivorous*, *omnis*, "all," and *voro*, "to eat"; hence eating up everything; voracious; or, figuratively, "devouring" everything, such as reading matter.

(6) MANDATORY: Obligatory; expressed as a positive command.

(7) PORTENTOUS: Ominous; significant; full of portents of ill.

(8) RIFE: An Old English word that means prevalent; common; numerous; current; widespread.

(9) COMATOSE: In Greek *koma* means "slumber"; hence, *comatose* means abnormally sleepy; lethargic; in a stupor.

(10) PROPITIOUS: Attended by favorable circumstances; kindly disposed; auspicious; favorable.

(11) INSUPERABLE: From the Latin *insuperabilis*, from *in-*, "not," and *super*, "above." Hence something that you "can't get above" and, therefore, something insurmountable and not to be overcome.

(12) IRREMEDIABLE: That cannot be remedied; incurable; irreparable.

Here are a few other useful adjectives. The sentences will reveal their meanings.

"He was *exultant* (overjoyed) at his victory."

"The gangster lived in a *pretentious* and *ostentatious* (showy) house."

"We spent several *halcyon* (calm and peaceful) days by the seashore."

"To this critic the works of Keats were *nonpareil* (without equal) in the field of poetry."

We are all born with a burning wish to learn. That, of course, is why children ask their innumerable questions. The very young have a voracious appetite for knowledge, an insatiable intellectual curiosity. But tragically, with maturity, much of this eagerness dies, and when it dies all mental growth stops. If, however, a person will sincerely and earnestly apply himself to building his vocabulary he will find that he is recapturing the powerful urge to learn.

> Words are the very stuff and
> process of thought.   *British*

32.   Adjectives in Fields of Writing and Speaking

WORDS about words are always interesting. We are presenting a few in this chapter that peculiarly belong to the fields of speaking and writing. We will approach these words by the indirect method where the meanings are not flashed on you but are revealed to you little by little.

I. You will meet them first in quotations from current newspapers and books.

1. "It is true that the occasion was a mournful one but his highly colored story about it was *lugubrious* (lū gū′brĭ us) in the extreme." Was his story
    (a) ridiculous?
    (b) exaggeratedly solemn?
    (c) sarcastic?

2. "The picture is *terse* (turse) with thrilling moments of incident and action." The picture is
    (a) short and to the point.
    (b) tense.
    (c) long drawn out.

3. "There is a handful of misguided fools who have been led astray by his *fatuous* (fat′ū us) theories." Were his theories
    (a) popular?
    (b) wicked?
    (c) stupidly silly?

4. "He has an *incisive* (in sī′siv) style, with the rare combination of a poetic imagination and an engineering precision." His style is
    (a) sarcastic.
    (b) sensitive.
    (c) clear cut and penetrating.

5. "It is a *scurrilous* (skur′ĭ lus) sheet that should have been put out of business long ago." Is the character of the newspaper in question
    (a) shallow?
    (b) offensively indecent?
    (c) politically unsound?

6. "His philosophy was no doubt profound and helpful but it was *esoteric* (es ō ter′ik) and hence impractical for the masses." Was his philosophy

(a) capable of being understood only by a select few?
(b) too severe in its discipline?
(c) too revolutionary?

7. "A *decadent* (dĕ kay′dent *or* dĕk′uh dent) aristocracy and a medieval school system could not dampen the charm of the city." What type of aristocracy are we dealing with—
    (a) decaying?
    (b) enormously wealthy?
    (c) ruthless?

8. "He was pretentious in his manner and his speech was filled with *magniloquent* (mag nil′ō kwent) phrases." The phrases he used were
    (a) boastful.
    (b) flattering.
    (c) humorous.

9. "He was notified of his dismissal by an *acrimonious* (ak rĭ mō′nē us) letter." What kind of letter was this—
    (a) brief?
    (b) bitter?
    (c) tactful?

10. "Voltaire attacked his age and its civilization with *iconoclastic* (ī kon ō klas′tik) writings."—This type of writing is essentially
    (a) angry.
    (b) amusing.
    (c) destructive to cherished beliefs.

Answers: 1—(b); 2—(a); 3—(c); 4—(c); 5—(b); 6—(a); 7—(a); 8—(a); 9—(b); 10—(c).

II. We will approach these words from a slightly different direction.

(1) Which one of the following authors would tend to be *esoteric?* A: Albert Einstein. B: William Makepeace Thackeray. C: Robert Louis Stevenson.

(2) Of the following three characters of fiction which one might be called *fatuous?* A: The Village Blacksmith. B: Don Quixote. C: Oliver Twist.

(3) One of these authors is noted for his *terse*, epigrammatic style. A: James Boswell. B: Benjamin Franklin. C: Charles Dickens.

(4) A writing style that is *incisive* and penetrating is called— A: florid. B: turbid. C: cutting.

(5) Which of these three authors could best be called *iconoclastic?* A: Tennyson. B: Shakespeare. C: Voltaire.

(6) Of these three political figures one could be definitely singled out as *magniloquent*. A: Thomas E. Dewey. B: Woodrow Wilson. C: Huey Long.

(7) The word *lugubrious* would most nearly apply to which of the following occasions? A: a wedding. B: a funeral. C: a christening.

(8) Which one of these writers could be most properly called *decadent?* A: Oscar Wilde. B: Emerson. C: Longfellow.

(9) *Scurrilous* language is—A: grossly vulgar. B: flattering. C: insincere.

(10) Of these three Presidents one stands out as a writer of *acrimonious* letters—A: Hoover. B: Truman. C: Harding.

Answers: 1—A; 2—B; 3—B; 4—C; 5—C; 6—C; 7—B; 8—A; 9—A; 10—B.

III. In the list that follows, match the 10 words with their synonyms or synonymic phrases.

1. acrimonious	*a.*	vulgar
2. scurrilous	*b.*	solemn
3. esoteric	*c.*	known to the few
4. decadent	*d.*	bitter

5.	lugubrious	e.	boasting
6.	iconoclastic	f.	destructive to beliefs
7.	magniloquent	g.	falling into decay
8.	terse	h.	foolish
9.	fatuous	i.	brief
10.	incisive	j.	clear cut and penetrating

Answers: 1—*d;* 2—*a;* 3—*c;* 4—*g;* 5—*b;* 6—*f;* 7—*e;* 8—*i;* 9—*h;* 10—*j.*

IV. If you did even approximately well with Section III you should be pleased. These are all words of high value, but if some of them are new to you, you may find it hard to master them on the first try. Now for their meanings.

(1) LUGUBRIOUS: You can have a *lugubrious* look on your face, or it can be a *lugubrious* occasion, or an author can write in a *lugubrious* fashion. It all means mournful, doleful, exaggeratedly solemn.

(2) TERSE: A *terse* style in speaking or writing is one that is short and to the point, but usually tasteful and finished. A synonym for *terse* is *SENTENTIOUS* (sen ten'shus), as, "His articles are *sententious* but never clipped." This means that he is saying much in few words; that what he writes is full of meaning.

(3) FATUOUS: Both this word and its Latin parent *fatuus* mean stubbornly blind and foolish; illusory; stupidly silly.

(4) INCISIVE: An *incisive* style is one that is penetrating and acute. It is trenchant and clear cut, for it comes from a Latin word that means "to cut in." Our word incision is from the same source. TRENCHANT (tren'shunt) is a synonym; but besides indicating that this certain style is sharp, keen, and clear, it emphasizes the fact that it

is also vigorous and effective. "It was stimulating to hear his *trenchant* observations on the current scene."

(5) SCURRILOUS: A biting word that means grossly offensive and vulgar in an indecent way.

(6) ESOTERIC: From the Greek *esoterikos*, "inner," and thus, the "inner" secrets of the temple. In this sense you can speak of the *esoteric* (secret) rites of the Masons. More broadly it can mean writings that are abstruse and difficult to understand. In this latter meaning it comes close to the term RECONDITE (rek'on dite *or* rĕ kon'dite). This word signifies too deep for ordinary comprehension; beyond ordinary perception, as we would say: "This book, in its clear thinking and simple phrases, clarifies a *recondite* subject."

(7) DECADENT: Anything decadent is characterized by a deterioration or decline; falling into ruin and decay.

(8) MAGNILOQUENT: In Latin *magniloquentia* literally means "big talk," and, in the same way, our English adjective means boasting; uttered in a boastful and vainglorious manner. Our English TURGID (tur'jid) is a close synonym. It essentially means swollen, but it now can apply to inflated and ostentatious speech or manners. "His mind is devoid of simplicity and his speeches are *turgid*."

(9) ACRIMONIOUS: The key Latin word is *acer*, "sharp." *Acrimonious* means sharp and bitter of speech or temper.

(10) ICONOCLASTIC: This is a colorful word that came to us from the Greek *eikonoklastes*. It is formed from *eikon*, "image" and *klaein*, "to break." Originally the *iconoclast* was opposed to the worship of idols. He "broke" the "images." Now the word has broadened. Anything *iconoclastic* is destructive to cherished beliefs and institutions.

With each chapter your wealth of words is growing. And this habit of word study you are forming is something that will never leave you. And what it will do for you is almost beyond description.

> Thoughts that breathe and words
> that burn. — GRAY

33. More Unpleasant Adjectives

YOU will be left pretty much to your own devices with this group of words. You have been going through quite a number of drills, and it might be restful and a change of pace to discuss the following words informally. They all are words with somewhat unpleasant implications.

I. Let's spell them and pronounce them first.

CHOLERIC—kol′ur ik

BELLICOSE—bel′ĭ kōs

BELLIGERENT—be lij′ur unt

OBSTREPEROUS—ob strep′ur us

INTRACTABLE—in trak′tă b'l

PREDATORY—pred′ă to rĭ

INSATIABLE—in say′shĭ ă b'l *or* in say′shuh b'l

USURIOUS—ū zūr′ĭ us

LAMENTABLE—lam′en tă b'l

POIGNANT—poin′yunt *or* poin′unt

VITRIOLIC—vit ri ol′ik

II. *Choleric* originally comes from the Greek word for "bile." The ancients thought bile was the cause of ill temper. The *choleric* person is hot-tempered and easily made angry. But if he is actually fond of fighting he is called *bellicose* or *belligerent*, as, "They grew *belligerent* or *bellicose* as the argument progressed." The key to both of these words is found in Latin *bellum*, "war."

There are other types of persons who, although possibly not fond of actual fighting, are nevertheless *obstreperous*, that is, noisy, disorderly, and unruly; or *intractable*, that is, unruly and difficult to manage. "The crowd was growing restless and *intractable*." And, "He was the most *obstreperous* patient ever admitted to the naval hospital."

The terms *predatory*, *insatiable*, and *usurious* all have the central idea of greed.

Predatory is probably the most important, or, at least, the most powerful of the three. We speak of the *predatory* nations. The word originally derives from the Latin *præda*, "booty," and hence, *predatory* powers plunder, rob, and destroy others. Let's put this word in a sentence: "In order to continue in power that hierarchy must lead their nation on to new *predatory* adventures."

Insatiable derives from a Latin combination meaning "not satisfied," and so our word means "that cannot be satisfied," as, "War has an *insatiable* appetite for materials." *Usurious* people have greed and *usury* in their hearts. They charge unfair interest for the use of money, as: "He now began to pay on his loan at the *usurious* rates demanded."

Lamentable things are things that are fitted to be lamented or mourned. They are regrettable or deplorable, as: "International relations are in a *lamentable* state."

Anything *poignant* is deeply moving, touching, painful. A *poignant* play is one that is emotionally affecting. We can say: "Even more *poignant* is the destruction we viewed a little later in Stepney."

Vitriol is a term for sulfuric acid. Hence, anything *vitriolic* burns and sears. If we say: "The report that he wrote was *vitriolic*," we mean that it is caustic and biting, sharp, and severely critical.

It would be almost impossible to test you on these words. Terms such as *choleric*, *bellicose*, *belligerent*, *obstreperous*, and *intractable*, for instance, all apply to troublemakers, and they are so near together in meaning that no sentences could be devised where one and only one of the words would fit.

Now that you have covered these 11 difficult adjectives you may be saying again: "They are good words, but how can I use them? Some of my friends wouldn't know what I was talking about. Others might think I was stuffy."

Once more I must emphasize that words are not only for the purposes of casual conversation or informal letter-writing, but also for reading and understanding. And for thinking. Short and simple words are the best for ordinary uses. They will serve most purposes. They will help you to speak and to write so that people will understand what you mean.

There is more to language than this, however, if you really want to become skilled in its use and in catching its fine meanings. Read Churchill's "Blood, Sweat, and Tears." Read Lincoln's "Gettysburg Address." These great masters will use words as simple as "The Sermon on the Mount." But they hold great words in reserve, and once in a while, when they have a truly great idea that they want to force into your mind, they will draw upon some magnificent verb or adjective or noun that will hit you with a physical impact. Words such as these are a necessary part of a cultured vocabulary.

> Words that may become alive
> and walk up and down in the
> hearts of men.   *British*

34.   Adjectives That Have to Do with Size

IN THIS WORLD of four dimensions that we live in (if we count time as the fourth), size has, of course, importance, and in this chapter you will have 12 adjectives that deal with it. Their full definitions will not be given to you at the moment, but you will be able to make a good guess at the meanings of the words that you don't already know.

I. Here are the 12 words with their pronunciations. All but two are words of four or more syllables, which tends to show that ideas or objects of large size almost demand big words to describe them.

1. Events that are *monumental* (mon ū men't'l) are impressive and notable and last "like a monument."

2. A *stentorian* (sten tō'rĭ an) voice is extremely loud and powerful.

3. Anything *gargantuan* (gahr gan'tū an) is enormous and is usually tied in with greed.

4. A *herculean* (hur kū lē'an) task is one that requires great effort.

5. *Astronomical* (as trō nom'ĭ k'l) figures are difficult to count because they are so huge.

6. A *momentous* (mō men'tus) occasion is one that is weighty and of great importance.

7. When we speak of a *catastrophic* (kat ă strŏf'ik) happening we are referring to an overwhelming and widespread misfortune.

8. When a person assumes a *grandiose* (gran'dĭ ōs) manner he is pompous and is trying to seem magnificent.

9. *Illimitable* (ĭ lim'ĭt ă b'l) just means "without limit."

10. An *august* (aw gust') manner is one that is majestic and imposing.

11. Those who are *omniscient* (om nish'ent) possess infinite knowledge.

12. Those who are *omnipotent* (om nip'ō tent) have unlimited power.

II. Be careful when you fill in the blank spaces that have been left in the following sentences. All these 12 adjectives have to do with a type of size, but there is one adjective that will best fit the meaning of each sentence. The initial letters will help you because the order of the words is changed.

1. The c_____ defeats on the eastern front did much to bring Germany to her knees.

2. The conceited official was explaining in a g_____ manner that he would be delighted to show us the institution.

3. This plain fact is a m_____ milestone on our onward march.

4. Leonardo da Vinci with his multiple skills and incredible wisdom could be truly said to have been o_____.

5. Japan's dreams of empire were modest in comparison with the g_____ aspirations of Germany.

6. They had too great a faith in his power and actually seemed to believe that he was o_____.

7. The referee announced the score in a s_____ voice.

8. It is time that the powers that be in Washington should rally to the h_____ task of stopping inflation.

9. Our national debt has reached a_____ figures.

10. Once again we come to one of those periods in history when m_____ decisions have to be made.

11. We are pouring out the world's savings and these savings are not i_____.

12. The crowd was hushed before his a_____ presence.

Answers: 1—catastrophic; 2—grandiose; 3—monumental; 4—omniscient; 5—gargantuan; 6—omnipotent; 7—stentorian; 8—herculean; 9—astronomical; 10—momentous; 11—illimitable; 12—august.

III. Some of these words are so near to each other in meaning that we had best turn to their derivations so that we will be able to draw a fine line between them.

(1) MONUMENTAL comes from the Latin *monumentum*, which means "that which is intended to preserve the recollection of any thing." That is, a *monumental* happening is some-

thing so tremendous and notable that we will always "remember" it.

(2) STENTORIAN: The man Stentor was a herald in the Trojan War who was famous for his clarion voice. Hence a *stentorian* voice is one that is uncommonly strong.

(3) GARGANTUAN: Gargantua was a giant in a satire by Rabelais, who had a phenomenal appetite. Hence the word *gargantuan* means anyone like Gargantua with his characteristics of size or greed. Another word with a similar derivation and meaning is TITANIC (tī tan'ik). In Greek mythology the Titans were giants, so anything *titanic* is of great size. Unlike *gargantuan*, greed is not implied in the meaning of *titanic*. This latter word would appear thus in a sentence: "We are giving everything we have in contributing our part to this *titanic* struggle."

(4) HERCULEAN: We know that Hercules was a hero of Greek mythology who was noted for his superhuman strength. Therefore a *herculean* task would be one that would require the strength of a Hercules.

(5) ASTRONOMICAL: Originally the Greek *astronomia*, from *astron*, "star," and *nemein*, "to distribute." So when we speak of the *astronomical* figures of our national debt we mean that it is as huge as the stars in numbers.

(6) MOMENTOUS: Here is a word that comes from the Late Latin term *momentosus*, meaning "of a moment." But our word refers to a "moment" of vast importance and great consequence, as "We have come to a period in history when *momentous* (weighty) decisions have to be made."

(7) CATASTROPHIC: This word pertains to a sudden and overwhelming misfortune or calamity. The Greek word *katastrophe*, "overturning," hints at the meaning. A *catastrophic* earthquake would carry the Greek sense of "turning over."

(8) GRANDIOSE: Originally from the Latin *grandis* meaning "large." But coming down to us through Italian and

French it grew to mean "large" or pompous and affected in manner, although occasionally it is used to mean imposing and impressive. A word close to this in meaning is GRANDILOQUENT (gran dil′ ō kwent), from the Latin *grandis,* "grand," and *loquor,* "to speak"—that is, "big talk." Unlike *grandiose* the term *grandiloquent* refers only to speech, to the using of lofty and pompous words.

(9) ILLIMITABLE: The *il-* part of this word (a form of *in* used before *l*) means "not" and *limit* is from the Latin *limes* which means "a cross-path or boundary line," so *illimitable* means "not able to be bounded," and thus, without limits; boundless.

(10) AUGUST: This is directly from the Latin *augustus,* "majestic."

(11) OMNISCIENT reveals its meaning in its Latin parts. *Omniscient* is made up of *omnis,* "all," and *scio,* "to know." Hence the *omniscient* "all-knowing."

(12) OMNIPOTENT: Here we have the whole story in the Latin word *omnipotens,* "all-powerful," from *omnis,* "all," and *potens,* "being able." So an *omnipotent* person is "able" to do "all" and so has unlimited and universal power.

IV. How many of these words can you recall? The order has been radically changed.

1. i_____   7. m_____

2. o_____   8. s_____

3. o_____   9. g_____

4. a_____   10. h_____

5. g_____   11. a_____

6. c_____   12. m_____

The intent of this book has been to save you, the reader, the bother of constantly turning to the dictionary. But the dictionary habit is a valuable one for you to form just the same. So many of the words you have been studying are rich in meanings, and all these shades of meanings cannot be given in the confines of this small volume.

> Clearness is the most important
> matter in the use of words.
>
> QUINTILLIAN

35. A Miscellany of Adjectives

YOUR VOCABULARY is the best single test of your IQ. Today there is no excuse for not improving it. The techniques for doing this are known. And if you make yourself rich in words your competition will be slight. Here is why.

From 1946 to 1949 seventy-five million people in the United States didn't read a single book; sixteen million read no magazine or newspaper. Ten million were completely illiterate.

How easy it is to stand above this crowd. There are so many ways of learning words.

Here is one hint that can be helpful. You can use outdoor advertising signs to aid you in adding to your vocabulary. Also the car cards in buses and subways and the advertisements in the magazines and newspapers can be used with profit to this end.

If the word *charming*, for instance, appears in an advertisement that you happen to be looking at, try to see how many synonyms you can find for it. Has the high-priced publicity man chosen the best word for the purpose? Would the word *attractive* be better, or *alluring*, *bewitching*, *lovely*, *captivating*, *enchanting*, *enrapturing*, *entrancing*, *winning*, or *fascinating?*

I. You can very often play this same game with the words in this list. Here is a group of 18 forceful adjectives to add to your

reservoir of words. You will first be introduced to their pronunciations. Of course it is more than possible that you are
already acquainted with them.

    (1) MARTIAL—mar′shul

    (2) PREMONITORY—pre mon′ĭ tō rĭ

    (3) STRIDENT—strī′dent

    (4) REPLETE—re pleet′

    (5) ACRID—ak′rid

    (6) INEXPLICABLE—in ex′plĭ kă b′l

    (7) EGREGIOUS—e gree′jus

    (8) LETHARGIC—lĕ thahr′jik (*th* as in *thin*)

    (9) LETHAL—lē′thal (*th* as in *thin*)

    (10) DOUGHTY—dow′tĭ

    (11) ACQUISITIVE—ă kwiz′ĭ tiv

    (12) INIMICAL—in im′ĭ kul

    (13) IRASCIBLE—ĭ ras′ĭ b′l

    (14) MALODOROUS—mal ō′dur us

    (15) STARK—stahrk

    (16) INELUCTABLE—in ē luk′tuh b′l

    (17) ABJECT—ab′jekt

    (18) IRATE—ī′rate

II. We will select the first 8 words in the above list. The test you
will receive on them is designed to show the power and economy
that can be gained by knowing the right word. One of the 8 terms
can be used in place of the italicized words that appear in the
parentheses in each sentence. Write in the word that you think
fits the definition.

a. acrid   *c.* inexplicable   *e.* martial   *g.* strident
b. egregious   *d.* lethargic   *f.* premonitory   *h.* replete

(1) The troops swung down the street to the strains of (*pertaining to or connected with military operations*) music.   _____

(2) The (*giving or containing an actual warning of something yet to occur*) signs of war are in the air.   _____

(3) The room was filled with the (*loud, shrill, and grating*) voices of children.   _____

(4) His speech was brilliant and colorful, (*abundantly supplied and filled to the uttermost*) with beautifully turned phrases.   _____

(5) He was almost suffocated by the stifling heat and (*stinging to the taste and nose*) smells.   _____

(6) His (*not capable of being explained*) actions caused his downfall.   _____

(7) The kindest thing that you could say of him is that he was an (*exceeding or towering above ordinary men*) ass.   _____

(8) He had been a person of great ambition, but whether through ill health or frustration he had become indifferent, inactive, (*unnaturally dull and sluggish*).   _____

Answers: 1—martial; 2—premonitory; 3—strident; 4—replete; 5—acrid; 6—inexplicable; 7—egregious; 8—lethargic.

III. It is one thing to know the meaning of a word when you see it. It is quite another to call it up when you want to use it. How many of these 8 words can you recapture?

    1. completely filled   r_____

    2. that cannot be accounted for   i_____

    3. sluggish and drowsy   l_____

    4. that surpasses all others   e_____

    5. giving warning ahead   p_____

6. pertaining to war   m_____

7. acid and biting to taste and smell   a_____

8. harsh and shrill   s_____

Answers: 1—replete; 2—inexplicable; 3—lethargic; 4—egregious; 5—premonitory; 6—martial; 7—acrid; 8—strident.

IV. These well-known speakers and writers have used these words in this fashion:

(1) "They have *martial* qualities, but they do not like to drill."— Winston Churchill.

(2) "The *premonitory* symptoms of despotism are upon us."— Hugo L. Black.

(3) "The world is menaced by brute force and *strident* ambition." —James F. Byrnes.

(4) "The book is *replete* with the details of just how the men advanced."—Cecil Brown.

(5) "Dark shapes loomed out of the steam and *acrid* fumes."— Elizabeth Fowler.

(6) "Her *inexplicable* rise is one of the great phenomena of history."—Jan Christiaan Smuts.

(7) "Such a person is cursed with *egregious* conceit."—Lloyd C. Douglas.

(8) "He was a heavy man, unwieldy in body and *lethargic* in mind."—Margery Wilson.

V. The second group of 10 adjectives in this chapter are of varying degrees of difficulty and value.

(1) You know the irritable type of man who is easily aroused to anger. He always has a chip on his shoulder.
He is *irascible*.

(2) Once such a touchy man is really stirred he becomes wrathful and enraged.

He is *irate*.

(3) Here is a difficult and unusual word but nevertheless one of great impact. It applies to something that is impossible to struggle against and that cannot be escaped. A girl, for example, can be said to have irresistible charm.

She has *ineluctable* charm.

(4) The one syllable word *stark* packs a punch. Scenery can be *stark*—that is, bare and unadorned. A person can be stark naked—that is, completely so and "unadorned" by clothes. Or there can be a tragedy that is bare, grim, and "unadorned."

That would be a *stark* tragedy.

(5) There are things in this world, such as the traffic in drugs, that are hurtful and unfriendly to man and to mankind and to his welfare.

They are *inimical* to man.

(6) Some people are more eager to gain money and possessions than others. They are grasping, greedy, and mercenary.

They are *acquisitive*.

(7) Lots of names exist for the brave man. He is valiant, formidable, courageous, and often strong and able.

He is *doughty*.

(8) A person can receive a deadly dose of poison.

It is a *lethal* dose.

(9) On occasion a person will be low in his spirits, sunk to a truly abased condition, where he can be called slavish, servile, and ignoble.

His condition is *abject*.

(10) There are substances that give off a very bad odor. They are obnoxious and evil-smelling.

They are *malodorous*.

VI. Review Section V and then see if you can remember the approximate meanings of the words that you covered.

  1. irascible   6. acquisitive

  2. irate   7. doughty

  3. ineluctable   8. lethal

  4. stark   9. abject

  5. inimical   10. malodorous

VII. These words have virtually been defined for you in Section V. If they are now shown to you in actual quotations it will bring the meanings into a sharper focus.

(1) "The strain of his long trial had made him *irascible*."—Robert G. Chaffee.

(2) "The comic strip was a normal one about a man and his *irate* mother-in-law."—Alexander Markey.

(3) "We are faced by a hard, *ineluctable* fact."—Samuel Hoare.

(4) "Not one word of comment is necessary; the *stark* facts speak for themselves."—Monroe E. Deutsch.

(5) "He was conscious of the strangeness of this cache in the snow, this mid-winter refuge in a world *inimical* to man."—John Buchan.

(6) "Suppose that strong, just men refused to take action against the *acquisitive*, unjust men."—Richard E. Byrd.

(7) "The *doughty* public servant assured the nation that the Navy was ready."—Wendell L. Willkie.

(8) "They equip their vigilantes with tin hats, gas masks, and *lethal* weapons."—John L. Lewis.

(9) "Europeans were terrorized into various forms of *abject* submission."—Winston Churchill.

(10) "The little flat was hot and stuffy, and from the road beat up a *malodorous* sultriness."—W. Somerset Maugham.

VIII. If you can call off 10 or 12 of these 18 words you will be well above average.

1. filled full   re_____

2. unexplainable   in_____

3. abnormally sluggish and dull   le_____

4. extraordinary and outrageous   eg_____

5. forewarning   pr_____

6. relating to war   ma_____

7. sharp and biting to the taste and smell   ac_____

8. harsh-sounding and shrill   st_____

9. easily angered   ir_____

10. wrathful   ir_____

11. irresistible   in_____

12. bare and grim   st_____

13. hurtful   in_____

14. greedy and grasping   ac_____

15. strong and valiant   do_____

16. deadly   le_____

17. cast down in spirit   ab_____

18. evil-smelling   ma_____

Answers: 1—replete; 2—inexplicable; 3—lethargic; 4—egregious; 5—premonitory; 6—martial; 7—acrid; 8—strident; 9—irascible; 10—irate; 11—ineluctable; 12—stark; 13—inimical; 14—acquisitive; 15—doughty; 16—lethal; 17—abject; 18—malodorous.

You can see that this language of ours is almost inexhaustible. And it is truly full of excitement and beauty.

FIFTH INTERMISSION

Odd Word Histories

WE HAVE spoken in this book of short, Old English words. They are usually words of simple form and are often of only one syllable. And yet at times it happens that these short and common words can be quite complicated. If you will place one of them under a microscope it will often break up into a phrase or even sometimes into a whole sentence.

Let's try a word like *barn*, for instance. Four letters, one syllable, and as solid as an oak beam. But is it?

If we look at *barn* under a reading glass we will see that it splits up into two words, *bere*, "barley," and *ærn*, "place." That is, the *bere-ærn*, our *barn*, was originally "a place for barley."

Again, there's hardly a day goes by that we don't use the word *about*. One time, long ago, somebody wrote it down and we have said it over and over "ever since." (Time out to consider the phrase "ever since." A thousand years ago we would have spelled these two words *æfre sithe*, and they would have meant literally "ever after" as they do now.)

But to return to our word *about*. Away back in Anglo-Saxon days you'll find *about* spelled *onbuton*, and this word is a sentence, *on*, "on," *be*, "by," and *utan*, "outside." So if you should remark "There is nobody *about*" you are really saying, "There is nobody nearby the outside of my house or wherever I am." Thus *about* got to be used in the sense of "near by," "nearly," "around," and so forth.

Alas is also a common word with a less complicated history. This little, old-fashioned number is just a sigh of weariness and sadness. It is made up of the Old French *"ah"* for the sigh, and the Latin word *lassum*, meaning "tired." So *alas* is merely a shortened form of *ah lassum*. You will recognize the Latin *lassum* in "lassitude," our English term that means "a condition of weariness."

When you are the *only* person at a party, you are literally "one-ly," the *ly* coming from the Old English term -*lĭc*, "like." So when you are the *only* one present you are "one-like" or "like one," which is about true.

The words *lonely* and *lone* both come from the term *alone* which, of course, is similar in meaning to *only*. The unpretentious word *alone* literally means "all one." And when one is by one's self, one is *alone*, or "all one," isn't one?

Then there are the two simple words *good-bye* and *Gospel*. We all know by this time that the first one is a telescoped version of the phrase "God be with you," and that the second one is derived from "God's spell." And since *spell* used to mean "story," its "God's story" we are talking about when we speak of the *Gospel*.

In our language the word *unless* used to be spelled "onless" these many centuries ago, but some smart scholar who was none too wise thought that the "on" should be "un," so he respelled it "unless." The meaning is still "on." For instance, if you were to say, "I'll work tomorrow *unless* I'm too tired," you really mean, *"On* any *less* event than being too tired I'll work tomorrow." Or you might demur and say that you have determined not to go to work *because* you are too tired, which actually means that you won't work "by cause" of the fact that you are too tired.

To carry this same anecdote a little further, you might remark that you would *rather* play golf than work. *Rather* comes from the Old English word *rathe*, which means "ahead of other things." So "ahead of other things" such as work you would prefer to play golf. Or, to put it another way, and with the same implication, you would "sooner" play golf than work.

There are many oddities among the plainer words of our language. *Naughty* is one such. You would hardly suspect such a common word as this of complications.

Back about a thousand years ago *naughty* was spelled by the English in several ways: *nauht, naht, noht,* or *nawhit*. And *nawhit* came from *ne,* "not," *a,* "ever," and *whit,* "thing." So *nawhit* meant "not ever a thing," or just plain "nothing." Even in the days of Miles Standish they spoke of "the *naughty* canoes." That is, the canoes were "good for *naught*." So if you are "good for naught" you are worthless, and worthless people are often bad, and that's what our word has finally come to mean.

But even the odd history of *naughty* is hardly as bizarre as that of the harmless four-letter word *nice*. What a chase that will lead us!

In the Middle Ages *nice* meant foolish or ignorant, for it comes from the Latin word *nescio,* which is made up of *ne,* "not," and *scio,* "to know." Then because ignorant people are very often silent, its meaning changed to "shy" or "coy." Later there came another shift in meaning. Sometimes shy folks get the reputation of being a little supercilious because of their offish ways. So with consequent changes *nice* came to mean "hard to please," "precise," "exacting." We use it today in that sense when we say: "That is a *nice* problem." Finally *nice* became general in its meaning and is now applied to many things, such as people of good taste and pleasant disposition.

So you can see that many of our simplest words are anything but simple after all.

SIXTH WEEK

Choice word and measure phrase
above the reach of ordinary men.
WORDSWORTH

36. Adjectives with Disagreeable Meanings

AS WE have said before, those words that deal with hate, crime, anger, vilification, invective, and such seem to have more sheer power than the kindlier terms. It is, perhaps, because they are surcharged with emotion, dynamic with passion. And they are often emphasized when spoken. As a matter of fact the sound of your voice can influence meaning. You can say "good-night" in a tone of surprise or disgust. And a girl can say it in a way that invites a kiss.

I. The adjectives listed in this chapter will have ominous or evil connotations. How many of them are familiar to you? How many can you define with a measure of accuracy?

(1) PERFIDIOUS—pur fid'ĭ us

(2) BALEFUL—bale'ful

(3) LARCENOUS—lahr'sĕ nus

(4) UNREGENERATE—un rĭ jen'ur it

(5) DIRE—dire

(6) GRUESOME—grōō'sum

(7) REPUGNANT—re pug'nant

(8) DEFAMATORY—de fam'ă to rĭ

(9) CLANDESTINE—klan des'tin

(10) VITUPERATIVE—vī tū'pur ā tiv

(11) ILLICIT—ĭ lis'ĭt

(12) SALACIOUS—să lay'shus

II. Let's approach these words with a general discussion, and without, at the moment, pointing up their exact and full definitions.

Perfidious actions are actions of treachery, and a *perfidious* man is one who is deliberately false to a trust. His actions can have a *baleful*—that is, a destructive and harmful influence on others.

A person who is *larcenous* at heart is thievish and given to defrauding others to his own profit. If he cannot be reformed he is *unregenerate*. He is at enmity with the higher virtues of life, and his evil ways can have *dire* consequences for himself and for those he has harmed.

We can speak of a *gruesome* crime such as murder, for things that are *gruesome* cause a kind of horror that makes one shudder. All crimes are *repugnant*—that is, repulsive to decent people.

Defamatory statements are those that *defame* a person, that blacken his character and reflect on his good name. *Clandestine* affairs are affairs that are kept secret. They are underhand and furtive. Lovers, for example, can have *clandestine* meetings.

When people are *vituperative* they are using abusive words. *Vituperative* language is angry, scolding language. *Illicit* acts are illegal acts. We read about the *illicit* traffic in drugs.

And *salacious* remarks or *salacious* books are those that are indecent and obscene.

III. In the last part of this chapter you will be given sentences with blank spaces to be filled in with the proper words. Before this happens it will be an aid to you if we first have a rehearsal.

There are tricks of association that can help somewhat in recalling at least a few of these words.

Fidelity, for instance, is a fairly common English word meaning faithfulness. It derives from the Latin *fides*, "faith." You find this Latin root, *fid-*, for "faith," in a number of our words. In*fid*elity, for example, is being "unfaithful" in marriage. An in*fid*el has no "faith" in God. And, in similar fashion, our word per*fid*ious that we are to remember, means someone who has been "unfaithful" to any trust.

Larcenous you can remember from *larceny*, since this is the legal term for stealing.

Unregenerate is a little harder to tie to anything. *Generate* means to produce or to give birth to; to bear. A person who is *regenerate* has been "born again" in a spiritual sense, and is good. The *unregenerate* are *un*, "not," *re*, "again," *generate*, "born"; that is, they have "not been born again," they have not been renewed in heart and are therefore wicked.

"Repel" can remind you of *repugnant* for you are repulsed and repelled by *repugnant* things. With *defamatory* you can think of the "fame" that is being taken "away" (*de-*) from someone.

When a person is *vituperative* you can almost hear the angry and offensive words that he is spitting out. "Illegal" will help you to recall *illicit*, and *salacious* is as slimy in its sound as the indecency that it suggests. You had also best refresh your memory about *baleful*, *dire*, *gruesome*, and *clandestine*.

IV. Please fit the right words in the blank spaces. The initial letters will be a help.

(1) The parents were greatly disturbed when they heard that their son was having c_____ meetings with the girl.

(2) He felt that his job was a sordid one and all the menial jobs he had to do were r_____ to him.

(3) They tried to ruin his reputation and hurt his good name with d_____ remarks.

(4) He was one of the most trusted members of the party, but in the end they were disillusioned for they learned of his disloyalty and p_____ acts.

(5) Those deep and haunting fears had a b_____ influence on his life.

(6) The i_____ traffic in narcotics has cost the American people five times the price of the Panama Canal.

(7) He blistered the ears of the man with a choice flow of v_____ English.

(8) The producers are yielding more and more to vulgar and s_____ plays.

(9) We are living in a wicked and godless and an u_____ age that is perhaps beyond salvation.

(10) Their armies are in d_____ peril.

(11) On the front line death never ended his g_____ harvest.

(12) America today is paying untold tribute to the greed of l_____ racketeers.

Answers: 1—clandestine; 2—repugnant; 3—defamatory; 4—perfidious; 5—baleful; 6—illicit; 7—vituperative; 8—salacious; 9—unregenerate; 10—dire; 11—gruesome; 12—larcenous.

Two of the above words have interesting synonyms. *Baleful* has a sister term, *baneful*. The latter is the stronger of the two. It comes from an Old English word, *bana*, "murderer," so it is not only harmful but death-dealing and deadly.

The word *salacious* has a host of synonyms. There are *lubricious* (loo brish′us), *licentious* (lĭ sen′shus), and *wanton*, which all mean lewd and lustful in varying degrees. And to these can be added *prurient* (prŭr′i ent), *libidinous* (lĭ bĭd′i nus), *lascivious* (lă siv′i us), and *lecherous* (lĕch′ur us), which parallel the meaning of *salacious*, but in addition they also mean "full of sexual and sensual desires."

All the terms in this chapter rank as words of strength and of color within their own realm.

> The only thing I would whip
> schoolboys for is not knowing
> English.   CHURCHILL

37. Adjectives That Describe Your Friends and Enemies

WE ARE now about to consider a sizeable group of words that describe the personalities and activities of some of the people who surround you.

May I suggest a trick to you? Try to identify each word with a friend of yours, or with a politician or an actor or some other public character. If you will dramatize the words in this way it will help to make them stick in your mind. Strangely enough, the more that you make a game out of this book, the better you will do at it.

I. Here are the first 5 adjectives:

(1) GARRULOUS (gar'uh lus): This type of girl is given to talking too much about trifles in a tedious, rambling way.

(2) MAUDLIN (mawd'lin): She cries easily at the movies and is sentimental and tearful in a silly way.

(3) LACONIC (lă kon'ik): You don't often meet her in the world of women. The definition of this word reads: "Using as few words as possible; bluntly brief."

(4) TYRANNICAL (tĭ ran'ĭ kul): If we wished to be libelous this word could apply to some despotic mothers-in-law.

(5) SUPERCILIOUS (soo pur sil'ē us): She's the social snob, scornfully superior in her manner and exhibiting a haughty contempt or indifference to her supposed inferiors.

II. Here are 5 more:

(6) RAPACIOUS (ră pay′shus): Such a man is excessively greedy and grasping. He wants all of everything he can get.

(7) PARSIMONIOUS (par sĭ mō′nĭ us): Another unpleasant type. He is stingy and niggardly and spends just as little money as he can.

(8) RECALCITRANT (re kal′sĭ trant): Both children and older people are *recalcitrant* when they are obstinate, rebellious, and defiant and stubbornly resist authority.

(9) DOUR (dōōr): You've seen the type with a *dour* look on his face. His expression is sullen, stern, and severe.

(10) EBULLIENT (ĕ bul′yent): Here is the opposite kind. If she's a girl she is happy and gay and literally "boiling over" with excitement and enthusiasm. For *ebullient* comes from the Latin *ebullio, e*, "out," and *bullio*, "to boil."

III. And 5 more:

(11) CARNAL (kahr′nal): Comes from a Latin word meaning "flesh," so such a *carnal* man is "fleshly"; he is interested in bodily and not spiritual things and is sensual and worldly.

(12) CENSORIOUS (sen saw′rĭ us): These people are always criticizing and finding fault and expressing censure and disapproval.

(13) IMPLACABLE (im play′kă b′l) *or* im plak′ă b′l): Such a man never forgives and is stubborn and constant in his enmity.

(14) RABELAISIAN (rab ĭ lay′zĭ un): A word that comes from Rabelais, the French satirist. Anyone who is *Rabelaisian* is coarsely satirical. He is humorous in a gross and earthy way.

(15) BRASH (brash): If this word should be applied to a girl it would mean that she is apt to be quick-tempered, saucy, pert, and impudent.

IV. And the last 5:

(16) ARROGANT (ăr′o gant): Here we have people who are boast-
    ful, overbearing, and offensively demanding.

(17) OBSEQUIOUS (ob see′kwi us): This fellow has the slavish and
    fawning manner of some headwaiters.

(18) PROFLIGATE (prof′li git) people are recklessly extravagant
    and wasteful.

(19) SLOTHFUL (slōth′ful): These folk are lazy, indolent, and
    sluggish about all they do.

(20) PERTINACIOUS (pur tĭ nay′shus): This word characterizes
    the man who is extremely persistent and tenacious of
    purpose. He will keep on and on until he finishes whatever
    he is doing.

V. Perhaps you should review these 20 adjectives, as you are now
going to be asked to write the proper one after each sentence.
What type of person is he or she?

1. She is gay and enthusiastic.   e_____

2. He is a despot.   t_____

3. He is an earthy and sensual type.   c_____

4. He never forgives.   i_____

5. He has a sullen and sour look.   d_____

6. He sticks to a job until he finishes it.   p_____

7. She is a society type of snob.   s_____

8. He is the type that resents authority.   r_____

9. She is always criticizing.   c_____

10. He is lazy as can be.   s_____

11. He is overbearing and offensively demanding.   a_____

12. She spends money recklessly.   p_____

13. He is humorous in a gross and coarse way.   R_____

14. She won't spend a penny she doesn't have to.   p_____

15. She is greedy and grasping.   r_____

16. He is the silent type.   l_____

17. She cries easily.   m_____

18. She is a pert and saucy lass.   b_____

19. She talks constantly about nothing at all.   g_____

20. He agrees in a fawning manner.   o_____

Answers: 1—ebullient; 2—tyrannical; 3—carnal; 4—implacable; 5—dour; 6—pertinacious; 7—supercilious; 8—
recalcitrant; 9—censorious; 10—slothful; 11—arrogant; 12—profligate; 13—Rabelaisian; 14—parsimonious; 15—rapacious; 16—laconic; 17—maudlin;
18—brash; 19—garrulous; 20—obsequious.

VI. In the next exercise you are supposed to fill each space with
the adjective that fits best. The initial letter again will be your
guide.

1. I resent your overbearing and a_____ manner.

2. The waiter made me a little sick with his o_____ bows.

3. Our nation is p_____ with its resources.

4. Work was something he heartily disliked. He seemed to have
been born s_____.

5. When you turn over a job to him, he is so p_____ that
you know it will be finished.

6. You can't resent her even though she is a bit brazen and
b_____ in her manner.

7. The old lady was shrewd, a little malicious, and sometimes
outright R_____ in her bawdy wit.

8. He has the most i_____ hatred for all forms of tyranny.

9. The Egyptian boatman stopped rowing in the middle of the
river and practically held us up with his r_____ demands for
more money.

10. He was a hard taskmaster and his children resented his c_____ attitude.

11. Religion centers upon the spiritual rather than the c_____ side of life.

12. She is young and gay, with one of the most e_____ personalities I have ever known.

13. He was obviously annoyed and turned his eyes on her in a d_____ fashion.

14. The teacher was trying to pull up some r_____ child from his seat.

15. She had wrung several small raises from her p_____ employer.

16. The great doctor saw to it that g_____ folk did not waste his time with senseless chatter.

17. When we try to apply intelligence it is often sidetracked by m_____ sentimentality.

18. They are suffering more from these attacks than is apparent in their clipped, l_____ reports.

19. In those days people lived under the brutal rule of t_____ kings.

20. She was a shallow and scornful society woman with a s_____ air.

Answers: 1—arrogant; 2—obsequious; 3—profligate; 4—slothful; 5—pertinacious; 6—brash; 7—Rabelaisian; 8—implacable; 9—rapacious; 10—censorious; 11—carnal; 12—ebullient; 13—dour; 14—recalcitrant; 15—parsimonious; 16—garrulous; 17—maudlin; 18—laconic; 19—tyrannical; 20—supercilious.

You will be surprised what confidence you will gain from these repeated drills. You don't need to be told that leaders of men have confidence in themselves and a command of words is one of the quickest ways to the self-confidence that they have. It is really true that those who speak well and write well have an almost unfair advantage over those who are poor in language.

Language is the dress of thought.
SAMUEL JOHNSON

38.   Adjectives That Suggest Strength

ONE OBJECT of this book, as we have stressed, is to encourage you to develop a burning curiosity about words. Once you have gained this you will be surprised to discover how many unusual words you have let go by unchallenged in your reading. Believe it or not, I personally have even found such words as *atavistic* and *Gargantuan* in the sports columns.

There is no intent to suggest that you stop every time you meet a strange word and look up the definition in a dictionary. After all the ideas and facts in whatever account you are reading are the important things. But you can still read with a pencil in your hand, and you can check the words that are new to you. Then, when you are through, you can look up their meanings and write down the definition that best fits the case in hand. It will be even better if you also copy the sentence in which the word in question is used.

I. Here are 14 selected adjectives that you will be apt to meet in your daily reading.

(1) INTREPID—in trep'id

(2) IMPREGNABLE—im preg'nă b'l

(3) INALTERABLE—in awl'tur ă b'l

(4) UNIMPEACHABLE—un im peech'ă b'l

   (5) UNMITIGATED—un mit′ĭ gate ed

   (6) SACROSANCT—sak′ro sangkt

   (7) CLARION—klăr′ĭ un

   (8) RIGOROUS—rig′o rus

   (9) IGNOMINIOUS—ig nō min′ĭ us

   (10) RAUCOUS—raw′kus

   (11) CALAMITOUS—kă lam′ĭ tus

   (12) CLIMACTIC—klī mak′tik

   (13) PEREMPTORY—pur emp′to rĭ

   (14) PARAMOUNT—par′ă mount

II. Most of these words no doubt have a meaning for you. Then concentrate on the strangers if there are any.

The Latin *intrepidus* gives us the meaning of the first word in our list, for *intrepidus* comes from *in-*, "not," and *trepido*, "to tremble." Those who are *intrepid* do "not tremble"; they are fearless, undaunted, and brave in the face of danger. And similarly, *impregnable* comes from Latin parts that mean literally "cannot be taken." Thus an *impregnable* fort or position is one that is proof against attack and is able to resist assaults.

With the word *inalterable* we again turn to the Latin for our source: *in-*, for "not," and *alter* for "other." Anything *inalterable* cannot be changed into "another" thing. It is unchangeable, incapable of being "altered" or modified.

Unimpeachable means faultless and blameless, as "he has an *unimpeachable* character." His character is irreproachable and cannot be called into question.

Unmitigated is wholly different in meaning. If you were to say that "he is an *unmitigated* liar" you would mean that he is an all-out liar. The word *mitigate* means to make less severe. So *unmitigated* means "not softened in any way."

Sacrosanct is a particularly interesting word. The Latin *sacrosanctus* gives it to us from *sacer*, "sacred," and *sanctus*, "sacred." So anything *sacrosanct* is twice over sacred and is peculiarly set apart, consecrated.

In Latin *clarus* means "clear," and in our language *clarion* means loud and clear as the sound of a trumpet. And once more in Latin *rigor* means "stiffness," and so in English *rigorous* means the characteristic that is marked by "stiffness" and sternness; uncompromising; exacting.

Ignominious is based on the Latin *ignominia*, from *in-*, "no," and *nomen*, "name." If you have lost your name you are humiliated and so *ignominious* means degrading. And *raucous*, from the Latin *raucus*, "hoarse," carries the meaning of "harsh-sounding"—"a *raucous* voice."

A *calamitous* event is, of course, a disastrous and deplorable one. But anything *climactic* pertains to a "climax" or critical period. This word, of course, is based on *climax*, from the Greek *klimax*, "ladder." When a thing is *climactic* you have climbed up the "ladder" until you have reached the highest point.

The last two words in the list are *peremptory* and *paramount*. Anything *peremptory* must be obeyed, and anything *paramount* is superior to all others. *Peremptory* orders express a command that admits of no refusal. I can speak of the *paramount* reason, the one of chief importance, that led me to a decision.

III. If all these words are known to you then this is merely a review. But if there are some that you are unsure about it might be well to go over Section II again, as you are about to be faced with a test.

Here are 14 sentences. Fill in each blank space with *the one word* that best fits the meaning. The wording of the sentences will always give you a hint. If you are in doubt about a word skip it for the moment and continue with the test. You may get it in the end by elimination.

1. The West was won by the ———— and courageous pioneers from the Atlantic States.

2. Fixed fortifications are no longer ————.

3. I take up my pen now to assure you of my ———— determination to adhere to my planned program.

4. He has an unchallenged and ———— reputation.

5. He is an unconscionable and ———— liar.

6. We sometimes think the military men are above criticism, but they are no more _____ than any other class.

7. The thing that is uppermost in our minds is the _____ call of democracy.

8. The plan was executed by the Air Ministry in a most forceful and _____ fashion.

9. He yelled at me in a _____ voice.

10. It would be a disaster, and nothing short of _____ to insist on cutting the budget any further.

11. The play rose in intensity to a _____ third act.

12. He was humiliated by his _____ dismissal.

13. One day a _____ order came to him to take over the office of Finance Minister.

14. I have duties in many directions but my _____ obligation is to him.

Answers: 1—intrepid; 2—impregnable; 3—inalterable; 4—un-impeachable; 5—unmitigated; 6—sacrosanct; 7—clarion; 8—rigorous; 9—raucous; 10—calamitous; 11—climactic; 12—ignominious; 13—peremptory; 14—paramount.

All these words you have just covered are of superb strength and can be used with telling effect.

Words are wise men counters.
HOBBES

39. Adjectives That Deal with Wickedness

THE WEALTH of adjectives that connote evil is a commentary on mankind. Every shade of sin is covered.

A few of these colorful words are gathered together in this chapter. As you read them you will recognize their tremendous power. After all, we fashion words in our own image, and they are the symbols of our bad characteristics.

I. Let's meet this little group of words the hard way. You will be introduced to them in short phrases and in many cases these phrases will not be sufficient to reveal the exact meanings of such of the words as may be strange to you. But, at the least, you start with the advantage of knowing that all of these adjectives are connected with some form of iniquity.

(1) UNCONSCIONABLE (un kon'shun ǎ b'l) medical practices

(2) REPREHENSIBLE (rep rē hen'sǐ b'l) acts

(3) MENDACIOUS (men day'shus) testimony

(4) INCORRIGIBLE (in kor'ǐ jǐ b'l) youths

(5) BESTIAL (bes'chul) savagery

(6) PHARISAICAL (far ǐ say'ǐ kul) reformers

(7) MERETRICIOUS (měr ě trish'us) manners

(8) IMPIOUS (im'pǐ us) deeds

(9) MACHIAVELLIAN (mak ǐ ǎ vel'ǐ an) statesmen

(10) SCABROUS (skay'brus) plays

(11) DESPICABLE (des'pǐ kǎ b'l) lives

II. We will now expose them in full sentences for a better understanding, although even this will not completely differentiate these terms.

1. He was horrified at the *unconscionable* practices of the popular physician.

2. Even his best friends agree that in this case his acts were *reprehensible*.

3. His testimony was pure fiction, *mendacious* from beginning to end.

4. They may not be completely *incorrigible* but they are certainly impenitent.

5. The *bestial* savagery of the man can be best compared with the acts of Attila the Hun.

6. These reformers, unclean in their own lives, were truly a *pharisaical* crowd.

7. She was a beautiful but a most dangerous girl, with a *meretricious* charm.

8. We are living without religion in an agnostic and *impious* world.

9. The thrones of Washington are occupied by unprincipled and *Machiavellian* planners.

10. The sailors started their *scabrous* tales of night life ashore.

11. There are many sins that people will condone, but the world draws aside its skirts from anyone whose acts are as *despicable* as his.

III. Some of the strangers among these words may be taking on more clarity, but on the whole, they are so similar in meaning that nothing short of the definitions themselves will keep them apart. In some ways they overlap but each one has an individuality of its own.

(1) *Unconscionable* acts are unreasonable and unscrupulous ones that go beyond ordinary bounds and limits. They are not governed by conscience. The word *unconscionable* would apply to a judge who had violated his oath of office. Or, in a gentler and more colloquial way, you can say: "She kept me waiting for an *unconscionable* time."

(2) *Reprehensible* emphasizes the blame angle. *Reprehensible* acts are those that deserve censure. They are blameworthy.

(3) Anyone who is *mendacious* is addicted to lying and his remarks are apt to be full of deceit.

(4) The *incorrigible* are those unmanageable persons who are too wicked to be reformed.

(5) *Bestial* is what it sounds like, "beastly." *Bestial* cruelty would be the brutish and savage cruelty of an animal.

(6) The *pharisaical* are self-righteous people. Like the Pharisees of the Bible, they observe the outward form but neglect the spirit of religion and ethics. They are hypocrites at heart.

(7) *Meretricious* means deceitfully or artificially attractive; having false charms; alluring by false or gaudy show. As a matter of fact this adjective derives from the Latin *meretrix,* "a public prostitute or harlot."

(8) Those who are *impious* are "not pious." They have no reverence for sacred things. They lack regard for the Supreme Being.

(9) *Machiavelli* was a Florentine statesman who, in *The Prince,* argued in behalf of politically unscrupulous doctrines. So the word *Machiavellian* refers to those schemers who are crafty and cruel in politics; who are treacherous and double-dealing.

(10) *Scabrous* is a strong word that means rough to the touch; scabby. But it now also applies to "rough," risqué, salacious writings.

(11) *Despicable* is from the Latin *despicio, de,* "down to" and *specio,* "to look." You "look down" on *despicable* things; they are contemptible, mean, and deserve to be despised.

IV. Five of these 11 adjectives are turned into nouns by the mere addition of "-ness." One is a proper name. Can you give the noun forms of the other 5 that are listed below?

1. mendacious		_____
2. incorrigible		_____
3. bestial		_____
4. impious		_____
5. reprehensible		_____

Answers: 1—mendacity; 2—incorrigibility; 3—bestiality; 4—impiety; 5—reprehensibility.

V. There are half a dozen other terms of this level that deal with the wickedness of man, but they are so near in meaning to several of the words in the foregoing list, and are often so near in meaning to each other, that it might be confusing to you to try to learn them at this time, if you don't already know them. They are given to you purely as a list for reference.

FLAGRANT (flay'grant), INFAMOUS (in'fă mus), FLAGITIOUS (flă jish'us) crimes are those that are notorious, glaring, shamefully wicked, and openly scandalous.

DIABOLICAL (dī ă bol'ĭ kal) acts are fiendish and infernal as though performed by the devil himself.

EXECRABLE (ex'ĭ kră b'l) comes from the Latin *execratus*, "accursed." With us our word means utterly detestable, abominable, damnable. It also can be used in a softer way, as: "The food and wine were *execrable*"—that is, very bad. Or, "Her taste in dress is *execrable*."

NEFARIOUS (ne fair'ĭ us) is based on the Latin word *nefarius*, that splits into *ne*, "not," and *fari*, "utter." That is, *nefarious* deeds are so wicked that they are "unutterable." They are too atrocious, heinous, and villainous to even be mentioned aloud.

Again I would suggest that you concentrate on the first 11 words in this chapter. To master the last 6 at this time might prove too much of a burden, unless you are an extraordinarily serious student. It is always possible to return to these words later on.

A word travels farther than a
man.   *German*

40. Adjectives We Should Remember

HERE IS a statement that may seem rather startling. And yet it is true.

If the words in this chapter should by any chance be new to you, and if you succeed in mastering them in one evening, you will be learning as many words in this one session as the average adult adds to his vocabulary in an entire year. After the age of 25 most grown-ups learn no more than 25 new words in 12 months. This number remains constant for the rest of their lives unless they plan and do what you are doing now.

You will now be faced with a list of 25 words that have not been covered in this book before. Try to fill in each blank space in the numbered sentences with that word (a), (b), (c), (d), or (e) that seems to make the most sense. You will meet some of the same words more than once in the 10 groups.

Don't let it concern you, when you check the answers, if you find that you have made mistakes in your choices, particularly in the first two or three tests. As you go on the strange words will become more familiar to you. With this method you are learning words by what might be called the "unfolding" process. The sentences suggest the meanings before the word is "opened" to you.

I. (a) TURBID (tur'bid)
    (b) RAMPANT (ram'pant)
    (c) AUSPICIOUS (aws pish'us)
    (d) STRINGENT (strin'jent)
    (e) OMINOUS (om'i nus)

1. The finishing school was carefully supervised and had _____ rules.

2. One couldn't see two feet down in the _____ waters.

3. The _____ threat of Russia hovers like a dark cloud.

4. In many parts of the world disease is _____.

5. All over the happy nation the flags were flying on that _____ day.

II.   (a) INDEFEASIBLE (in de fē′zi b'l)
     (b) LUCRATIVE (lōō′kră tiv)
     (c) AUSPICIOUS (aws pish′us)
     (d) FURTIVE (fur′tiv)
     (e) ARDUOUS (ar′dū us)

1. As a rule teachers are in modest circumstances since their profession was never a _____ one.

2. It was the end of a most exhausting campaign filled with long and _____ tasks.

3. The omens were bright and the times _____ for his new career.

4. His sly ways and _____ looks aroused suspicion.

5. In democracies we believe that we have an _____ right to free speech.

Answers: I—1—(d); 2—(a); 3—(e); 4—(b); 5—(c).
           II—1—(b); 2—(e); 3—(c); 4—(d); 5—(a).

III.   (a) ARRANT (ăr′ant)
     (b) OMINOUS (om′ĭ nus)
     (c) PALTRY (pawl′trĭ)
     (d) STRINGENT (strin′jent)
     (e) GRATUITOUS (gră tū′ĭ tus)

1. He was a hopeless knave and an _____ fool.

2. The _____ threat of Russia hovers like a dark cloud.

3. All of them together could raise only a _____ sum.

4. This was the most _____ and binding curb that legislation had ever put on tyranny.

5. He was officious with all of his _____ advice.

IV.   (a) UNWONTED (un wunt′id)
     (b) ONEROUS (on′ur us)

    (c) SPURIOUS (spū′rĭ us)

    (d) INDEFEASIBLE (in de fē′zĭ b'l)

    (e) FRACTIOUS (frak′shus)

1. There was an _____ crowd in the streets.

2. They had to relieve him of some of his responsibilities as his duties had become too _____.

3. He thought that he had purchased a genuine diamond but he discovered later that it was _____.

4. He was trying to herd together a lot of _____ calves.

5. The doctrine of hereditary right does by no means imply an _____ right to the throne.

Answers: III—1—(a); 2—(b); 3—(c); 4—(d); 5—(e).
           IV—1—(a); 2—(b); 3—(c); 4—(e); 5—(d).

V. (a) TURBID (tŭr′bid)

    (b) INORDINATE (in or′dĭ nit)

    (c) ECSTATIC (ek stat′ik)

    (d) LIVID (liv′id)

    (e) IRREPARABLE (ĭ rep′uh rŭ b'l)

1. One couldn't see two feet down in the _____ waters.

2. I saw a sick and _____ face staring at me from the window with white, hollow eyes.

3. They were bubbling and _____ about their European trip.

4. This will require an _____ amount of patience.

5. The damage was heavy, there was no insurance, and the loss was therefore _____.

VI. (a) LUCRATIVE (lōō′kră tiv)

    (b) BLATANT (blay′tent)

    (c) PALTRY (pawl′trĭ)

    (d) FLACCID (flak′sid)

    (e) RAMPANT (ram′pant)

1. I resented the _____ amount he gave me for all my services.

2. The weeds were running _____ over the lawn.

3. His muscles were as _____ as India rubber.

4. Many millionaires were made in the _____ 1920's.

5. He is a bellowing and _____ reformer.

Answers: V—1—(a); 2—(d); 3—(c); 4—(b); 5—(e).
         VI—1—(c); 2—(e); 3—(d); 4—(a); 5—(b).

VII. (a) GRATUITOUS (grǎ tū'ĭ tus)
      (b) TRANSCENDENT (tran sen'dent)
      (c) INEXORABLE (in ek'so rǎ b'l)
      (d) TURBULENT (tur'bū lent)
      (e) LIVID (liv'id)

1. The _____ river boiled white over the falls.

2. We looked upon the calm and _____ beauty of the Grand Canyon.

3. His face turned _____ with rage.

4. The shore was giving way to the _____ inroads of the sea.

5. He gave me a _____ insult.

VIII. (a) UNWONTED (un wunt'id)
      (b) CATACLYSMIC (kat ǎ kliz'mik)
      (c) ECSTATIC (ek stat'ik)
      (d) FRACTIOUS (frak'shus)
      (e) ARDUOUS (ar'dū us)

1. The bombers brought their _____ ruin.

2. These tribes have queer and _____ customs.

3. His labors have been long and _____ for his party.

4. Youth can be so _____ over little joys.

5. The disorderly and _____ pupils wouldn't keep their seats.

Answers: VII—1—(d); 2—(b); 3—(e); 4—(c); 5—(a).
VIII—1—(b); 2—(a); 3—(e); 4—(c); 5—(d).

IX.   (a) IRREPARABLE (ĭ rep′uh rŭ b′l)
(b) ARRANT (ar′rant)
(c) TURBULENT (tur′bū lent)
(d) FLACCID (flak′sid)
(e) INEXORABLE (in ek′so ră b′l)

1. He was completely out of condition and his flesh hung
_____ on his body.

2. He was a wicked and _____ crook.

3. These times are troubled and _____ with disorders.

4. The harm he did to the nation was _____.

5. Our universe is governed by _____ and unchangeable laws.

X.   (a) TRANSCENDENT (tran sen′dent)
(b) SPURIOUS (spū′rĭ us)
(c) INORDINATE (in or′dĭ nit)
(d) CATACLYSMIC (kat ă kliz′mik)
(e) ONEROUS (on′ur us)

1. The racketeers flooded the city with _____ money.

2. The king was weary of his _____ duties.

3. The price was _____ and most outrageous.

4. And then came the _____ disaster of the market crash
of 1929.

5. We were awed by the _____ beauty of the scene.

Answers: IX—1—(d); 2—(b); 3—(c); 4—(a); 5—(e).
X—1—(b); 2—(e); 3—(c); 4—(d); 5—(a).

XI. We will now list the 25 different words that you have
covered above and with each one we will give you three choices.

Check that one of the three that you believe to be nearest in meaning to the key word.

(1) TURBID—A: provoked. B: muddy. C: worried.

(2) RAMPANT—A: unchecked. B: bored. C: sharp.

(3) AUSPICIOUS—A: favorable. B: beautiful. C: trustful.

(4) STRINGENT—A: long drawn out. B: strict. C: burdensome.

(5) OMINOUS—A: sad. B: threatening. C: all-inclusive.

(6) INDEFEASIBLE—A: incapable of being carried out. B: unbelievable. C: incapable of being made void.

(7) LUCRATIVE—A: happy. B: highly profitable. C: amusing.

(8) FURTIVE—A: intense. B: absurd. C: stealthy.

(9) ARDUOUS—A: strong. B: proud. C: requiring effort.

(10) ARRANT—A: roving. B: out-and-out. C: foolish.

(11) PALTRY—A: showy. B: almost worthless. C: boring.

(12) GRATUITOUS—A: resentful. B: freely given. C: thankful.

(13) UNWONTED—A: unusual. B: unwished for. C: unpopular.

(14) ONEROUS—A: dishonest. B: mean. C: burdensome.

(15) SPURIOUS—A: scornful. B: false. C: widespread.

(16) FRACTIOUS—A: perverse. B: clownish. C: broken.

(17) INORDINATE—A: selfish. B: in confusion. C: excessive.

(18) ECSTATIC—A: foolish. B: enraptured. C: unhappy.

(19) LIVID—A: enraged. B: red. C: ashy-pale.

(20) IRREPARABLE—A: disreputable. B: that cannot be controlled. C: that cannot be repaired.

(21) FLACCID—A: calm. B: flabby. C: strong.

(22) TRANSCENDENT—A: shining. B: surpassing. C: hopeful.

(23) INEXORABLE—A: relentless. B: angry. C: puzzling.

(24) TURBULENT—A: quiet. B: tempestuous. C: muddy.

(25) CATACLYSMIC—A: extremely sudden and violent. B: enthusiastic. C: depressing.

Answers: 1—B; 2—A; 3—A; 4—B; 5—B; 6—C; 7—B; 8—C; 9—C; 10—B; 11—B; 12—B; 13—A; 14—C; 15—B; 16—A; 17—C; 18—B; 19—C; 20—C; 21—B; 22—B; 23—A; 24—B; 25—A.

If you happen to have a high vocabulary rating this test will have been comparatively easy. If, however, your vocabulary is limited, the test probably seemed hard to you. Words like *indefeasible, inordinate, transcendent, flaccid,* and *inexorable* are valuable to know but they are not apt to be a part of ordinary vocabularies.

> Language is the archives of history.   EMERSON

41. Adjectives That Deal with Personalities

AT THIS POINT in the book you should be able to handle a harder assignment than you did at the beginning.

I. You will now be faced with 20 words. These are warm and human words and are not too hard to remember. In almost every case the sentence will help reveal the meaning.

1. We have tried to get along with them but they are a rebellious and·*intransigent* (in tran′si jent) crowd.

2. The play repelled us with its *mawkish* (mawk′ish) sentimentality.

3. The *imperturbable* (im pur tur′bă b’l) officer lined up the lot and calmly collected their knives.

4. We will have no *pusillanimous* (pū sĭ lan'ĭ mus) crying for peace at any price.

5. Waves of savages, *demoniacal* (dē mo nī'ă k'l) in their ferocity, hit our lines day after day.

6. You know I am not one of your *dolorous* (dol'ur us *or* dōl'ur us) gentlemen; so now let us laugh again.

7. The employees are a pitifully low-paid group, but somehow they stay on in spite of the *penurious* (pe nū'rĭ us) attitude of their employers.

8. He is a dramatic critic who is pleased at nothing and writes a *captious* (kap'shus) review of every play he sees.

9. Those who have been victorious should not be *vindictive* (vin dik'tiv).

10. The *unctuous* (unk'tū us) manner in which he served us was slightly sickening.

11. She possessed an *indomitable* (in dom'ĭ tă b'l) will.

12. We asked him a list of leading questions, but he was wise and *taciturn* (tas'ĭ turn) and we learned nothing.

13. We hope to keep *inviolate* (in vī'ō let) the sacred concepts of liberty we so cherish.

14. There are some men whose *imperious* (im pēr'ĭ us) mien commands obedience.

15. He was a depressive type with a grim and *saturnine* (sat'ur nine) expression.

16. His *sardonic* (sar don'ik) criticism hurt the success of the play.

17. With an eloquence too *fervid* (fur'vid) to concern itself with the niceties of metaphor, he called upon the city to wipe out crime.

18. The feasts of the Emperor Nero were always attended by a *gluttonous* (glut'tun nus) crowd.

19. Each test case was backed by *irrefutable* (ir ref′ū tă b′l) evidence of blood guilt.

20. The racketeers are not satisfied with little gains but are *avaricious* (av ă rish′us) for unholy profits.

II. Each of the 20 words that you have just covered will now be paired with another word that will be the same or the opposite in meaning. In making this list you may find it necessary to refer back to Section I.

1. intransigent—docile	Same	Opposite
2. mawkish—sickening	Same	Opposite
3. imperturbable—excited	Same	Opposite
4. pusillanimous—brave	Same	Opposite
5. demoniacal—raging	Same	Opposite
6. dolorous—cheerful	Same	Opposite
7. penurious—stingy	Same	Opposite
8. captious—faultfinding	Same	Opposite
9. vindictive—revengeful	Same	Opposite
10. unctuous—oily	Same	Opposite
11. indomitable—yielding	Same	Opposite
12. taciturn—talkative	Same	Opposite
13. inviolate—impure	Same	Opposite
14. imperious—commanding	Same	Opposite
15. saturnine—gloomy	Same	Opposite
16. sardonic—sarcastic	Same	Opposite
17. fervid—unenthusiastic	Same	Opposite
18. gluttonous—piggish	Same	Opposite
19. irrefutable—disprovable	Same	Opposite
20. avaricious—grasping	Same	Opposite

Answers: 1—Opposite;   2—Same;   3—Opposite;   4—Opposite;
5—Same; 6—Opposite; 7—Same; 8—Same; 9—Same;
10—Same; 11—Opposite; 12—Opposite; 13—Opposite; 14—Same; 15—Same; 16—Same; 17—Opposite;
18—Same; 19—Opposite; 20—Same.

III. By now you probably have a reasonably clear idea as to the
meanings of such of these words that may have been unknown
to you. But since a few of them are slightly close together in
meanings it will be best if we run over their dictionary definitions.

(1) INTRANSIGENT: Irreconcilable; refusing to agree or compromise. Another word of similar meaning is *contumacious*
(kon tū may'shus). If we were to say that "she is a
restless, roving, disobedient, *contumacious* female" we
would mean that she was insolently disobedient and
contemptuous of all authority.

(2) MAWKISH: Sickeningly sentimental.

(3) IMPERTURBABLE: Calm and unexcitable; incapable of being
disturbed.

(4) PUSILLANIMOUS: Cowardly.

(5) DEMONIACAL: Devilish; fiendish; like demons; frenzied.

(6) DOLOROUS: Sorrowful; mournful; doleful.

(7) PENURIOUS: Mean and miserly in the use of money.

(8) CAPTIOUS: Faultfinding; cross and critical; hard to please.

(9) VINDICTIVE: Revengeful; bearing a grudge.

(10) UNCTUOUS: Oily and persuasive; unduly suave; polite in
a fawning way.

(11) INDOMITABLE: Unconquerable; unyielding; not to be sub-
dued; stubbornly determined.

(12) TACITURN: Disinclined to talk.

(13) INVIOLATE: Pure; unprofaned; unbroken; uninjured.

(14) IMPERIOUS: Commanding; compelling; requiring implicit
obedience.

(15) SATURNINE: Gloomy; heavy; morose; grave; dull; sullen.

(16) SARDONIC: Derisive; sneering; scornful; bitterly sarcastic.

(17) FERVID: Ardent; zealous; spirited; enthusiastic; full of fervor and eagerness.

(18) GLUTTONOUS: Greedy; voracious; inclined to feast and eat too much; apt to gormandize.

(19) IRREFUTABLE: Not able to be disproved; that cannot be refuted or proved false; that cannot be repelled by argument.

(20) AVARICIOUS: Greedy for gain or wealth; keen to get and to keep; grasping.

The adjective *ravening* (rav'en ing) belongs in this list but it might have been confusing. It means greedy and hungry, eagerly seeking for prey, as "the *ravening* wolves."

You may feel that these drills are merely adding a certain mathematical number of new words to your vocabulary. But word study is immeasurably more important than this. Words touch all the far-distant shores of knowledge, and anybody who becomes a serious student of words will inevitably receive a liberal education.

> Words are the dress of our thoughts which should no more be presented in rags, tatters and dirt than your person should.
> CHESTERFIELD

42. Adjectives in the Higher Brackets

THESE will be truly high-level words. They are introduced largely to show you to what an extent a vocabulary can be developed. We will hardly call this an assignment unless you wish to accept it as such. You could scarcely be considered as handicapped if you are unaware of their meanings. You will occasionally meet these words in your reading. More rarely in conversation. Yet they have a true value that is not entirely to be overlooked.

I. Here they are:

    (1) MINATORY—min'a to rĭ

    (2) SONOROUS—so naw'rus *or* so nō'rus

    (3) FRENETIC—frĕ net'ik

    (4) HEINOUS—hay'nus

    (5) COGENT—kō'jent

    (6) CONDIGN—kon dine'

    (7) RECREANT—rek'rē ant

    (8) MACABRE—mă kah'bruh

    (9) REDOUBTABLE—re dowt'uh b'l

    (10) TEMERARIOUS—tem ur air'ĭ us

II. If your vocabulary is average, or even above average, it is my opinion that it would still be best for you to read about these words and not to try as yet to definitely add them to your vocabulary unless the majority of them should already be known to you. For this reason we will merely discuss them and their meanings and you will not be tested on them.

(1) MINATORY: Anything *minatory* is menacing and portends either punishment or destruction. It is a word that contains a threat. We can say, "The nations faced one another as before, each pointing a *minatory* finger at one of its neighbors."

(2) SONOROUS: Here we have the Latin *sonorus* from *sonus*, "sound." Things that are *sonorous* give out a loud "sound," as: "We listened to the *sonorous* voice of the

orator." His voice was full-sounding and resonant. Another word similar to this is *orotund* (or'ŏ tund). The word *sonorous* could apply to a loud-sounding bell but *orotund* refers only to the human voice. It comes from a combination of Latin words that mean "round mouth." The speaker has opened his mouth wide and his words are full, rich, and strong in sound. "In *orotund* tones the preacher announced their marriage."

(3) FRENETIC: This means frenzied, frantic, and violently agitated. You could speak of the *frenetic* mob or could remark on the *frenetic* oppression of the South after the Civil War.

(4) HEINOUS: A *heinous* act is one that is atrocious and extremely wicked. Here is a quotation that will illustrate its use: "How *heinous* it would be to send overseas armies of our men which we could not supply."

(5) COGENT: If a person advances *cogent* reasons in support of a certain action, his reasons are powerful and convincing and tend to compel belief and assent.

(6) CONDIGN: Well-deserved; merited. "We will never cease to strike until their crimes have been brought to *condign* and exemplary justice."

(7) RECREANT: "He was *recreant* to freedom and to humanity." That is, he was unfaithful to a cause to which he was pledged. A *recreant* is false to his loyalties and to his professed faith.

(8) MACABRE: Relating to the dance of death in which a skeleton led a bevy of laughing maidens to the grave; hence symbolizing the power of death. In common language *macabre* is used to mean ghastly; horrible; gruesome; as: "The newspapers were filled with the *macabre* details of the murder."

(9) REDOUBTABLE: A slightly more common word meaning formidable; inspiring fear; valiant; as: "John Henry Newman was a *redoubtable* champion of Christian principles against contemporary evils."

(10) TEMERARIOUS: Unreasonably adventurous; very rash and
    reckless. "I don't call that bravery; I call it insanely
    temerarious."

These may be difficult words, but they are strong words,
and some day, if not now, they will be valuable to add
to your arsenal.

THIRD TEST

A Test for You on Your Adjectives

YOU are meeting your third and last test in this book. It is to your credit that you have gone this far.

I.
1. furtive	a. lying
2. portentous	b. giving offense because unfair
3. omnivorous	c. eating up
4. blatant	d. at the point of death
5. invidious	e. favorable
6. moribund	f. stealthy
7. recreant	g. ominous
8. propitious	h. offensively loud
9. salacious	i. lustful
10. mendacious	j. false to a cause

Answers: 1—*f;* 2—*g;* 3—*c;* 4—*h;* 5—*b;* 6—*d;* 7—*j;* 8—*e;* 9—*i;* 10—*a.*

II. You are to fill in each blank space with that one of the 10 words that fits best. The sense of the sentences will be the guide.

1. He was a sneaking fellow with a _____ look.

2. It was pleasant to see how large his library was and to learn he was such an _____ reader.

3. With such grim talk of war, the times are _____.

4. He was the most loudmouthed, _____ braggart I have ever had to listen to.

5. The _____ favoritism he shows for his oldest child is damaging and cruel.

6. Our _____ civilization is truly come upon its last days.

7. He is traitor and _____ to the cause of liberty.

8. The times are _____ for a religious revival.

9. The stage is corrupt and the plays are wickedly _____.

10. He is a _____ character, and falsifies by habit.

Answers: 1—furtive; 2—omnivorous; 3—portentous; 4—blatant; 5—invidious; 6—moribund; 7—recreant; 8—propitious; 9—salacious; 10—mendacious.

III. Can you recall these 10 new review words and their meanings?

1. incisive	6. laconic
2. decadent	7. arrogant
3. perfidious	8. intrepid
4. stentorian	9. penurious
5. adamant	10. poignant

IV. These phrases are not definitions but each suggests one of the above words.

1. Rome in the days just before its fall _____

2. the announcer's voice at a prize fight   _____

3. the spirit of the early pioneers   _____

4. the miser   _____

5. sorrow   _____

6. the attitude of the overbearing salesman   _____

7. a certain sharp style of wit   _____

8. an uncommunicative Yankee farmer   _____

9. a term that could be applied to Aaron Burr   _____

10. the attitude of a father to an unwelcome suitor   _____

Answers: 1—decadent; 2—stentorian; 3—intrepid; 4—penurious; 5—poignant; 6—arrogant; 7—incisive; 8—laconic; 9—perfidious; 10—adamant.

V. Some of the below pairs are similar in meaning. Some are nearly opposite. Check which is which.

1. decadent—growing	Same	Opposite
2. intrepid—trembling	Same	Opposite
3. penurious—stingy	Same	Opposite
4. incisive—cutting	Same	Opposite
5. arrogant—modest	Same	Opposite
6. laconic—talkative	Same	Opposite
7. perfidious—treacherous	Same	Opposite
8. adamant—unyielding	Same	Opposite
9. stentorian—loud	Same	Opposite
10. poignant—piercing	Same	Opposite

Answers: 1—Opposite; 2—Opposite; 3—Same; 4—Same; 5—Opposite; 6—Opposite; 7—Same; 8—Same; 9—Same; 10—Same.

VI. Here are the last test words in the book. Match each one with its synonymic word or phrase.

1. turbid	*a.*	extremely wicked
2. redoubtable	*b.*	disdainful
3. grandiose	*c.*	cowardly
4. heinous	*d.*	shameful
5. auspicious	*e.*	favorable
6. predatory	*f.*	roiled and muddy
7. pusillanimous	*g.*	affecting grandeur
8. ignominious	*h.*	inspiring respect or fear
9. supercilious	*i.*	inclined to plundering
10. didactic	*j.*	instructive

Answers: 1—*f;* 2—*h;* 3—*g;* 4—*a;* 5—*e;* 6—*i;* 7—*c;* 8—*d;* 9—*b;*
10—*j.*

VII. Now fill each blank space with the right word. The sentences are so phrased that they will act as guides.

1. The stream was so _____ that we couldn't see the bottom.

2. It was a _____ series of fortifications, so powerful that they resisted all attacks.

3. He gave a party in the elaborate and _____ style of a *nouveau riche.*

4. It was such a _____ and inhuman crime that it made one shudder.

5. It was an _____ day for the outdoor celebration.

6. The _____ hordes of Attila the Hun burned what they could not carry away.

7. I would hate to call him _____ but his knees were certainly shaking.

8. The general was broken to a colonel after his overwhelming and _____ defeat.

9. She lifted her lorgnette to her eyes and surveyed the audience with the grand and _____ air of a duchess.

10. Throughout his lecture he talked down to his audience in _____ terms.

Answers: 1—turbid; 2—redoubtable; 3—grandiose; 4—heinous; 5—auspicious; 6—predatory; 7—pusillanimous; 8—ignominious; 9—supercilious; 10—didactic.

Twenty-two correct answers to the test in Section VI and VII would be excellent; 19, very good.

You are now through with your tests. Have you done reasonably well with them all? Good. If on the other hand your record has been somewhat poor, remember this: You are one of the comparatively few who have had enough determination to plan to improve your vocabulary. Also, while many thousands will start this book, the majority will not have the pertinacity to finish it as you have. This is something that actually sets you apart.

YOUR COMMENCEMENT

Now You Are Beginning

WHEN our young folk graduate from high school or college they are apt to think that this is the end of their education. We who are older know that neither college nor high school is a terminus. This is only the beginning of our schooling.

My hope is that you will feel the same way about this book.

A volume of this size can cover only the most minuscule part of the subject of the world of words. But its purpose is to tempt you to go on with this exciting adventure.

No wonder English is a required subject in the schools of many foreign countries. Never has it been so important to be a master of this language. As a matter of fact, never has it been so critically important to be a master of words, for this is the age of words. They run by electric couriers along the wires of our telephones. The air is alive with them as they flow into our living rooms from radio and television sets. They pour in Niagaras from the presses and are spewed from platforms. They are hurled over the ether of the seven seas and are piped under the oceans to far-off shores.

The foreigner has to learn English words by dint of hard effort. We are more fortunate. English is our inheritance. But the vast majority of Americans remain virtually illiterate in their own language.

It is hard to believe, but 9 native words carry one fourth of the burden of our letter writing and our conversation. Would you like to know what these words are? Here is the list: *and, the, be, to, have, will, it, you, of.*

Add 34 more and you have half the words actually used in American speech. That is how bankrupt we are.

It is really true that most people, when the impulse moves them, open their mouths and speak almost as a dog barks. The idea of choosing words to fit the occasion never crosses their minds.

If it were a difficult and dreary job to acquire an adequate vocabulary this bankrupt state of the average American would be more understandable. But building a vocabulary is intensely interesting, and the rewards are prodigal.

So train your ear to the beauty of words. Learn to be enthusiastic in your desire for accurate, forceful expression. It's fun. And as we said at the beginning of this book, a game can be made of it. And it can.

Here is some advice that was given earlier in this book, but it is so important that it bears repetition.

As you walk along the street look at the outdoor ads. This space costs money and experts are hired to fill it with the most telling words. You may see some wares that are advertised as having "rare value." Is "rare" the best word to use? How many other words of similar meaning can you think of?

This merchandise could be of *exceptional, unique, excellent, unusual,* or *superior* value. The value could be *fine, select, genuine, choice, superlative, prime, unprecedented.*

This practice in thinking up synonyms is a wonderful exercise and will stretch a vocabulary no end.

Why not try to make your letters and your conversation more interesting?

You don't always have to say that you admire a man because he tells the "truth." You can speak of his *frankness, sincerity, candor.* You can recall his *openness,* his *honesty* and *straightforwardness* in speech; his reputation for *veracity*. All these words touch upon the quality of truth.

You can even make a family game out of words. It will help you and it will help the young people around you.

Words become commonplace and hackneyed from too much use. They wear out, like anything else, and you need constantly to replenish your supply. If your words are dull and fuzzy, your ideas will be fuzzy and dull. And if your vocabulary has stopped growing, so has your mind. This you can depend upon.

But when we speak of a rich and varied vocabulary we don't mean that you should use long and ponderous words in your conversation. This would be silly and stuffy.

I received a letter one time from a man returning a previous book of mine. He said: "I'm sending your book back. If I used the words you give here nobody would understand me." That's probably true. To use difficult words in the average and ordinary conversation is stilted and stupid. The important thing is that it will give you a sense of power and superior confidence to have these valuable words at your command to read with, to understand with, to think with. And you may find, to your surprise, that as your vocabulary improves, the intellectual level of your friendships will improve also, and you may be able to use some of these words after all in your conversations.

The dynamic and expressive words that you have learned in this book are not generally found in a mediocre vocabulary. The mere fact that you have made them your possession will have automatically raised your intellectual level, for, curiously, it has been discovered that an IQ test and vocabulary test are almost identical as measures of the mind. That is, the size of a person's vocabulary is a telltale as to his mental level.

Now you have finished this book. Most people who have arrived at this point will be filled with good resolves. Unfortunately, the good resolutions of the vast majority will disappear like water in the sands. Why not be the exception? The future belongs to those who prepare for it.

A LAGNIAPPE FOR YOU

THE TITLE of this last chapter gives us a pleasant word from New Orleans. A truly Creole word that breaks up into the French *la*, "the," and the Spanish *napa*, "gratuity." When a Louisiana tradesman makes a sale to a customer he often presents the buyer with a *lagniappe* (lan yap')—that is, a gratuity or present as a reward for having been so gracious as to have placed an order. The hope is that the customer will be properly grateful at having an unexpected gift! So this addendum to our book is your lagniappe.

The selection of the power vocabulary that appears in this book was made by going through many thousands of words. Some were of a borderline type. They didn't seem important enough to include in the main body of the volume. And yet I considered them to be too important to omit them entirely from the book. I have listed such words as these in the pages that follow, each one with its pronunciation, its most common meaning, its derivation, when it is helpful, and an illustrative sentence to show it in use.

You may easily differ with me about the importance of these words. You may think that some of them have as much or more power than some of the words in the body of this book. If you think this you are quite correct; for no single word holds the identical amount of power for you that it does for me.

As I explained in the Introduction, you have learned each word in your vocabulary at a different time in your life than I have learned it. You have had different experiences with it. The connotations that have crystallized around it in your mind are apt to be different from those that have crystallized around it in my mind.

You see, a great portion of the meanings of words are in our minds and not in the dictionaries. The impact of a given word upon you and upon me is purely a personal affair. Therefore there can be no important dispute between us.

If you have the time and the wish you can add the following 63 additional words to your vocabulary, and I'm inclined to think that you will be happier if you do. Where it is helpful, the etymology of a word has been included.

ABORTIVE (ă bore'tiv): Born prematurely; hence, coming to nothing; vain; useless. "An *abortive* attempt was made to capture the city."—Roy Chapman Andrews. The Latin *abortus*, "a miscarriage."

ACERBITY (ă sur'bĭ tĭ): Bitterness of language; harshness; sharpness; as: "There was a cruel *acerbity* to his tongue." From the Latin *acerbus*, "harsh."

AMUCK (ă muck'): Making frenzied attacks on everyone in sight. "The simple folk hid Jews in their homes because the persecutors had run amuck."—George N. Shuster. Malay *amoq*, "engaging furiously in battle."

APOTHEOSIS (ă poth ĭ ō'sis: *th* as in *thin*): An exaltation or raising in rank to divine honors. "To put the Kingdom of God above nationalism would not be the denial of patriotism but its *apotheosis*."—Harry Emerson Fosdick. Latin *apo*, "from," and *theos*, "god."

ARDENT (ar'dent): Intense; fervent; glowing. "He animated an *ardent* philanthropy with the keenest and brightest intellectual powers."—Winston Churchill. Originally from the Latin *ardeo*, "to burn."

ASTUTE (as tute'): Keen in discernment; shrewd; sagacious. "I think there is a general feeling that bankers are *astute*."—Charles L. Kaufman. The Latin *astutus*, from *astus*, "cunning."

CADAVEROUS (kă dav'ur us): Like a corpse; looking like a dead person. "These birds had bald *cadaverous* heads and long wrinkled necks."—Arthur Koestler. Latin *cadaverosus*, "like a corpse."

CAUSTIC (kawce′tik): Sarcastic; satirical; sharp and biting; as: "He made bitter, *caustic* remarks." The Greek *kaustikos*, from *kaiein*, "to burn."

CAVIL (kav′il): To find fault with; to raise petty and trivial objections; as: "He knew that his failure was his own fault and he didn't *cavil* at fate." Originally from the Latin word *cavillor*, "to make captious objections."

CHURLISH (chur′lish): Mean; crabbed; rude in manner; uncivil in speech. "To enquire why he had not thought of it in the first place seemed like *churlish* quibbling."—Ellen Lewis Buell. Old English *ceorl*, "a freeman of low rank."

CONTENTIOUS (kon ten′shus): Quarrelsome; disputatious; fond of argument or strife; persistently starting disputes. "When a man reaches 70 he is conventionally supposed to become less *contentious* and more philosophical."—Harold L. Ickes. Latin *contentiosus*, "quarrelsome."

CONTORTION (kon tor′shun): A "twisting" together or upon itself; or an unnatural wryness of face or limbs caused by this "twisting." "He was asked how he prevented the efforts of *contortion* from intruding upon the difficult speeches."—Gene Fowler. The Latin *contortus* from *con-*, "with," and *torqueo*, "to twist."

CORROSIVE (kor rō′siv): Having the power to gradually eat away, rust, or disintegrate. "Due to the *corrosive* effects of water, more careful inspections must be made."—Theodore P. Hall. The Latin *corrosus*, from *corrodo*, "to gnaw away."

CRAFTILY (kraft′i li): Cunningly; cleverly and deceptively; guilefully; artfully. "They say every human being who writes an autobiography exposes himself, no matter how *craftily* he tries to make out a good case."—Irvin S. Cobb. Old English *craeft*, "skill."

CRASS (krass): Dense; dull; obtuse; lacking refinement; coarse. "Both parties typified the spirit of a *crass* and godless age." —Edmund A. Walsh. Latin *crassus*, "thick."

CRAVEN (kray′ven): Cowardly; full of fear. "Idle and futile is the voice of the weak nation, or the *craven* nation, when it clamors for peace."—Frank Knox.

DELETERIOUS (del ĕ tir′i us): Causing moral or physical injury.

"This particular article is not *deleterious*, but it is inferior in food value."—Fiorello H. La Guardia. Greek *dēlētērios*, from *dēleomai*, "to spoil."

DENIGRATE (den'i grate): To defame; to blacken; to make an attack on the reputation; as: "During the life of Abraham Lincoln many newspapers tried to *denigrate* him." The Latin *denigratus*, from *denigro*, "to blacken."

DESPOILER (de spoil'ur): Plunderer; robber; one who seizes the belongings of others. "They would welcome the opportunity to put a bayonet into the *despoiler* of their ancestral homeland."—George E. Sokolsky. The Latin *de*, "thoroughly," and *spolium*, "spoil."

DISTORTION (dis tor'shun): A "twisting" away from or out of shape. If mentally, it is a false interpretation; if morally, a perversion; if physically, a misshapen condition. "There can be no greater misinterpretation and no greater *distortion* of the truth."—John L. Lewis. Latin *dis-*, "apart," and *torqueo*, "to twist."

DYNAMICS (di nam'iks): The movements of physical and other forces; the forces producing or governing activity. "The *dynamics* of his personality had been directed into channels different from mine."—Roy Chapman Andrews. Greek *dynamikos*, "powerful."

EXACT (eg zakt'): To demand by authority; to insist upon as a right; as: "The new ruler was determined to *exact* obedience from his subjects."

EXECRATED (ek'se krate id): Cursed; detested; abhorred; denounced; as: "Few presidents in history have been so *execrated* and so glorified." From the Latin *execro*, "to call down evil upon."

FACTIOUS (fak'shus): Causing strife or stirring up disputes; seditious; given to opposition; as: "There is a *factious* element in every labor union."

FETID (fĕt'id): Giving out an offensive odor; stinking; smelling like something rotten. "These monstrous plans have hatched from the *fetid* brain of the Dictator."—Wallace L. Ware. The Latin *fetidus*, from *feteo*, "to smell badly."

FURTIVE (fur'tiv): Stealthy; secret; illusive; sly. "Somewhere in Washington a *furtive* little group of men are craftily erecting agency after agency."—Wayne Coy. Latin *furtivus*, "stolen."

GHOULS (gōōlz): Persons who rob dead bodies; hence, people who act like them; as: "The most despicable of all charlatans are the *ghouls* who prey on the bodies of cancer victims." From the Arabic, *ghul*, the name of an Oriental demon who was supposed to feed on corpses.

IMPECCABLE (im pek'ă b'l): Not capable of doing wrong; free from sin and error; as: "We think of Ingres, whose technique in pencil was *impeccable*." From the Latin *impeccabilis*, *im-*, "not" and *pecco*, "to sin."

IMPRECATIONS (im prĕ kay'shunz): Curses; invocations of evil on someone; maledictions; execrations; words calling forth calamities. "As he stumbled on through the darkness, the raging *imprecations* followed him as far as the old gate."— Lloyd C. Douglas. The Latin *imprecatus*, from *imprecor*, "to curse."

IMPUTE (im pūte'): To attribute; to charge; to blame; as: "They *impute* the offenses of a few doctors to the profession as a whole." From the Latin *imputo*, "to ascribe as a fault."

INALIENABLE (in ale'yen a b'l): That cannot be rightfully taken away; as: "Americans have an *inalienable* right to freedom of speech."

MAGNANIMITY (mag nă nim'ĭ tĭ): Greatness of soul or heart; generosity in feeling or behavior toward others; nobility of mind; elevation above what is petty. "To effect this settlement requires moral resolution and great *magnanimity*."— Walter Lippmann. The Latin *magnus*, "great," and *animus*, "soul."

MALEDICTIONS (mal uh dik'shunz): Invocations of evil; curses. "The political party heaped *maledictions* upon the existing order."—William Allen White. From the Latin *male*, "evilly," and *dico*, "to speak."

MALICIOUS (mă lish'us): Harboring malice or ill will; spiteful. "The *malicious*, interfering action of the board is designed to prolong the controversy."—John L. Lewis. Latin *malitia*, "badness."

NIGGARDLY (nig'urd lĭ): Stingy; scanty; miserly; meanly small. "They only got a *niggardly* handout of some square miles of territory."—Baruch Braunstein. Scandinavian *hnoggr*, "stingy."

NOXIOUS (nŏk'shus): Causing injury to health; morally harmful. "The use of *noxious* gases in war is a hideous commentary on civilization."—Franklin Delano Roosevelt. Latin *noxius*, "injurious."

OBDURATE (ob'dū rit): Unyielding; stubborn; obstinately pursuing a purpose in spite of appeals; as: "She was *obdurate* in her refusal to accompany him." The Latin *obduratus*, from *obduro*, "to hold out."

OBLIQUITY (ob lik'wĭ tĭ): Crooked conduct; deviation from that which is moral and right; indirectness of sound thinking or upright behavior; deceit. "The whole affair was tainted with moral *obliquity*."—John J. Green. Latin *obliquus*, "covert."

OBTUSENESS (ob tūs'ness): Dullness; lack of perception; insensitivity; stupidity. "She marvelled once more at the *obtuseness* of the most brilliant men."—Edith Wharton. Latin *obtusus*, "dulled."

ODIUM (ō'dĭ um): A feeling of extreme disgust; something hated; as: "Impeachment brought the office to its lowest point, and Grant added the *odium* of corruption." From the Latin *odi*, "hate."

PANEGYRICS (pan ĕ jir'iks): Elaborate eulogies; orations expressing great praise. "When panaceas are offered on one side, only to be answered by *panegyrics* on the other, the argument lacks in conclusiveness."—John W. Davis. Greek *panēgyrikos*, "of an assembly."

PERVERSE (pur verse'): From the Latin *perversus*, "turned the wrong way." Hence obstinate; unreasonable; willful; wrong and erring; as: "He is so *perverse* that he likes to show his independence by doing just the opposite of what you tell him to do."

PRESUMPTUOUS (prē zump'chu us): Unduly confident; venturesome; overbold; daring and forward; audacious. "His grandfather had been incautious or *presumptuous* enough to build this metropolitan house amid a world of wretched huts."—Franz Werfel. Latin *praesumtus*, "taken for granted."

PROVOCATIVE (prō vok'ĭ tiv): Serving to stimulate or excite; arousing; as: "His book is filled with *provocative* ideas." Originally from the Latin *provoco*, "to call forth."

RABID (rab'id): Furious; raging; violent; fanatical. "We use our sweat and blood to shatter the *rabid* attempt of our enemies." —Generalissimo Chiang Kai-shek. Latin *rabidus*, "raging."

RADIANT (ray'dĭ ant): Brightly shining; beaming with joy; as:

"It was pleasant to look at the *radiant* faces of the little children." From the Latin *radius*, "ray."

RAMPAGE (ram'pāj): Boisterous agitation; a dashing about with anger or violence; a wild and reckless outbreak. "Everything he was doing meant he would pretty soon go on a *rampage*." —Cordell Hull.

REFUTATION (ref ū tay'shun): Proof of error or falsehood; disproof; as: "His *refutation* of the charges against him was complete." Originally from the Latin *refuto*, "to repel."

REMORSELESSLY (rē morse'less lĭ): Pitilessly; cruelly; mercilessly; without compassion. "The criminals are being hunted down *remorselessly*."—Douglas E. Lurton. The Latin *remorsus*, "suffering," from *re-*, "back," and *mordeo*, "to bite."

ROISTERER (roise'tur ur): A noisy reveler; a bulstering, boisterous merrymaker. "In this rural community one *roisterer* can make enough disturbance to sound like a whole battalion."— Frederick Lewis Allen. From the Old French *ruistre*, "rude."

SCATHING (skāthe'ing: *th* as in *the*): Withering; searing; as: "His government has never drawn more *scathing* criticism." From the Scandinavian *scathi*, "injury."

SEARED (seer'd): Withered; parched; shriveled or scorched as by heat; as: "The land was cracked and *seared* by the blazing sun." From the Old English *serian*, "to wither."

SEDULOUSLY (sed'ū lus lĭ): Busily; untiringly; industriously; assiduously; unrelentingly; perseveringly. "Our enemies have *sedulously* propagated these misapprehensions."—Carlton J. H. Hayes. Latin *sedulus*, "diligent."

SKULKING (skulk'ing): Lurking; moving furtively from place to place; lying hidden. "He has decreed the death of our citizens wherever his *skulking* assassins of the sea may send them to a watery grave."—Tom Connally. From the Scandinavian *skulke*, "skulk."

SPEWS (spūze): Pours forth; is forcibly ejected; as: "It rides the radio waves, *spews* from the presses." From the Old English word *spiwan*, "spit."

SPLENETIC (splē net'ik): Suffering from spleen; hence, peevishly malicious; spitefully stern and harsh. "Driven constantly to write for bread, it was easy to be gossipy, *splenetic*, to make anecdote do for substance."—Ludwig Lewisohn. From the

Latin *splen*, "spleen," since this organ was supposed to be the seat of ill will.

TIRADES (ti'rād'z): Prolonged, declamatory speeches, generally censuring or complaining. "It is little use uttering *tirades* against anti-Semitism."—Cardinal Hinsley. Originally from the Italian *tirare*, "to shoot."

VAINGLORIOUS (vain glaw'ri us): Boastful; extremely vain or proud; puffed up by vanity; vaunted; ostentatious. "They will withdraw before it is too late from a *vainglorious* enterprise."—Winston Churchill.

VAPID (vap'id): Insipid; inane; dull; without life; spiritless; flat and without spirit or zest. "You could not ignore the *vapid* backing on the other side of the record, but were forced to play it through."—Jan Struther. Latin *vapidus*, "insipid."

VENAL (vee'nul): Ready to sell honor or principles; mercenary; open to bribery and corruption. "These revolutionary movements are based on the assumption that human beings are *venal* and criminal."—Dorothy Thompson. Latin *venalis*, "that can be bought with bribes."

VENGEFUL (venj'ful): Vindictive; exhibiting a strong desire for revenge; as: "He was warped by a *vengeful* and malicious spirit." Through the French *venger* from the Latin *vindico*, "to avenge."

VENOMOUS (ven'um us): Poisonous; harmful; malignant; spiteful; as: "He was capable of a *venomous* hatred for those who opposed him." From the Latin *venenum*, "poison."

WANTONLY (won'tun li): Without check or restraint; recklessly; waywardly; heartlessly. "Has the rubber program *wantonly* or unnecessarily stood athwart other essential programs?"—Guy M. Gillette.

A FEW WORD BOOKS FROM
MY LIBRARY

I HAVE listed several books here that may be helpful to those who wish to carry their word explorations further.

Johnson O'Connor's English Vocabulary Builder. Human Engineering Laboratory, Hoboken, New Jersey
This book presents a real challenge and is a genuine vocabulary stretcher. It begins with words that are known to all literate people and then gradually increases in difficulty until it faces the reader with words that are unknown to 98 percent of all adults. When the reader starts to miss he has found his word level and from that point on his study begins.

Word Power Made Easy, Norman Lewis. Doubleday & Company, Garden City, New York
A comprehensive volume on vocabulary building done in an engaging style. It also covers grammar, spelling, etymologies and the like.

The Latin Key to Better English, Archibald Hart, Ph.D., and F. Arnold Lejune. E. P. Dutton & Co., New York
Over 60 percent of our English language is derived from the Latin directly or by way of the Romance languages. This book shows us the Latin roots and gives us the English words that have come from these roots. It is a helpful book and no knowledge of Latin is needed to understand it.

English Synonyms, Antonyms and Prepositions, James C. Fernald. Funk & Wagnalls Co., New York

Webster's Dictionary of Synonyms, G. & C. Merriam Co., Springfield, Mass.

Books of synonyms are basic aids in vocabulary expansion. They spread the prodigal riches of the English language before us and they even contain high excitement for the lover of words. Dr. Fernald's book is a classic of many years' standing and recently revised. The Webster volume is a comparatively recent publication.

The Wonder of Words, Isaac Goldberg. D. Appleton-Century Co., New York

This work is not a vocabulary builder in the textbook sense, but it is an introduction to language. It is written with beauty and imagination and it opens up the gates to all the bright avenues of language.

The Tyranny of Words, Stuart Chase. Harcourt, Brace & Co., New York

Language in Action, S. I. Hayakawa. Harcourt, Brace & Co., New York

People in Quandaries, Wendell Johnson. Harper & Row, New York

Possibly your interest in the subject of words is not yet intense enough to have carried you to the level of these three books. You will be the judge. These volumes deal with semantics, the study of the meanings and the development of the meanings of words, and they take up the great difficulty we human beings have in making ourselves understood. They are far more fascinating than they sound. The authors know how to deal with the subject in a popular and most readable fashion. I would say that your best beginning would be with Stuart Chase.

"It Pays to Increase Your Word Power"

This is a magazine feature that I have conducted in *The Reader's Digest* for a number of years. Each month it gives you an exercise in vocabulary building in the form of a game.

INDEX

All references are to pages. Power words that are fully discussed in the chapters are indicated by SMALL CAPITAL letters.

269